NEEDED RESEARCH
IN AMERICAN DIALECTS

NEEDED RESEARCH
IN AMERICAN DIALECTS

DENNIS R. PRESTON

Michigan State University

Publication of the

American Dialect Society

·

Number 88

·

Published by Duke University Press

for the American Dialect Society

Annual Supplement to American Speech

PUBLICATION OF THE AMERICAN DIALECT SOCIETY

RONALD R. BUTTERS, Editor, *Duke University*
CHARLES E. CARSON, Managing Editor, *Duke University*

Number 88
Copyright © 2003
American Dialect Society
ISBN: 0-8223-6594-4

Library of Congress Cataloging-in-Publication Data

Needed research in American dialects / [edited by] Dennis R. Preston.
    p. cm. — (Publication of the American Dialect Society ; no. 88)
    Annual supplement to American Speech
    Includes bibliographical references.
    ISBN 0-8223-6594-4
      1. English language—Dialects—North America. 2. English language—Variation—North America. 3. English language—Dialects—United States. 4. English language—Variation–United States. 5. English language—Dialects—Canada. 6. English language—Variation—Canada.
    I. Preston, Dennis Richard. II. American Speech. III. Series.
PE2841.N44 2003
427'.973—dc22   2003062715k

British Library Cataloguing-in-Publication Data available

CONTENTS

INTRODUCTION

DENNIS R. PRESTON

Michigan State University

IN 1943, PROCEEDINGS FROM A SYMPOSIUM held at a meeting of the American Dialect Society (ADS) Executive Council were published. The symposium consisted of reports from the chairs of the various ADS committees: "Regional Speech and Localisms" (George P. Wilson), "Place Names" (Harold W. Bentley), "Linguistic Geography" (Hans Kurath), "Usage" (Robert C. Pooley), "Non-English Dialects" (J. M. Carrière), "New Words" (Dwight L. Bolinger), and "Semantics" (S. I. Hayakawa). These proceedings were published separately and, since they were quickly out of print, reprinted in PADS 41 (Apr. 1964, 42–54). The title of the original and the reprint was *Needed Research in American English*.

Wilson's report focused heavily on the need for bibliographies of dialect work and of works containing and related to dialect. Bentley's was primarily concerned with suggestions of topics for place-name research; Kurath's report outlined work on the Linguistic Atlas project and contained a plea for volunteer fieldworkers to record even single persons in areas where the work had not yet progressed. The report on usage emphasized the need for data collection and offered the Usage Committee of ADS as a "clearing house" for usage findings. The work on non-English dialects applauded recent use of "the standards of the most exacting scholarship"; further collection was recommended, and the area's importance to an understanding of the English of the United States and Canada was pointed out. The "New Words" entry noted the efficacy of treating students to linguistic instruction with words from their own generation, and "Semantics" was greeted as an area of concern not traditionally associated with dialect study but was urged on the profession as an important and growing area of theoretical linguistics that should not be overlooked.

Twenty years later, ADS President Albert C. Marckwardt acquired funds from the American Council of Learned Societies (ACLS) to support a meeting of the Executive Council of ADS to assess what had happened in ADS research areas in the 20 years since the first report. Marckwardt's summary of the meeting appeared in the *Report of the Commission on the Humanities*, published by ACLS, the Council of Graduate Schools in the United States, and the United Chapters of Phi Beta Kappa (1964), but the reports themselves (with revisions from committee chairs in some cases) were published as *Needed Research in American English* in PADS 41 (Apr. 1964, 22–41). The contents were as follows: "Linguistic Geography" (Allen F. Hubbell), "Usage" (Francis L. Utley), "Place Names" (Frederic G. Cassidy), "New Words" (I. Willis Russell), "Non-English Dialects" (Einar Haugen), and "Proverbs and Proverbial Sayings" (James B. McMillan).

Hubbell's work noted progress on the Linguistic Atlas project, studies derived from it, the perennial need for funds, and the progress made in bringing dialect awareness to public schools. He also praised dialect initiatives in England and Scotland and wondered if the Society might not hold an annual meeting. The "Usage" section spoke very directly about social class and status as important issues in the study of dialect and praised usage surveys and their publication. Utley also called for intense cooperation with the National Council of Teachers of English. Cassidy's "Place Names" entry welcomed the foundation of the American Name Society and its journal *Names* but called for continued interest in names in ADS and urged a state-by-state national survey. Russell pointed out the creation of the now long-standing *American Speech* department "Among the New Words," founded by Dwight Bolinger after the first *Needed Research* report. Haugen urged continued attention to non-English varieties by the ADS and mentioned the appearance of PADS 26, *Bilingualism in the Americas: A Bibliography and Research Guide*, by Einar Haugen. Finally, McMillan called attention to the formation of a committee on proverbs and proverbial sayings in 1944 and hoped ADS would serve as a central archive for collections.

By 1983 the 20-year plan for a volume of *Needed Research* was in place, and PADS 71 (although it actually appeared in 1984) was

PE
1702
AS
A071

1983
#71

entitled *Needed Research in American English (1983)*. The contributions were as follows: "Historical Perspective" (Thomas L. Clark), "Linguistic Geography" (Raven I. McDavid, Jr.), "Regional Speech and Localisms" (Frederic G. Cassidy), "Usage" (John Algeo), "New Words" (I. Willis Russell), "Proverbs and Proverbial Sayings" (Kelsie B. Harder), "Non-English American Languages" (Juergan Eichoff), and "Computer Needs" (William A. Kretzschmar, Jr.).

Clark's piece is introductory and summarizing; McDavid's is a thorough treatment of Linguistic Atlas projects to date and a critical assessment of difficulties in financing, housing, processing, and publishing Atlas work. He included a bibliography of research and a summary appendix of Atlas projects. Cassidy, of course, updated readers on progress on the long-awaited *Dictionary of American Regional English* (*DARE*), fieldwork for which had been entirely completed in the 20 years between the 1963 and 1983 reports. (It is interesting that the "Secretary's Report," published in the same PADS 41 where the 1963 and 1943 *Needed Research* accounts appear, cited the appointment of Cassidy to the editorship of a "Dictionary of American Regional Speech" [57].) Algeo's report on "Usage" is not only an account of work which had been done but a careful outline of goals, methods, and means of dissemination for future studies. His contribution also contained a useful bibliography. Russell's report on "New Words" emphasized the need for careful etymologizing in this area and dealt with the ticklish business of "slang." In calling for archiving of the numerous citations of new words which ADS handles, particularly in its "Among the New Words" department, Russell emphasized the need for electronic preservation. Harder noted that, although work had gone on in the area of proverbs and proverbial sayings, a dictionary of American proverbs was still only a desideratum. His contribution also identified such ignored areas as African American proverbs. Eichoff's contribution is somewhat pessimistic; like Haugen's of 20 years earlier, it cited the importance of other languages in the Americas but found that little careful work had been done, that there was a lack of communication among scholars carrying out such research, and that basic works (e.g., PADS 26) needed to be updated. (Eichoff also raised the interesting question of the distinction between "dialectology" and "sociolinguistics.") Finally, and doubtless surprising to the 2003 reader, Kretzschmar pointed out the usefulness (and hazards) of electronic data storage and handling, and that is surely an appropriate cutoff point for the next 20 years.

By chance, however, a volume that might qualify as a midpoint "Needed Research" volume appeared in only ten years. The Society celebrated its centennial in 1989, and ADS committee chairs and others were asked to find ways to mark this anniversary. As chair of the Research Committee, I proposed a volume of research representative of the Society's interests. Authors were recruited, and *American Dialect Research* was designated one of the official publications celebrating the Society's centennial. Since it appeared in 1993 (Amsterdam: Benjamins), it came at just the mid-point of the usual 20-year wait for *Needed Research*. I include mention of it here since the authors and their topics will provide an interesting contrast with the earlier volumes: "The Historical and Cultural Interpretation of Dialects" (W. Nelson Francis), "An Approach to Linguistic Geography: The Linguistic Atlas of the Gulf States" (Lee Pederson), "Area Lexicon: The Making of DARE" (Frederic G. Cassidy), "Some Applications of Mathematical and Statistical Models in Dialect Geography" (Dennis Girard and Donald Larmouth), "Sociolinguistic Dialectology" (J. K. Chambers), "Adapting Dialectology: The Conduct of Community Language Studies" (John Baugh), "Identifying and Interpreting Variables" (Walt Wolfram), "The Quantitative Analysis of Language Variation" (Gregory R. Guy), "Variation Theory and Language Contact: Concepts, Methods, and Data" (Shana Poplack), "A Perspective on African-American English" (Guy Bailey), "Professional Varieties: The Case of Language and Law" (William M. O'Barr), "Folk Dialectology" (Dennis R. Preston), and "The Patterning of Variation in Performance" (Charles Briggs). (Chapters on gender and pidgin and creole varieties were solicited but were not available in time to be included in the book.) An appendix, "Resources for Research," was provided by Michael D. Linn and included recorded as well as print resources. Even a casual reading of this list will show the emergence of sociolinguistic, attitudinal, and discoursal concerns, which continue to engage the society's members.

That brings us to the present and this volume. When this installment was planned, I was president of the society and was asked to see this version of *Needed Research* into print. I will not bore the reader here with my summary of the chapters; they stand on their own, but it may be interesting to some readers to compare the topics treated here with ones dealt with in earlier installments. Although this 2003 edition is perhaps more like the 1993 extra, it contains entries on linguistic theory, the likes of which have not been seen since the earliest version's entry on "Semantics." That is no accident; ADS work and the work of sociolinguists, perhaps particularly in North America, have established much closer ties to general and theoretical linguistics over the last twenty years, and both the 1993 volume and the current version reflect that.

On the other hand, those who fear any diluting of ADS's main interest should be reassured by this volume that the study of the regional character of English language variation is still prominent. While it is true that sociolinguistic, discoursal, and theoretical concerns have been added, dialect atlas and dictionary making are still fully represented, and one hopes that entries on performance, ideology, attitudes, and other topics represent emerging sophistication in the study of what has been ADS's objective all along, one perhaps best summarized by our instructions to authors in *American Speech*, which note that we are ". . . concerned principally with the English language in the Western Hemisphere, . . . with English in other parts of the world, with other languages influencing English or influenced by it,[1] and with general linguistic theory." That editorial policy goes on to note that we welcome ". . . articles dealing with current usage, dialectology, and the history and structure of English."

In short, ADS as it is now constituted has taken several pretty big bites out of the linguistic apple. I hope this 2003 version of *Needed Research* will show that we have been vigorously chewing on those bites for the last 20 years but that there is plenty of apple to feed on for the next 20 and that, given the very nature of our subject, even the 2023 report will find that not everything has been done.

NOTE

1. I take the editor's prerogative in calling this version of the *Needed Research* volumes *Needed Research in American Dialects*. Non-English languages in the Americas were, have been, and continue to be important, not only for their internal diversity, which makes them "American dialects," but also for their two-way contact influence with English. It is interesting to note that this same change has surfaced from time to time in the designation of "NWAV" (New Ways of Analyzing Variation), originally "NWAVE" (New Ways of Analyzing Variation in English), the principal North American sociolinguistics conference.

1. THE HISTORY
OF AMERICAN ENGLISH

MICHAEL MONTGOMERY

University of South Carolina

THIS ESSAY OUTLINES some needs and considerations for historical research on American English (AE) from the seventeenth through the nineteenth century, a period of great dynamism, a time of extensive contact with other languages and between varieties of English, and indeed the formative period of most major regional and social varieties of present-day AE. In recent decades researchers have shown that quantitative variation within synchronic data sets often indicates ongoing change, even when that change does not proceed to completion, and in this regard, variation in AE over the past three to four generations of living Americans identifies important questions and issues for historical linguists. To exercise control, however, the ensuing discussion focuses on only the first three centuries in the part of North America that became the United States, except when research on present-day varieties has direct relevance for earlier ones. Our age has witnessed how thoroughly English penetrated other languages in the twentieth century and assumes that was the time of its most dramatic spread. While perhaps true for AE or for vocabulary, Bailey (1996) has shown that the English language dispersed, if anything, more widely in the nineteenth century. The eighteenth century likewise saw it spread, as English reached beyond the American littoral well into the interior, and also to Australasia and South Africa by the 1790s. Already in the seventeenth century, English was planted in the Caribbean and much of coastal North America, established a beachhead in India, and penetrated many parts of the east and north of Ireland.

For the first two and one-half centuries of the period of focus, little more is understood today about the character or formation of AE than 40 years ago, despite it being a model testing ground for issues of language contact (cf. especially Mufwene 2001) and text-based sociohistorical linguistics (cf. Kytö 1991). Many factors have coincided with and helped bring this situation about, more than anything else the attraction of speech records to the neglect of written texts and knowledge of how to interpret them. As long ago as the 1920s Hans Kurath, director of the Linguistic Atlas of the United States and Canada, posited that interviews with older, less-traveled speakers in the Atlantic states would offer the best basis for approximating the AE of the formative period and outlining transatlantic linguistic connections and for mapping major dialect areas (Kurath 1928). More recent quantitative research has also exploited speech records, that is, of older speakers in conservative communities, especially to examine morphological features. However, by using speech records internal reconstruction can proceed no farther back than the mid-nineteenth century at the very outer limit. For earlier periods, researchers must use commentary from travelers, grammarians, and lexicographers, representations of speech in plays and fiction, manuscripts such as private letters, and other elements of the written record (see Montgomery 2001, 96–104), collectively the only record for varieties of English beyond a century and a half ago. Beyond finding and utilizing older recordings more thoroughly and carefully, progress in reconstructing earlier AE depends to a large extent on pinpointing and interpreting speech-based documents of likely value. It is easy enough to say that we need more, larger, and earlier data sources, but two other research needs are equally important:

1. To identify and respect the limitations as well as the advantages of one's chosen methodology and data and to avoid unwarranted assumptions regarding them.

Linguistic studies, like pharmaceuticals, need to be labeled for potential side effects. Whether for convenience or otherwise, such caveats have often been neglected for research on African American English (AAE), as when researchers label data from a small, disparate sample or from a single small community as a sociohistorical "variety" (Poplack and Tagliamonte 1989, inter alia), use dichotomous social categories such as "black" versus "white" that obscure the complexity of rural communities, or divide and compare speakers by state (Schneider 1989; Rickford 1999; inter alia) rather than by cultural region (i.e., reflecting internal migration) or physiographic region (but cf. linguistic geography, especially Pederson 1986–92). Researchers need to be self-critical of their methodologies, their categories, and the generalizability of their findings. Too often social and linguistic categories and variables are adopted because they are dichotomous and permit binomial analysis.

2. To utilize knowledge of social history and the history of the English language.

Otherwise studies risk being overly enamored of their own methodologies, imposing modern linguistic categories and distinctions on historical data and making false starts rather than laying a secure foundation for further research. A great strength of linguistic geography, for example, has been its practitioners' willingness to learn from geographers. Too often the field of American English has seen a simplistic use of history or social profiles of communities, produced when linguists consult the work of historians only cursorily for a convenient quotation or summary to frame an argument. Labov (1972) notwithstanding, historians have been much better in understanding that each type of evidence has its problems and what those problems are. By comparison, linguists have much to learn (Fischer 1970).

As is evident, discussion of needed research is inseparable from a critique of existing research. Because ADS's previous *Needed Research* collections lacked coverage of history, this chapter will attempt a perspective somewhat broader than the past two decades. It will take "history" to refer to both internal and external developments, that is, changes within AE and how historical events and periods intersect with these. American English may be one of the most thoroughly documented language varieties (or collections of varieties) in the world, but the proportion of scholarship on its historical dimensions remains relatively small.

USING SPEECH RECORDS

A convenient division of language change research using speech records is that between cross-generational and cross-variety comparisons. The first approach has been used quantitatively and fruitfully, as by Bailey (1997) to posit that some features of "Southern American English" diffused rapidly both socially and geographically beginning around 1880. Even so, it remains premature to characterize many grammatical and phonological features of that and other varieties of AE as late-nineteenth-century innovations, inasmuch as few speech records predate that time and intensive manuscript research has hardly begun (cf. Schneider and Montgomery 2001; Montgomery and Eble forthcoming). The cross-generational approach needs much further development to enable researchers to move from apparent-time (e.g., that the speech of people born in 1850 but recorded in the 1930s represents that of their youth) to real-time analysis. The second approach is older and more established and dates back more than a century (Bailey 1992). It is premised on the use of conservative data from one or more speech communities or varieties.

CROSS-VARIETY COMPARISON. This approach proposes an inferential triangulation between two or more varieties that from historical sources are thought to have shared an origin or earlier history, though demonstrating the precursor(s) may not always be relevant. It uses data from interviews (usually with older, less literate speakers) to capture details of variation, takes apparent time for granted, and rarely compares generations of speakers. Adopted by linguistic atlas research on lexical and phonetic differences in AE, cross-variety comparison for phonological and morphological features was pioneered more recently by sociolinguistic and creole research, the best examples of which involve explicitly specifying contexts of variation, tabulating variant forms, and considering the distribution of forms in relation to other features. However, in equating conservative twentieth-century varieties with ones that existed one or more generations earlier, cross-variety comparison avoids using written records, undertaking instead comparative reconstruction before internal reconstruction beyond that permitted by apparent time. As previously suggested, to posit input patterns from the eighteenth-century settlement period, extreme versions of this approach have sometimes been used, from early linguistic atlas work as conceived by Hans Kurath (1949) to Tagliamonte and Smith (2000), who use late-twentieth-century material collected and analyzed in the British Isles and Canada. The privileging of data from sociolinguistic interviews (and the exclusion of other data from consideration; cf. Myhill 1995) not only to quantify variation but also to claim that certain features did NOT exist is one result. But the absence of evidence is not necessarily the evidence of absence. Pragmatic conditions may always be at work screening grammatical features that are highly charged emotionally out of the written record as well as most conversations, but to date we have no principled account of what to expect to show up in a sociolinguistic interview and what not to.

In other cases, as when speech communities are not at issue, cross-variety comparison is more appropriate, as in comparing vowel systems of colonial varieties of English (Lass 1990). This is also the case for inventories of British and American speech relations (Laird 1970, 163–74; Ellis 1984; Schneider forthcoming) that use dialect dictionaries, linguistic atlas materials, and so on; even though the time-depth of a common ancestor is relatively shallow for such studies (usually the eighteenth century), the presumption of staticness needs to be recognized and calls for corroborative evidence from the written record whenever possible.

AFRICAN AMERICAN ENGLISH. Most often cross-variety comparisons of pre-twentieth-century AE have involved AAE, one of many varieties whose historical development is still very much open to exploration. Three decades of work on AAE have produced mainly studies of verbal morphology but left many areas of grammar and phonology unknown, even with the publication of Mufwene et al. (1998). The research to date has been driven overwhelmingly by one overarching issue—the so-called creolist-versus-dialectologist origin of AAE, a large and important question that is now somewhat outmoded because most linguists accept a position somewhere between these extremes often used to frame arguments.

To make further progress, the "origins issue" would benefit enormously from a more thorough descriptive base, such as a comprehensive grammatical account along the lines of Schneider (1989) for nineteenth-century AAE (such a resource is needed for other varieties of AE as well). The WPA Ex-Slave Narratives (Rawick 1972) are the first quasi-speech documents on nineteenth-century AAE given to large-scale quantitative analysis, a process which required Brewer (1974) and Schneider (1989, 1997) to develop explicit methodologies and assess the utility of such texts for linguistic purposes. More researchers should follow their self-critical approach to the relative merits of the data they use. Kautzsch (2002), the only major work using and comparing written and spoken records, is also exemplary in this way.

English creoles and nineteenth-century AAE are not necessarily comparable entities (but see the arguments of Mufwene 1996). One can posit a common ancestor for Anglophone creoles in the Western Hemisphere on external grounds, but can the same be said for AAE and other varieties of nineteenth-century AE? The creoles have been in situ for generations and are the tongues of majority communities. AAE varieties, in contrast, have undergone profound changes in the past century and a half and, as spoken by minority communities, have been in constant contact with mainstream communities.

Recent work on emigre communities founded by African Americans in the late eighteenth or early nineteenth century in Nova Scotia and the Dominican Republic (Poplack 2000; Poplack and Tagliamonte 2001) and in Liberia (Singler 1991) has attempted to approximate African American speech of a century and a half or more ago. Poplack and Tagliamonte's ambitious, sophisticated research argues that people of African descent formed socially and linguistically distinct "enclave" communities abroad after leaving the United States. To extend the validity of data collected from speakers in these places in the 1980s and 1990s, they have likened linguistic patterns there to those found in the WPA Ex-Slave Recordings (Bailey, Maynor, and Cukor-Avila 1991) from the rural American South dating from two generations earlier. This effort to validate more recent data through cross-variety comparison offers a welcome model. Nonetheless, two of their presumptions that need more critical evaluation are the monolithicness of geographically very dispersed nineteenth-century AAE (a view shared, it must be said, by many other researchers) and the staticness of diasporan varieties of AAE over the past two centuries (Afro-Nova Scotian English is not a "transplanted variety" but a descendant of one). Generational comparisons, not pursued by them but shown in the recent work of Wolfram and Thomas (2002) to reveal large-scale change in an "enclave community" in coastal North Carolina, suggest the dynamism at work between consecutive generations even in very rural areas. Thus, the reification of diasporan varieties as representing mid-nineteenth-century AAE is problematic. Though Poplack and Tagliamonte (2001, 39–66) do not mention it, the Nova Scotian communities featured intermarriage with whites in the first generation (Carol W. Troxler, pers. com., 21 June 2002), the implications of which need to be explored. In the crucial formative period, black and white communities there may not have been as distinct as they are now.

In editing transcripts and analytical essays on 11 interviews with former slaves, Bailey, Maynor, and Cukor-Avila (1991) made valuable use of recordings in the Archive of Folk Culture at the Library of Congress. Despite clamors for more such material, few researchers have seriously taken up the call to locate it. The same archive holds hundreds of stories, sermons, interviews, and other texts recorded in the 1930s yet to be consulted by linguists; they just happen not to be from ex-slaves. Two examples are "Hoodoo Story" (AFC 115 A1, recorded from an African American by John A. and Alan Lomax in New Orleans in 1935) and "The Capture of John Hardy" (AFC 2742 B3, recorded from a white by Herbert Halpert in Ferrum, Virginia, in 1939). Many texts come from speakers comparable in birth date with former slaves and can be strategically employed to enlarge the corpus of recorded material from speakers born in the mid-nineteenth century. In fact, the Ex-Slave Recordings have often forced those who have used them to generalize from an unhappily small sample of 11 speakers dispersed over five states, making it suspect to treat their speech as a coherent variety or to conclude that features did not exist in nineteenth-century AAE because these few speakers did not use them.

One large corpus is transcripts of interviews conducted mainly in the late 1930s by Harry Middleton Hyatt with hoodoo doctors in towns and cities across much of the eastern United States (Hyatt 1970–75). Heretofore they have been analyzed for only the verb *be* (Viereck 1988; Ewers 1996), though the main title of the latter author's book (*The Origin of American Black English*) implies a broader-based analysis, not to mention one using earlier material. The Hyatt transcripts form, after the WPA Ex-Slave Narratives, the largest corpus of material from speakers of AAE born in the nineteenth century and deserve a book-length treatment comparable to Schneider (1989). They are of considerable value for features such as verb principal parts, noun plurals, and others. Questions about their validity (and indeed that of other transcripts) can be explored by internal validation with reference to other data sources rather than only by external validation with reference to the circumstances in which they were produced. How can one explain, for example, the fact that habitual *be* (and *bes*) is often found in the Hyatt materials, but apparently not at all in "enclave" varieties? Can this be attributed entirely to wholesale change at the end of the nineteenth century? If AAE allegedly changed so much from the late nineteenth to the late twentieth century, would we not have expected it to have done so in other ways in the nineteenth century? Is it sufficient to claim that it was "insular" or spoken only in "enclave" communities during that time? Should data other than that from interviews from such communities be in effect discounted even though it cannot be analyzed with the same methodology? How do we reconcile it with nineteenth-century evidence in the *Dictionary of American Regional English* (*DARE* 1985–) on habitual *be*, for example?

Other collections of early AAE speech records, including interviews, are not hard to find. Typically data from linguistic atlases, because of its inventorial nature (Montgomery 1993), has been used for correlational (Dorrill 1986) rather than quantitative variationist analysis. The Linguistic Atlas of the Gulf States (LAGS) project, however, is fundamentally different, in that all interviews were recorded, contain significant amounts of free conversation, and are archived at Emory University and the University of Georgia. The oldest African American speaker in LAGS was born in 1884 (an 88-year-old man from Edwards, Mississippi, who was interviewed for four hours and ten minutes); 13 others were also born in the 1880s (Pederson 1986–92, vol. 1).

The lack of work using recordings to explore other nineteenth-century varieties, especially white ones, has meant little progress on a host of major questions, some to be identified below. In some ways, then, the consuming interest in reconstructing AAE has been a mixed blessing.

FROM SPEECH RECORDS TO WRITTEN RECORDS

Interest in twentieth-century varieties has been fueled by diverse, often large collections of technologically produced and analyzed data, but research using speech records often raises issues that can be productively pursued for earlier stages of AE. For example, acoustic equipment certainly permits the measurement of details of vowel articulation that can rarely be guessed at from the written record (Thomas 2001; Labov, Ash, and Boberg forthcoming), but it also lays the groundwork for much further work on vowel changes as revealed in good impressionistic phonetics (Boberg 2001) and in occasional spellings found in manuscripts (Stephenson 1967).

Written records rarely, if ever, feature the vernacular language that linguists most prize, but to the extent that they exhibit non-standard forms, they can provide many insights to the spoken AE of former days. Despite the fact that literary attestations involve perhaps the most uncertainties of assessment because their relation to real-life models is uncertain, they have been used routinely, but uncritically, in attempts to document and reconstruct AAE (e.g., Stewart 1970b; Dillard 1972). Nonetheless, evidence from literary dialect in the speech of stock characters in drama and fiction can be used in an appropriate, principled, and restrained manner. In fact, the study of eighteenth-century ethnic varieties of AE relies largely on such material, which is extensive for several ethnic character types, including Irish, German, Scottish, African American, Amerindian, and Yiddish (Cooley 1995). By the mid-

1700s, when it began in the American colonies, literary dialect drew on British traditions of comic stereotypes. It probably often reflected conventions imported from Britain rather than native to the United States, but this has been investigated in only one case (Cooley 1997).

Another way to reach beyond the time limitations of tape recordings is to extract commentary from accounts by the extraordinary variety of people (clergymen, journalists, explorers, etc.) who toured or sojourned in the American colonies or the young nation and then wrote of their experiences and impressions of local people, occasionally citing or evaluating the speech they heard. Read (1933) pioneered this research from sources being read for the *Dictionary of American English,* but few linguists other than Dillard (1972) have invested much effort in digging such commentary out. As shown in Clark's *Travels in the Old South* (1956), it dates from the early seventeenth century and is particularly voluminous for the antebellum period. Though limited and often reflecting prejudices and misconceptions, such popular observations complement other types of period evidence on speech patterns. In them lie not only citations of linguistic forms, but labels and perceptions of local and regional speech. They are perhaps the best sources for undertaking perceptual dialectology of pre-twentieth-century AE, but nineteenth-century schoolbooks, usage manuals, and the like can also be mined in this regard (e.g., the extensive section on "Provincialisms" in Kirkham 1829). Manuals describing the uncertain English of minority-language communities should also be of interest.

As already suggested, however, it is manuscript documents—in particular, letters from semiliterate writers—that hold the most value. They include personal letters, petitions, depositions (Wright 2003), and so on that have single authorship and preferably no amanuensis. Despite some manifest limitations (e.g., the lack of personal information about the writers), such documents often offer the only data with time-depth greater than a century and a half. Montgomery (1999) and Schneider and Montgomery (2001) show that it is untenable to argue that the effects of standard spelling and grammar inevitably obscure or distort the speech of a writer and make semiliterate writing too problematic to analyze. Manuscript documents are often speech-based, that is, writers compose and spell by ear rather than by written model. Beyond their direct evidence, they are invaluable for corroborating inferences from establishing the input of Irish and British English to American colonies in the seventeenth and eighteenth centuries.

Just as sociolinguists must grapple with the all-too-familiar "observer's paradox" (Labov 1972), sociohistorical linguists face two analogous paradoxes regarding the vernacular in written records. First, it is much more difficult to find evidence of it antedating the twentieth century, yet to rely solely on data collected in the twentieth century and inferences from that leads to scholarship that is easily overstated and possibly unreliable. Second, individuals of lower social stations whose speech intruded more directly into their writing usually wrote infrequently and were less likely to have their writing preserved.

TYPOLOGY OF LETTER WRITERS. One way to overcome the latter paradox, or at least to reduce considerably the necessary time in locating appropriate documents, is to identify persons of little education having a compelling reason to write (preferably with some frequency, to a government official or an estate, for example) and thus who might have their letters preserved in collections of official or family papers. A tentative typology (Montgomery 1997) includes at least three kinds of individuals: functionaries (those who were required by their occupation to submit periodic reports), lonely hearts (who were separated from loved ones), and desperadoes (who needed help). An example of a lonely heart is the farm boy who became a Civil War private, left his family for the first time, and wrote home to dispel the pain of separation. A typical desperado was a Civil War soldier who, unjustly arrested, punished, or deprived of pay or privilege, wrote to a military or governmental official for assistance. A functionary was a plantation overseer who supervised slaves in the field and reported periodically on the progress of crops and other affairs to an absentee plantation owner. Though linguists have recently begun to use recordings of Civil War veterans (Thomas 2001), they have yet to exploit the primary source on the language of the day, letters from privates. In a classic essay, "Dear Folks," Wiley (1978) suggests how rich they are. We know very little about the status of dialect boundaries in the nineteenth century except by extrapolating from twentieth-century linguistic atlas records, though the availability of Civil War letters and diaries, among other documents, makes this question quite approachable. Profitable comparisons could be made between the letters of white and black Civil War soldiers, who were sometimes from the same areas. How did AE migrate as a result of the war and other large-scale demographic and social events of the nineteenth century?

These three situations cut sharply across the social spectrum because people of various social stations faced loneliness, deprivation, or the requirement to inform others of their work. More important, they motivated people to write for themselves and put words to paper regardless of their literacy. Someone pleading for mercy or relief may well pay little attention to the form (spelling, capitalization, grammar, etc.) of his or her writing, being more concerned with getting a message across. The written version of the observer's paradox is accordingly mitigated.

Beyond collecting such letters and analyzing them in case studies, historians of AE need to take the next logical step: assembling corpora of them using principled criteria (work has begun with Schneider and Montgomery 2001 and Van Herk and Poplack forthcoming). The challenge is quite different from that faced by other historical corpora of English because of the very different nature of "representativeness" of the texts of interest.

INPUT VARIETIES AND EMIGRANT LETTERS. The study of donor or input varieties to AE has come a long way since becoming an interest to American linguists in the 1920s (Krapp 1925; Kurath 1928; for a review, see Montgomery 2001). Collectively written records enable researchers to detail, not only approximate, aspects of input varieties. Research to date has little utilized early letters and other contemporary documents, though they afford more reliable internal reconstruction and can often be used to confirm or disconfirm connections arrived at by cross-variety comparison alone. For example, habitual *be* has been attributed by Stewart (1970a), Rickford (1986), and others to contact between Irish emigrants and African slaves in the antebellum South because it is found in strikingly similar patterns in modern Irish English and AAE. Manuscript evidence from Irish emigrant letters, however, shows that habitual *be* arose in Ireland almost certainly too late for input or transfer to AAE (Montgomery and Kirk 1996). Emigrant letters indicate that it spread rapidly as a result of language shift from Irish to English in Ireland in the mid-nineteenth century.

Emigrant letters especially hold promise for documenting input varieties to AE because they date to the early eighteenth century (Miller et al. 2003), are numerous, and provide the most continuous record of the language of lesser-educated individuals from the British Isles (Montgomery 1995). Research using them requires an understanding of emigration history, however, because not all regions contributed significant numbers of emigrants and not all varieties came to North America or to the same parts of the continent in the same proportion. Emigrant letters from New England have never been analyzed or, apparently, even collected. The settlement of the region by East Anglians is well documented, but very little had survived there by the time New England speech was first described in the late nineteenth century. What are the possible explanations for this? Was it lack of transfer, due to heterogeneous input that was quickly leveled, the standardizing influence of a highly literate society, or something else? Was it lack of evidence, due to lack of documentation? We do not know, perhaps because to date no one has scoured the archives and county record offices in Essex and Sussex in search of letters of local, often ephemeral, literature such as promotional and other propagandistic tracts and letters. Nor has anyone done this in the north Midlands of England to document the language of thousands of Quakers who came from there to the Delaware Valley between 1680 and 1720, or in southwestern England to document the input varieties to the mid-seventeenth-century Chesapeake (Fischer 1989). The vast collections of the Colonial Office at the British Public Record Office could occupy a team of researchers to ferret out documents.

A long-range goal of the study of Old World/New World linguistic relations, involving languages and varieties from the British Isles, continental Europe, and Africa, is a predictive model for which linguistic features, on linguistic and extralinguistic grounds, would have survived and which would not have. In this regard, historians of AE have much to learn from creole studies, as shown by Mufwene (2001).

EARLY AFRICAN AMERICAN ENGLISH. Interest in reconstructing the earlier history of AAE has motivated fruitful research for more than three decades and not a few assessments of the state of knowledge and calls for more data. Rickford (1998, 157–63), for example, cites seven types of useful information: (1) sociohistorical conditions; (2) textual attestations of AAE from earlier times (examples from fiction, drama, poetry, travelers' accounts, and court proceedings, as well as interviews with former slaves and other African Americans); (3) diaspora recordings; (4) creole/AAE similarities; (5) African language/AAE similarities; (6) English dialect/AAE differences; and (7) comparisons across age groups of African American speakers. He rightly contends that the reconstruction of AAE has often fallen short because linguists have been content to draw inferences from only twentieth-century data and have done too little to identify and use earlier data sources.

Rickford advocates quantitative analysis of dialect representations found in literary texts for features such as zero copula but makes no mention of manuscripts from semiliterate writers. The usefulness of the latter has in recent years been demonstrated for African Americans who were Civil War soldiers from the 1860s (Montgomery, Fuller, and DeMarse 1993), who migrated from North America to Sierra Leone in the 1790s (Montgomery 1999), and who left the American South to found Liberia in the 1830s–1850s (Van Herk and Poplack forthcoming). How clearly evidence from such documents supports or fails to support a creole background to AAE has only begun to be determined. Such material can be found in both American and British archives. A number of reliable transcripts have been published (Starobin 1974; Miller 1978; inter alia).

DESCRIPTIVE STUDIES

Interest in basic description has waned considerably in research on early AE, partly as a result of emphasis on quantitative approaches, which consider narrowly circumscribed sets of variable features and deem others unworthy of examination. The long-term result of this is the lack of comprehensive works such as Krapp (1925) (yet to be superseded for the history of American pronunciation, but badly needing updating) or Eliason (1956), an exemplary account of the diverse linguistic landscape of one state, drawing on the widest range of written records. Such work has been replaced by newer scholarship that is often sociologically richer but culturally much poorer.

LANGUAGE CONTACT AND SPEECH COMMUNITIES. Given recent advances in the field of language contact, it is time to consider afresh issues of borrowing from other languages into AE. To date research has dealt with lexis, except for the influence of German in Pennsylvania and a few similar cases. This is not to say that lexical borrowing from other languages has been adequately assessed (not since Marckwardt 1958 has the field had a general overview), but *DARE* offers extraordinary new possibilities for investigating the topic. In tandem with the two indexes produced for its first three volumes (von Schneidemesser and Metcalf 1993; von Schneidemesser 1999), many studies of items labeled by *DARE* as having a particular language source are possible, especially lexis and semantics having nonnative sources. Hamilton (1998) shows brilliantly how *DARE* can be exploited in one case study. Other possibilities include Spanish, German (inside and outside Pennsylvania), Dutch, and Algonquian. The influence of other languages is ripe for investigation using approaches and sources other than *DARE*. The Cherokee, for example, contributed much to the culture of southern Appalachia, but next to nothing to the English of western North Carolina—apparently. Many Cherokee borrowings may in fact lurk as loan translations in the names of local plants and other items there. In this case and others, too little language contact research has been undertaken by those who know the donor language well. This includes influence from African languages, which because of the numerous and varied inputs, remains inadequately understood and still a subject for much conjecture. The influences of some languages having contact with English in the colonial period (e.g., Scottish Gaelic in eastern North Carolina, Irish Gaelic in eastern ports) has never been researched, but there is little point in investigating these and many others if researchers are not adequately schooled about what groups settled where, what language(s) they spoke (speakers from Ireland or Scotland were frequently bilingual), the types of communities they formed, how intact these communities were, what contacts communities had with others, what social networks they participated in, what role(s) the emigrant language played in educational, religious, and community functions, and so on. They should begin with case studies of locales by detailing the order of arrival and numbers of speaker groups and what language(s) they spoke. What interactions did people have with different language and dialect groups? How important was linguistic solidarity with members of one's own linguistic group?

How or when did a generalized version of AE develop? Did regional varieties exist at the time of the American Revolution? To what extent can we detect in early AE principles of dialect contact presented by Trudgill (1986)? Such broad questions require the introduction of concepts and analytical tools from language contact and sociolinguistic research to scenarios of early AE. The work of one scholar in particular has confronted such questions. Dillard (1992) has argued that regional British English contributed next to nothing to early AE because emigrants spoke contact varieties like Maritime Pidgin English before departing. Dialect contact after arrival leveled input varieties further and produced a koiné by the mid–eighteenth century (modern regional varieties of AE arose in the early national period from social factors and other types of language contact). While Dillard's stressing of the fluidity of colonial life is a healthy corrective to presumptions about transatlantic connections made by linguists such as Kurath, leveling did not occur uniformly everywhere, nor almost certainly did a single leveled variety of AE develop in the eighteenth century. Some of the counteracting factors would have included the following: (1) Americans were multistyle speakers from the beginning, and dialect rivalry and contact may have reinforced if not increased their range of styles. If newcomers learned a new variety, they did not necessarily discard their old one(s). Koinéization may have affected more public styles of language but probably left private ones more or less unaffected. (2) Covert prestige probably became associated with many linguistic forms in colonial times, screening them from the written record. (3) New arrivals tended to seek their national or ethnic group and to reinforce existing communities. (4) Rivalry between regions and colonies was common in the eighteenth century and has remained strong ever since. The perception, and most likely the reality, of regionally distinct speech must have been based in part on selective maintenance of British regional patterns. (5) American colonies were autonomous from one another—they were founded separately, had lives of their own, and were usually bound by commercial and cultural ties more closely to Britain than to one another. And (6) each colony would have had its dynamics, if not its distinct inputs, producing different dialect mixtures. In short, the complexity of early American speech communities, which always involved contact and were often multilingual, needs much scholarly attention.

OTHER NEEDS AND POSSIBILITIES. As suggested above, more work needs to use the written record to seek a historical perspective on sound changes, many of which may not be twentieth-century phenomena. Thomas (2001) has made a splendid start on this, but his coverage, often with only one speaker for a large territory, is not deep. More intensive studies can exploit the extraordinary wealth of recordings from the 1930s to the 1960s by folklorists and oral historians, many of whose speakers were born in the latter half of the nineteenth century. Nor does Thomas analyze consonants. Reconstruction of rudiments of the intonation of AE and its varieties has hardly been contemplated, but perhaps it is time to consider what the appropriate research questions would be. Popular commentary in the eighteenth and nineteenth century frequently made reference to voice quality (e.g., the "whine" of New England or the "twang" of the South), offering possible starting points.

In tandem with the two *DARE* indexes, one can explore the development of many regional vocabularies. For example, the first three volumes of the dictionary label 228 items "Appalachian" or "southern Appalachian." The English of these regions is widely believed to be among the most conservative in the country, yet only a fairly small portion of items now concentrated there (e.g., *budget* 'pouch, valise') are evidently archaisms. This suggests that, at least for vocabulary, Appalachian English is strikingly and fundamentally a new variety of AE.

CONCLUSIONS

Good research on early AE begins with well-informed questions and the willingness to employ a variety of methods and sources. Just as diachrony and synchrony need one another, so do speech records and written records. The latter dichotomy is in any case a false one, because the records overlap chronologically and intersect in numerous ways, and some sources (e.g., historical dictionaries) draw on both. As often as feasible, researchers of AE should utilize both speech records and written records to prompt questions, to seek the broadest (in type of source) and widest (in time period) support for their projects, and to confirm their findings.

Good research on early AE is motivated by larger comparative and historical questions concerning language and identity, language status, and language evolution. Much more than at the time of the last report on *Needed Research* twenty years ago, the empirical perspective, basic research tools, and refined, diverse methodologies are at hand to tackle such questions. More than for most other research areas in our field, however, good research on early AE is interdisciplinary. The work of Schneider and Montgomery (2001) on overseer letters would have been impossible without the help of historians to identify documents, help decipher them, and offer assistance in other ways. Collaboration between linguists and their colleagues in other disciplines is the lifeblood of such research.

REFERENCES

Bailey, Guy. 1997. "When Did Southern American English Begin?" In *Englishes around the World: Studies in Honour of Manfred Görlach*, ed. Edgar W. Schneider, 1: 255–75. Amsterdam: Benjamins.

Bailey, Guy, Natalie Maynor, and Patricia Cukor-Avila, eds. 1991. *The Emergence of Black English: Text and Commentary.* Amsterdam: Benjamins.

Bailey, Richard W. 1992. "The First North American Dialect Survey." In *Old English and New: Studies in Language and Linguistics in Honor of Frederic G. Cassidy*, ed. Joan H. Hall, Nick Doane, and Dick Ringler, 305–26. New York: Garland.

———. 1996. *Nineteenth-Century English.* Ann Arbor: Univ. of Michigan Press.

Boberg, Charles. 2001. "The Phonological Status of Western New England." *American Speech* 76: 3–29.

Brewer, Jeutonne Patton. 1974. "The Verb 'be' in Early Black English: A Study Based on the WPA Ex-Slave Narratives." Ph.D. diss., Univ. of North Carolina at Chapel Hill.

Clark, Thomas D. 1956. *Travels in the Old South: A Bibliography.* 3 vols. Norman: Univ. of Oklahoma Press.

Cooley, Marianne. 1995. "Sources for the Study of Eighteenth-Century Literary Dialect." Unpublished MS.

———. 1997. "An Early Representation of African American English." In *Language Variety in the South Revisited*, ed. Cynthia Bernstein, Thomas Nunnally, and Robin Sabino, 51–58. Tuscaloosa: Univ. of Alabama Press.

DARE. *Dictionary of American Regional English.* 1985–. Vol. 1 (A–C), ed. Frederic G. Cassidy. Vols. 2 (D–H) and 3 (I–O), ed. Frederic G. Cassidy and Joan Houston Hall. Vol. 4 (P–Sk), ed. Joan Houston Hall. 4 vols. to date. Cambridge, Mass.: Belknap Press of Harvard Univ. Press.

Dillard, J. L. 1972. *Black English: Its History and Usage in the United States.* New York: Random House.

———. 1992. *A History of American English.* London: Longman.

Dorrill, George T. 1986. *Black and White Speech in the South: Evidence from the Linguistic Atlas of the Middle and South Atlantic States.* Bamberger Beiträge zur englischen Sprachwissenschaft 19. New York: Lang.

Eliason, Norman E. 1956. *Tarheel Talk: An Historical Study of the English Language in North Carolina to 1860.* Chapel Hill: Univ. of North Carolina Press.

Ellis, Michael E. 1984. "The Relationship of Appalachian English with the British Regional Dialects." M.A. thesis, East Tennessee State Univ.

Ewers, Traute. 1996. *The Origin of American Black English: "Be"-Forms in the HOODOO Texts*. Berlin: de Gruyter.

Fischer, David Hackett. 1970. *Historians' Fallacies: Toward a Logic of Historical Thought*. New York: Harper and Row.

———. 1989. *Albion's Seed: Four British Folkways in America*. New York: Oxford Univ. Press.

Hamilton, Anne-Marie. 1998. "The Endurance of Scots in the United States." *Scottish Language* 17: 108–18.

Hyatt, Harry Middleton. 1970–75. *Hoodoo—Witchcraft—Conjuration—Rootwork: Beliefs Accepted by Many Negroes and White Persons, These Being Orally Recorded among Blacks and Whites*. Memoirs of the Alma Egan Hyatt Foundation. 5 vols. Hannibal, Mo.: Western.

Kautzsch, Alexander. 2002. *The Historical Evolution of Earlier African American English: An Empirical Comparison of Early Sources*. Berlin: de Gruyter.

Kirkham, Samuel. 1829. *English Grammar, in Familiar Lectures*. New York: Collins.

Krapp, George Philip. 1925. *The English Language in America*. 2 vols. New York: Ungar.

Kurath, Hans. 1928. "The Origin of the Dialectal Differences in Spoken American English." *Modern Philology* 25: 385–95.

———. 1949. *Word Geography of the Eastern United States*. Ann Arbor: Univ. of Michigan Press.

Kytö, Merja. 1991. *Variation and Diachrony, with Early American English in Focus: Studies on CAN/MAY and SHALL/WILL*. Bamberger Beiträge zur englischen Sprachwissenschaft 28. Frankfurt am Main: Lang.

Labov, William. 1972. "Some Principles of Linguistic Methodology." *Language and Society* 1: 1–20

Labov, William, Sharon Ash, and Charles Boberg, eds. Forthcoming. *Atlas of North American English: Phonetics, Phonology, and Sound Change*. Berlin: de Gruyter.

Laird, Charlton. 1970. *Language in America*. Englewood Cliffs, N.J.: Prentice-Hall.

Lass, Roger. 1990. "Where Do Extraterritorial Englishes Come From? Dialect Input and Recodification in Transported Englishes." In *Papers from the Fifth International Conference on English Historical Linguistics, Cambridge, 6–9 April 1987*, ed. Sylvia M. Adamson, Vivien A. Law, Nigel Vincent, and Susan Wright, 245–80. Amsterdam: Benjamins.

Marckwardt, Albert H. 1958. *American English*. New York: Oxford Univ. Press.

Miller, Kerby A., Arnold Schrier, Bruce D. Boling, and David N. Doyle. 2003. *Irish Immigrants in the Land of Canaan: Letters and Memoirs from Colonial and Revolutionary America, 1675–1815.* Oxford: Oxford Univ. Press.

Miller, Randall M., ed. 1978. *"Dear Master": Letters of a Slave Family.* Ithaca, N.Y.: Cornell Univ. Press.

Montgomery, Michael. 1993. "Review Article: The Linguistic Atlas of the Gulf States." *American Speech* 68: 263–318.

———. 1995. "The Linguistic Value of Ulster Emigrant Letters." *Ulster Folklife* 41: 26–41.

———. 1997. "A Tale of Two Georges: The Language of Irish Indian Traders in Colonial North America." In *Focus on Ireland*, ed. Jeffrey Kallen, 227–54. Amsterdam: Benjamins.

———. 1999. "Eighteenth-Century Sierra Leone Settler English: Another Exported Variety of African American English." *English World-Wide* 20: 1–34.

———. 2001. "British and Irish Antecedents." In *Cambridge History of the English Language*, vol. 6, *American English*, ed. John Algeo, 86–153. Cambridge: Cambridge Univ. Press.

Montgomery, Michael, and Connie C. Eble. Forthcoming. "Historical Perspectives on the *pen/pin* Merger in Southern American English." In *Studies in the History of the English Language II: Conversations between Past and Present*, ed. Anne Curzan. Berlin: de Gruyter.

Montgomery, Michael, Janet M. Fuller, and Sharon DeMarse. 1993. "'The Black Men Has Wives and Sweet Harts [and Third Person Plural *-s*] Jest Like the White Men': Evidence for Verbal *-s* from Written Documents on Nineteenth-Century African American Speech." *Language Variation and Change* 5: 335–54.

Montgomery, Michael, and John M. Kirk. 1996. "The Origin of the Habitual Verb *be* in American Black English: Irish or English or What?" *Belfast Working Papers in Linguistics* 11: 308–33.

Mufwene, Salikoko S. 1996. "The Development of American Englishes: Some Questions from a Creole Genesis Perspective." In *Focus on the USA*, ed. Edgar W. Schneider, 231–64. Amsterdam: Benjamins.

———. 2001. *The Ecology of Language Evolution.* Cambridge: Cambridge Univ. Press.

Mufwene, Salikoko S., John R. Rickford, Guy Bailey, and John Baugh, eds. 1998. *African-American English: Structure, History, and Use.* London: Routledge.

Myhill, John. 1995. "The Use of Features of Present-Day AAVE in the Ex-Slave Recordings." *American Speech* 70: 115–47.

Pederson, Lee, ed. 1986–92. *Linguistic Atlas of the Gulf States.* 7 vols. Athens: Univ. of Georgia Press.

Poplack, Shana, ed. 2000. *The English History of African American English.* Malden, Mass.: Blackwell.

Poplack, Shana, and Sali Tagliamonte. 1989. "There's No Tense Like the Present: Verbal -*s* Inflection in Early Black English." *Language Variation and Change* 1: 47–84.

———. 2001. *African American English in the Diaspora.* Malden, Mass.: Blackwell.

Rawick, George. 1972. *The American Slave: A Composite Autobiography.* 19 vols. Westport, Conn.: Greenwood. Supp., ser. 1, 1977. Supp., ser. 2, 1979.

Read, Allen Walker. 1933. "British Recognition of American Speech in the Eighteenth Century." *Dialect Notes* 6: 313–34. Repr. in *Milestones in the History of English in America,* Publication of the American Dialect Society 86, 37–54, Durham, N.C.: Duke Univ. Press, 2002.

Rickford, John R. 1986. "Social Contact and Linguistic Diffusion." *Language* 62: 245–90.

———. 1998. "The Creole Origins of African-American Vernacular English: Evidence from Copula Absence." In Mufwene et al., 154–200.

———. 1999. *African American Vernacular English: Features, Evolution, Educational Implications.* Malden, Mass.: Blackwell.

Schneider, Edgar W. 1989. *American Earlier Black English: Morphological and Syntactic Variables.* Tuscaloosa: Univ. of Alabama Press.

———. 1997. "Earlier Black English Revisited." In *Language Variety in the South Revisited,* ed. Cynthia Bernstein, Thomas Nunnally, and Robin Sabino, 35–50. Tuscaloosa: Univ. of Alabama Press.

———. Forthcoming. "The English of the Lower South." In *The Legacy of Colonial English: The Study of Transported Dialects,* ed. Raymond Hickey. Cambridge: Cambridge Univ. Press.

Schneider, Edgar W., and Michael Montgomery. 2001. "On the Trail of Early Nonstandard Grammar: An Electronic Corpus of Southern U.S. Antebellum Overseers' Letters." *American Speech* 76: 388–409.

Singler, John Victor. 1991. "Copula Variation in Liberian Settler English and American Black English." In *Verb Phrase Patterns in Black English and Creole,* ed. Walter F. Edwards and Donald Winford, 129–64. Detroit: Wayne State Univ. Press.

Starobin, Robert S., ed. 1974. *Blacks in Bondage: Letters of American Slaves.* New York: New Viewpoint. Repr. New York: Wiener, 1988.

Stephenson, Edward A. 1967. "On the Interpretation of Occasional Spellings." *Publication of the American Dialect Society* 48: 33–50.

Stewart, William A. 1970a. "Historical and Structural Bases for the Recognition of Negro Dialect." In *Linguistics and the Teaching of Standard English to Speakers of Other Languages and Dialects,* ed. James E. Alatis, 239–47. Washington, D.C.: Georgetown Univ. Press.

———. 1970b. "Toward a History of American Negro Dialect." In *Language and Poverty: Perspectives on a Theme,* ed. Frederick Williams, 351–79. Chicago: Markham.

Tagliamonte, Sali, and Jennifer Smith. 2000. "Old *was,* New Ecology: Viewing English through the Sociolinguistic Filter." In Poplack, 141–71.

Thomas, Erik. 2001. *An Acoustic Analysis of Vowel Variation in New World English.* Publication of the American Dialect Society 85. Durham, N.C.: Duke Univ. Press.

Trudgill, Peter. 1986. *Dialects in Contact.* Oxford: Blackwell.

Van Herk, Gerard, and Shana Poplack. Forthcoming. "Rewriting the Past: Bare Verbs in the Ottawa Repository of Early African American Correspondence." *Journal of Pidgin and Creole Languages.*

Viereck, Wolfgang. 1988. "Invariant *be* in an Unnoticed Source of American Early Black English." *American Speech* 63: 291–303.

von Schneidemesser, Luanne, ed. 1999. *An Index by Region, Usage, and Etymology to the "Dictionary of American Regional English," Volumes III.* Publication of the American Dialect Society 82. Durham, N.C.: Duke Univ. Press.

von Schneidemesser, Luanne, and Allan Metcalf, eds. 1993. *An Index by Region, Usage, and Etymology to the "Dictionary of American Regional English," Volumes I and II.* Publication of the American Dialect Society 77. Tuscaloosa: Univ. of Alabama Press.

Wiley, Bell Irwin. 1978. *The Life of Johnny Reb: The Common Soldier of the Confederacy.* Baton Rouge: Louisiana State Univ. Press.

Wolfram, Walt, and Erik R. Thomas. 2002. *The Development of African American English.* Malden, Mass.: Blackwell.

Wright, Laura. 2003. "Eight Grammatical Features of Southern United States Speech Present in Early Modern London Prison Narratives." In *English in the Southern United States,* ed. Stephen J. Nagle and Sara L. Sanders, 36–63. Cambridge: Cambridge Univ. Press.

2. LINGUISTIC ATLASES
OF THE UNITED STATES
AND CANADA

WILLIAM A. KRETZSCHMAR, JR.
University of Georgia

In his report on "Linguistic Geography" for the 1983 *Needed Research* session (McDavid 1984), Raven I. McDavid, Jr., began with an uncharacteristically pessimistic view of the condition of the American Linguistic Atlas projects in American academic life, in brief that they were underappreciated and insecurely housed. He then, more characteristically, admitted that some progress had been made in the previous 20 years, and he described accurately and with some optimism the problems and prospects of each of the major regional projects. Finally, McDavid made recommendations for the future: (1) provision of safe and secure quarters for the field records; (2) microfilm copies of the field records; (3) improved processing of the field materials; (4) completion of the initial regional surveys; and (5) follow-up operations. It is possible to report, now 20 years later, that we are well advanced toward every one of McDavid's recommendations, though not without risk and loss along the way.

The year 1984 was when many of the American Linguistic Atlas projects were nearly lost. When McDavid suddenly died late in that year, less than twelve months after delivering the assessment just described, the University of Chicago made it known that the collections that McDavid had assembled were no longer welcome there. The Chicago decision threatened the materials from the linguistic atlases of the Middle and South Atlantic States (LAMSAS), the North-Central States (LANCS), and New England (LANE), as well as many smaller collections like Guy Lowman's records from Southern England, Lorenzo Turner's Gullah interviews, and materials from disparate places like Oklahoma and the Maritime Provinces. Of course some regional projects would have survived, certainly Lee Pederson's Gulf States (LAGS) project, which was then in the midst of vigorous editorial work, but the archival center of the American Linguistic Atlas effort could literally have ended up in the dumpster. Lest this be thought mere hyperbole, McDavid (1984) described the loss at Harvard in the 1940s of the American Dialect Society's (ADS) early materials for preparation of a dialect dictionary, and the accidental disposal of some of the original LAMSAS records at Chicago in the early 1980s. David Carlson had to rescue what he could from the Linguistic Atlas of the Pacific Northwest (LAPNW) on short notice before its disposal following the death of Carroll Reed. Harold Allen, another pillar of the Atlas effort, in the mid-1980s was fighting cancer in Minnesota and himself looking for a home for the Upper Midwest materials (originals are now in the Newberry Library in Chicago). David Reed and Allan Metcalf were also looking for a home for the Pacific Coast materials. It would have been easy in 1984 and shortly thereafter for the product of so much labor in the American Linguistic Atlas movement to lapse from real existence into memory.

But it did not. Through the good offices of John Algeo, the University of Georgia came forward to receive the Chicago collections (and the new editor-in-chief as well), the only institution among the many that were contacted that expressed its interest in becoming the new archival and editorial site. The collections could more easily be moved because Raven McDavid had set in motion the administrative means for continuing maintenance of the Linguistic Atlas Projects (LAP), and the financial means for baseline editorial expenses for LAMSAS (as described in the appendix). The agreement with Georgia falls into two parts. First, Georgia and the ADS have an agreement that creates a LAP archive, under which Georgia provides adequate space and the ADS retains title to the materials. Arrangements for the Atlas editorial operation are part of the agreement to hire the editor-in-chief, and thus tied to the person and not to the project. By the end of the 1980s the Chicago LAP collection had been augmented by the Linguistic Atlas of the Pacific Coast (LAPC) materials, copies of the surviving materials from the LAPNW, and large quantities of material on both paper and tape (copies of original audio field records) from

LAGS. In later years the collections grew slowly, notably with the addition of materials from Michael Miller's (1999) Savannah River study, tape recordings from Roger Shuy's northern Illinois project whose interviews were included in LANCS, and recordings and other materials from Lee Pederson's Rocky Mountain project. All of these materials follow Atlas protocols. The Georgia site has also occasionally received supporting materials, such as the aluminum platters from early dialect recordings after the Library of Congress had finished recovering their sound, and Howard Dunlap's (1977) important collection of recordings of Atlanta schoolchildren from the 1960s. We continue to maintain an unpublished finding aid for the collections, originally prepared by Ellen Johnson (1997). Thus, by the fall of 1986, McDavid's first recommendation for the future of the LAP had been achieved, safe and secure quarters, and McDavid's administrative and financial planning has permitted formation of an Atlas archive at Georgia of national scope.

McDavid's second recommendation had been substantially accomplished for the materials in his collection before they left Chicago. LAMSAS, LANCS, and some smaller collections were microfilmed in 1983 and 1984 by Regenstein Library of the University of Chicago (McDavid et al. 1982–86). This set of microfilms may no longer be available (the Regenstein Photoduplication Department has not been easy to contact regarding the Atlas series), but a number of copies were purchased and now exist in libraries around the country. The LAPC collection was also microfilmed at the same period, at Bancroft Library of the University of California. Best of all, not just basic materials but a concordance for LAGS was created by University Microfilms (Pederson 1981, 1986). These microfilms protect against accidents in the archives and provide some means (though expensive and limited) of distribution for the materials.

There is much to report about processing of Atlas materials and completion of the regional surveys. The locus of development in the 1980s was Pederson's (1986–92) LAGS project. Michael Montgomery's (1993) review article on LAGS asserts, conservatively in my view, that "LAGS constitutes one of the half-dozen most important scholarly achievements in American English linguistics in the twentieth century" (264). LAGS is much larger than any other regional Atlas except the still-incomplete LAMSAS, and much more complex. It is the first American survey to balance region, social characteristics, and population in a true quota sample. It is the first American survey fully to embrace technological advances, such as the portable Uher tape recorder for fieldwork in the late 1960s and early 1970s, and then computer assistance for editorial work in the 1980s and thereafter, the mainframe early and later personal computers. It is the first American survey to integrate descriptive maps with full presentation of the data and to make descriptive quantitative assessments of the data. Finally, LAGS is the first American survey to publish its data as digital files, along with programs to aid in the visualization and analysis of the data, as the Automatic Atlas in Microform (AAM) (see McDaniel 1989; AAM files are now available from the LAP Web site, http://us.english.uga.edu). Pederson not only finished his Atlas, a claim that only Hans Kurath and Harold Allen could share in America, but revolutionized and thoroughly modernized the practice of linguistic geography along the way, all the while maintaining comparability with earlier Atlas research. That practically nobody, whether in the ADS or outside it, appeared to notice this remarkable achievement (as Montgomery points out) has much to do with the changing currents of academic politics. Good work will out, and we can trust that Pederson will receive the recognition that he deserves from users of LAGS over many decades to come. In his review article Montgomery provides a valuable overview of the seven volumes of LAGS, plus microfilm and computer materials, and so no repetition is needed here. He also comments on the "limitations of LAGS," chief among which was his judgment of the potential difficulty of its use by readers.[1]

Montgomery has materially assisted LAGS users in other parts of his review, and especially in his description of the LAGS electronic materials (offered for downloading on the LAP Web site with the LAGS electronic files), and so it would be inappropriate to take him too much to task. The point to take home about LAGS is that it retained comparability of its data with the data collected for other American atlases, which by necessity meant the continuation of many traditional practices, and at the same time greatly advanced the methods of collection and presentation of the data. Its only real limitations are those of any very large and well-accomplished project: it is what it is, which is perhaps not what every user might want it to be, and it takes time and effort to become familiar with LAGS and to use it well.

The LAMSAS project had to wait until the late 1980s, while the Georgia archive was being established and while the editor-in-chief developed computer methods, to resume active editorial work. The first two fascicles of LAMSAS data were edited by McDavid and O'Cain and published by the University of Chicago Press (McDavid and O'Cain 1980), and another fascicle was completed with the same production methods but was supposed to remain unpublished until steady production could be resumed with new computer methods (it did not and will not now appear). Thus, unlike Pederson's computer innovations for LAGS, which did not have to address any preexisting format, mine for LAMSAS had to be focused on resumption of publication of the fascicle series. This required a means to manipulate detailed Atlas phonetic transcriptions on computer, and these tools were in hand by the late 1980s, with assistance from the National Science Foundation (NSF), after three years of work on computer type founding (Kretzschmar 1987, 1989) and programming for a suitable database (Kretzschmar and Konopka 1996). Unfortunately, shortly after the tools were ready, the University of Chicago Press canceled the fascicle series. The press did, however, agree to publish the LAMSAS handbook, which was printed from camera-ready copy prepared with the typographic systems intended for the fascicle series (Kretzschmar et al. 1993). The typographic and database systems supported work with National Endowment for the Humanities (NEH) funding for two years in the early 1990s to begin to keyboard LAMSAS data for the fascicle series, and so a significant quantity of LAMSAS data was converted to digital form. When it came time to reapply for funding the application was not approved, and neither were many subsequent NEH applications in the following years. NEH has also declined to fund proposals to digitize LANE and LANCS data from the Georgia archive. However, NSF did fund the keyboarding of all of the data collected from African Americans interviewed for LAMSAS, plus the Gullah data collected by Lorenzo Turner with the Atlas questionnaire. Today, therefore, nearly 25% of overall LAMSAS data has been keyboarded, all of the African American data and a smaller portion for the rest of the informants. All of the data in digital form contains responses in standard orthography; all of the files keyboarded during the original NEH grant also contain phonetic transcriptions; files for African American speakers contain phonetic transcriptions for only about eighty items deemed valuable for phonological analysis and comparisons; and files for all LAMSAS speakers, which we have continued to keyboard as limited funding has been available, contain only orthographic, not phonetic, renderings of responses.

When the University of Chicago Press canceled the fascicle series and no other publisher could be persuaded to take it up, we began to investigate electronic means of publication. As early as 1993 we were experimenting with electronic file transfer methods, notably "gopher," working especially to make access to the data interactive and user friendly. The first LAP system administrator, Rafal Konopka, one day commented on a new technology, the World Wide Web. We immediately began work to implement a Web site, and by 1995 Konopka had built the first version of a comprehensive LAP Web site. Not only did the site make it possible for users to get information about different regional projects, it enabled complete interactive access to LAMSAS (for a brief description in print, see Kretzschmar 1999). Users could browse and search the database of speakers and all the digitized files of data. Moreover, users could generate maps interactively which plotted the occurrence of a linguistic feature in the survey area, plus where some other variant was found or where no data was elicited for the feature (for the development of interactive mapping techniques, see Kirk and Kretzschmar 1992; Kretzschmar 1992). The site, http://us.english.uga.edu, has been maintained and enhanced ever since, including a major revision in 1998. Another major revision is in the works (see http://us.english.uga.edu/new). We may still offer electronic access only to data that we hold in electronic form, which consists of some LAMSAS data, the LAGS electronic files and programs, and electronic versions of the LAPNW data prepared by David Carlson. We would be happy to offer electronic data from LANE, LANCS, LAPC, and other projects as soon as they become available in digital form (we have been in contact with Beverly Flanigan at Ohio University about possible digitizing of some LANCS material, following the recent donation of copies of the LANCS materials there). The LAP Web site offers the framework for, though not as yet the substance of, Hans Kurath's dream of an American Atlas that covers the entire country.

After the completion of LAGS fieldwork, Lee Pederson turned to the Rocky Mountain region and continued to send field-workers there as editorial work on LAGS proceeded (Pederson and Madsen 1989). During the next decade Pederson oversaw the collection of interviews according to a grid plan (Pederson 1996a); the planned number of interviews was completed in Wyoming and Utah, and substantial progress was made in Colorado. These interviews were conducted with a modified set of worksheets designed to create a three-hour interview, as opposed to the six-hour or longer interviews with the traditional questionnaire (Pederson 1996b). The approximately 300 targets of Western worksheets carried over much from the 800+ items investigated in the East, but the changing times demanded a shorter interview. Recently, as Georgia students have shown an interest in carrying on Western fieldwork, Pederson and I have agreed to work together toward a Linguistic Atlas of the Western States. At this writing, additional Western States interviews have been conducted in West Texas (El Paso), Colorado (with assistance from NSF), and California. It is our view that it is worthwhile trying to complete national coverage with Atlas methods as resources permit, even though these Western States interviews will have been conducted at a substantially later time than the first interviews on the East Coast; the difference in time will look small to posterity.

While we are still interested in completion of primary national coverage, secondary studies are beginning to be made. Perhaps first among them is Ellen Johnson's return in 1990 to communities first visited by Guy Lowman in the 1930s (Johnson

1996). Johnson elicited responses for 150 lexical items from speakers with the same social characteristics as those that Lowman had interviewed. Contrary to what many consider common sense, Johnson found that the vocabulary in the region is richer now than it was in the 1930s. She also found that fewer responses from the contemporary data could be correlated with regional and social variables than from the 1930s data.[2] A dissertation and article by Burkette (2001a, 2001b) and a master's thesis by Hoover (2001) both compare Atlas results with new contemporary fieldwork. We may expect many more such studies, both full-scale comparisons and use of LAP data as historical evidence in more focused studies (such as Thomas 2003, which inspects LAMSAS data in an otherwise acoustical-phonetic analysis of change in Southern vowel glides), since earlier Atlas interviews offer fine opportunities for investigation of linguistic change in real time.

The future bodes well for LAP. The work of the last two decades has been described as a "resurgence" by Chambers and Trudgill (1998, 20), an accurate name for intense activity in the LAP which is not yet complete, indeed still in process of radical redevelopment. Several publications in recent years have established new theoretical expectations for LAP (e.g., Pederson 1995, 1996b; Kretzschmar and Schneider 1996; Kretzschmar 1995, 1996, 1998, 2002; Kretzschmar and Tamasi forthcoming). Taking impetus from the work of Gilliéron, the new approach does not simply submerge Atlas work beneath the tide of sociolinguistics (as Chambers and Trudgill 1998 appears to suggest) but instead promotes it for its own special qualities and affiliates it with other empirical approaches to linguistics such as corpus linguistics (Kretzschmar 1999). Both Pederson and Kretzschmar (especially as a result of consultation with Edgar Schneider in the late 1980s) paid particular attention to modern ideas about sampling in survey research; the LAGS grid was established from the beginning as a valid quota sample, and chapter 2 of Kretzschmar et al. (1993) describes LAMSAS methods in terms of modern survey practices and shows that, within limits, it may be interpreted as such a sample. Both in LAGS and now in the Western states, the interview style has become more conversational, more in line with interview practices in sociolinguistics, though, of course, the need to elicit particular targets will not allow for completely undirected conversation. Some of the best conversational passages in the Western states interviews, for instance, have been submitted for inclusion in the spoken language section of the American National Corpus.

The most recent work at the Georgia editorial site, in addition to maintenance of the archives and extension of the fieldwork in the Western states, seeks to carry the Atlas effort even further in the next generation. For presentation of data, this means multimedia on the Internet, including transcripts, sound, and analytical information all linked together so that users can read and hear and make generalizations about interviews interactively. This will require substantial developmental work in text encoding and multimedia programming. We are, for instance, working toward a digital archive of Southern speech by converting LAGS audio tapes into digital sound files (we have over 60Gb of sound already on CDs). We are also testing, with NSF funding, a new one-hour interview format which collects many targets from the traditional and Western states questionnaires, but in addition includes fixed-format elicitation of the kind favored by speech scientists and perceptual data about local speech. The new format has been designed to provide data for many consumers of linguistic information, according to the following goals:

1. Interviews must yield information that addresses the needs of speech science.
2. Interviews must yield information that addresses the needs of Natural Language Processing.
3. Interviews must be compatible, to the extent possible, with both previous Linguistic Atlas data and with contemporary sociolinguistic research.
4. Interviews must take advantage of contemporary practices in survey research and must be planned in expectation of quantitative processing.
5. Interviews must be presented fully and fairly for analysis.
6. It must be possible to conduct the interviews, transcribe them, and publish them on the Web with moderate funding and within a reasonable time.

These goals will be difficult to achieve, but not impossible. In the last two decades work on the LAP has successfully met the challenge of new technology, and its practitioners have shown that they are willing, while honoring and drawing value from the work of their predecessors, to change with the times. In a way, the times have caught up with the original goals of Atlas work, in that technology has now truly made it possible to store and process large enough quantities of real talk so that we can deal effectively with variation in language in use.

APPENDIX

Report to the American Dialect Society Executive Council
on the Hans Kurath Fund and Linguistic Atlas Projects, Fall 2002

BILL KRETZSCHMAR, *Editor-in-Chief, LAP*

After questions were raised at the 2002 American Dialect Society (ADS) Executive Council meeting, I was asked to prepare a report on the origin and present status of the Hans Kurath Fund. This is that report. Because the Fund was established in support of the Linguistic Atlas Projects, I have taken the liberty of also reporting on the origin and current status of the Atlas.

FUND FOR SUPPORT OF LINGUISTIC ATLAS PROJECTS. Attachment 1 is a transcript of the founding document of the Hans Kurath Fund for the Linguistic Atlas (hereafter Kurath Fund), which was drafted and later approved by the ADS Executive Council. It clearly delineates the purposes and management of the Kurath Fund. There are two beneficiaries: first, "editing and publication of the Linguistic Atlas of the Middle and South Atlantic States" (LAMSAS), and secondarily "research for and publication of other works dealing with American linguistic geography." Administrative oversight is granted to the ADS, whose Executive Council approves the appointments of the Kurath Fund Trustees and whose Executive Secretary disburses the funds. The "ultimate authority over the fund" is vested in the Kurath Fund Trustees, whose instructions control the receipt, investment, and disbursement of funds. The other person with an official function in the founding document is the editor-in-chief of LAMSAS, who is empowered to nominate trustees in consultation with the current trustees, prior to the approval of the nomination by the ADS Executive Council.

This elegantly simple document has served well over the years. In practice, the Trustees have from the beginning delegated the creation of the annual report and budget mentioned in the founding document to the editor-in-chief of LAMSAS (see below), but have reserved their right to comment on and approve the report. Neither the Trustees nor the editor-in-chief of LAMSAS has taken an active role in the investment of the capital of the Kurath Fund, which has largely been monitored by the ADS Executive Secretary. Because the ADS has an IRS 501c3 tax-exempt ruling, the Kurath Fund is officially a part of ADS rather than a separate entity, which would have required a separate ruling. Trustees have been nominated and approved each year as provided in the founding document; the current Trustees are Ellen Johnson, Mike Linn, and Lee Pederson. In addition to the formally-approved trustees, Virginia McDavid has always been included in consultation and reporting associated with the Kurath Fund.

The funds disbursed each year have consistently been provided to the editor-in-chief of LAMSAS through the agency of a subcontract agreement with the University of Georgia (UGA). Each year the Executive Secretary writes a letter to UGA to establish the spending limit for the year ($8000/year in the late 1980s, $10000/year in the early 1990s, more recently $12000/year). UGA handles the day-to-day accounting for actual expenditures without any charge for indirect costs, and bills the Executive Secretary periodically for money actually spent. The cumulative total expenditure from the subcontract between July 1989 and September 30, 2002, is as follows:

Salaries	$110,645.64
Operating Expenses	$ 22,230.57
Equipment	$ 1,157.24
Other	$ 2,092.43
TOTAL	$136,125.88

Over the years the vast majority of expenditures have paid salaries for student workers. Most of the expenses were in support of editing and publication of LAMSAS, although other major efforts have included copying LAGS audio tapes, and receiving and archiving Linguistic Atlas collections from other parts of the country such as the Pacific Coast and Pacific Northwest. Allocation of funds to projects other than LAMSAS has occurred by mutual agreement between the editor-in-chief of LAMSAS and the editor of the other project, within the scope of the annual budget approved by the Trustees. A much smaller portion of expenses over the years has provided matching funds for an NEH grant ($20,000 not routed through the subcontract), bought or provided matching funds for software and equipment, and provided equipment maintenance and repair, copying services, shipping costs, and supplies ("operating expenses"). Currently, the largest part of the annual budget pays for one-half of a graduate assistantship used for system administration of the computer server on which the Linguistic Atlas projects web site and ADS web site are maintained; the lion's share of the remainder pays for student assistants who continue to digitize LAMSAS data and maintain the archive of Atlas materials (notably through creation of digital audio files in recent years). Formal annual reports and budgets have not been generated in every fiscal year by the editor-in-chief of LAMSAS because the pattern of expenditure has been essentially similar every year for nearly ten years, but the editor-in-chief has provided periodic comprehensive accounting to the Trustees and sought their approval for any divergence from the normal pattern.

During the years since the inception of the Kurath Fund, LAMSAS and Linguistic Atlas Projects archive have relied on the Fund for a baseline of dependable support. However, the editor-in-chief has consistently sought additional funding. Since 1986 UGA has provided office and archival space, office supplies and services, travel and occasional supplemental funding, grant matching funds, and the salary of a part-time secretary and the editor-in-chief. Federal agencies such as NEH and NSF have awarded several grants for Linguistic Atlas Projects research during the same period; such grant funding has provided essentially all of the computers and other equipment in use for LAP. While UGA and grant funding have provided many times the dollar contribution of the Kurath Fund to LAP, it is certainly true that the Kurath Fund has provided the key funding that has made possible the effective use of other resources. It would not be possible to operate the current UGA editorial and archival site without the support of the Kurath Fund, at or near the levels of expenditure currently in place.

LINGUISTIC ATLAS PROJECTS AND THE ADS. In 1984, the year after the creation of the Kurath Fund and the same year in which we later suffered the sudden and premature death of Raven McDavid, the relationship between the Linguistic Atlas Projects and ADS was finally made official. The founding document for the relationship is provided as attachment 2. It too is elegantly simple.

By the early 1980s, many of the autonomous regional projects which made up the Linguistic Atlas Projects (LAP) had come under the care of Raven McDavid at the University of Chicago, this without any formal agreement about title or management of the records or any provision for their maintenance. By executing the document of relationship, McDavid vested title for "all materials belonging to the project" in the ADS, and also created a management structure for "the project" consisting of an editor-in-chief, advised by an Advisory Committee, whose members were to be nominated by the editor-in-chief and confirmed in office by the ADS Executive Council. While heretofore every Atlas project had been autonomous, the document of relationship created a central entity with an editor-in-chief, under which the different regional atlases could be maintained. Clearly, any regional project which was still independently managed at the time of the document of relationship, such as the Upper Midwest and Gulf States Atlases, were not bound by it. However, the new entity called "Linguistic Atlas Projects" provided a mechanism under which additional collections of atlas materials besides LAMSAS and the North-Central materials (the core of McDavid's collections) could later be maintained.

While ADS holds title to materials in the LAP, the editor-in-chief is empowered to determine "practices and policies." Unlike the Trustees of the Kurath Fund, the members of the LAP Advisory Board were given only an advisory role, not "ultimate authority." The process for appointments to Advisory Board memberships and to editorships is similar to the process for Trustee appointments: the editor-in-chief is empowered to nominate, in consultation with the Advisory Board, before ratification by the ADS Executive Council. However, if a new editor-in-chief should be needed, the Advisory Board is empowered to make the nomination before ratification by the ADS Executive Council.

There is a special clause in the agreement on budget and financial matters, which are "the responsibility of the editor-in-chief," subject only to the condition that the Advisory Board should be consulted for "major changes." This clause mentions the Kurath Fund as having been "established to support LAMSAS and other Linguistic Atlas projects." This clause could potentially be seen to create a conflict between the Trustees of the Kurath Fund and the editor-in-chief, who are granted "authority" and "responsibility," respectively. However, the "authority" of the Trustees specifically governs investment and disbursement of the money in the Kurath Fund, while the "responsibility" of the editor-in-chief governs the planning and execution of expenditures for LAMSAS and other parts of the LAP. Thus the evolution of the current practice for use of the Kurath Fund: the editor-in-chief creates a budget based on practices and policies, and the Trustees consider and approve funding for disbursements.

Over the years additional Atlas collections have joined the LAP, including the Pacific Coast, copies of the Pacific Northwest materials, copies of the Gulf States materials, Western States materials, Miller's Augusta materials, and others. Still other materials from the Upper Midwest and Iron Range will eventually join the archive. In every case where an editor for a project remains active and interested in project materials, the editor-in-chief has arranged for maintenance of the collection jointly with the project editor, while also accepting responsibility for the collection's safekeeping under the LAP structure.

The editor-in-chief has not been as diligent about the maintenance of the Advisory Board. Many of those who were originally named as editors or as members of the Advisory Committee are now retired from active participation in the field, or deceased. However, the following people have at one point been ratified as Atlas editors or members of the Advisory Committee and remain active in linguistic geography and the ADS: besides Bill Kretzschmar (currently editor-in-chief), Virginia McDavid, Ron Butters, Allan Metcalf, Michael Linn, Lee Pederson, David Carlson, and Ellen Johnson. These people de facto constitute the standing LAP Advisory Committee, and should be acknowledged as such by the ADS Executive Council.

The simple and elegant structure established in 1984 has worked well over the years because of the collegial relations between practitioners and ADS members interested in the field. LAP continues as an active venture of the ADS in large part because we all cooperate, not because authority has been vested in one or another person. We can hope that such a heritage of cooperation continues into the future. At the same time, it is also a good thing for us, while we are cooperating, to have a central structure like LAP around which we can rally and develop new ventures. This in fact has always been the common practice among Atlas editors, first in association with Hans Kurath at Brown and Michigan and later in association with Raven McDavid at Chicago, even before the formal creation of the LAP structure in 1984.

LINGUISTIC ATLAS PROJECTS AND UGA. After the death of Raven McDavid in 1984, the University of Chicago made it clear that it would not continue to provide space for LAP. I immediately began to make inquiries about a new home for the project. Through the good offices of John Algeo and others at Georgia, LAP was able to be relocated at UGA. Attachment 3 shows the agreement that was reached. ADS retains title to all materials, in line with the creation of the LAP structure. The agreement with UGA makes no mention of any provision for active work on the materials, only archival space under suitable conditions. UGA's substantial support for LAP has occurred under the auspices of my faculty employment agreement, which specified a location for editorial work in the English Department's building, and made provision for a part-time secretary and for LAP access to the normal office supplies and services of the department. Thus, the archival agreement between UGA and ADS for LAP materials can survive my tenure as a faculty member, but, unless additional arrangements are made, the working editorial operation of LAP will not.

ATTACHMENT 1
Fund for Support of Linguistic Atlas Projects
(Approved October 17, 1983, by the ADS Executive Council)

1. This fund is named the Hans Kurath Fund for the Linguistic Atlas, in honor of the initiator of the Linguistic Atlas of the United States and Canada.

2. It supports, first, the editing and publication of the Linguistic Atlas of the Middle and South Atlantic States (now under the editorship of Raven I. McDavid, Jr.),* and second, research for and publication of other works dealing with American linguistic geography.

3. It is administered by the American Dialect Society under the direction of three trustees, serving three-year staggered terms, eligible for reappointment.

4. The first trustees (nominated by McDavid) are Thomas Creswell, Michigan City, Indiana; A. M. Kinloch, University of New Brunswick; Glenn T. McDavid, Chicago. They will draw lots to determine who will have the one-year, two-year, and three-year terms.*

5. Subsequent appointments to the trustees will be made by nomination of the editor-in-chief of LAMSAS, in consultation with the current trustees, and with approval of the ADS Executive Council.

6. The trustees have ultimate authority over the fund. Following their instructions (usually in an annual report and budget), the ADS Executive Secretary will receive and invest contributions, royalties, and other sources of funds; and will disburse funds to the editor-in-chief of LAMSAS and others.

7. ADS general funds are not liable for support of the Kurath Fund, and the Kurath Fund is not liable for support of ADS operations. Administrative expenses for the Kurath Fund, such as bank service charges and brokerage fees, will be paid by the Kurath Fund.

*These provisions apply to circumstances at the time of establishment of the Kurath Fund.

ATTACHMENT 2
Linguistic Atlas Projects and the American Dialect Society
July 17, 1984

When it was begun half a century ago, the Linguistic Atlas of the United States and Canada obtained the sponsorship of the American Council of Learned Societies, the national association of the chief learned societies in the humanities. The ACLS itself served as publisher of the first of the regional projects to be completed, the *Linguistic Atlas of New England* (Providence, 1939–43).

Originally the LAUSC was envisioned as a single continent-wide project under the direction of Hans Kurath. Practical limitations on resources available for the project (to survey the whole United States would have cost $664,000 in 1930) made it necessary to proceed region by region. After starting with New England, Kurath entrusted the other regional projects to scholars in those regions who could obtain the necessary local support. Though coordinated with each other, the regional projects thus developed independently.

Kurath himself continued work on the atlas of the Middle and South Atlantic States, eventually entrusting the editorship to Raven I. McDavid, Jr. Meanwhile, Albert H. Marckwardt had undertaken the Linguistic Atlas of the North-Central States; after Marckwardt's untimely death, McDavid had to assume direction of that project too.

Safekeeping of these two projects, LAMSAS and LANCS, together with Kurath's original records for New England, the Maritimes, and southern England, has now been entrusted by McDavid to the American Dialect Society, which was admitted as a constituent society of ACLS in 1962.

This is the nature of the relationship for each of the projects:

1. The ADS retains title to all materials belonging to the project, unless otherwise specified.

2. The project is under the direction of an editor in chief (currently Raven I. McDavid, Jr.), who determines practices and policies.

3. The project has an Advisory Committee, which advises the editor in chief on practices and policies.

4. Members of the Advisory Committee are proposed by the editor in chief, approved by current members of the Advisory Committee, and confirmed in office by the ADS Executive Council.

5. Appointments to editorships are made by the editor in chief with approval by the Advisory Committee and ratification by the ADS Executive Council. Minor appointments (to assistantships, etc.) do not require approval.

6. Appointment of a new editor in chief is made on recommendation of the Advisory Committee with ratification by the ADS Executive Council.

7. Budget and finances are the responsibility of the editor in chief, who will consult with the Advisory Committee concerning major changes. ADS general funds do not support LAMSAS, and LAMSAS resources do not support ADS. The special Kurath Fund for the Linguistic Atlas has been established to support LAMSAS and other Linguistic Atlas projects.

8. Relocation of the archives, gifts of the materials, or changes in this agreement require the approval of the editor in chief, the Advisory Committee, and the ADS Executive Council.

9. A local advisory committee may be established to act as liaison with local authorities where the project is housed. Members of this committee are nominated by the editor in chief, with approval of the Advisory Committee and ratification by the ADS Executive Council. They are ex officio members of the Advisory Committee.

Current staffing and membership of LAMSAS:
Editor in chief, Raven I. McDavid, Jr.
Associate editor, Virginia G. McDavid
Assistant editor and designated successor as editor in chief, William A. Kretzschmar, Jr.
Advisory Committee: John Fisher, Eric Hamp, Archibald Hill, Robert Hogan, James McMillan, William Moulton, Herbert Penzl, Randolph Quirk, Ronald Butters, Lurline Coltharp, Larry Davis, Allan Metcalf.
Local advisory committee (U. of South Carolina): Milledge Seigler, Kenneth Toombs, William Workman.

Current staffing of LANCS:
Editor in chief, Raven I. McDavid, Jr.
Pronunciation volume, Alva L. Davis
Grammatical volume, Virginia G. McDavid and Michael D. Linn.
Vocabulary volume, William A. Kretzschmar, Jr.

ATTACHMENT 3
Agreement between ADS and UGA regarding Linguistic Atlas Projects

AGREEMENT. This agreement specifies the terms and conditions under which certain collections of materials for dialect research under control of the American Dialect Society (hereafter ADS) may be moved to and maintained at the University of Georgia Library (hereafter UGL).

ADS GOALS. The ADS is interested to provide for the secure maintenance of dialect collections under its control, to promote active work on those collections, and to expand the coverage of its collections, all in order to move towards a more complete and comprehensive description of English dialects, in particular American English dialects. In furtherance of these goals, the ADS is willing to assist in the establishment of an active editorial site for dialect research at the University of Georgia, especially in conjunction with the hiring by the University of a faculty on-site editor who is associated with and acceptable to the ADS.

NATURE OF ADS COLLECTIONS. The ADS holds title to the fieldrecords and associated materials of several of the autonomous regional divisions of the American Linguistic Atlas Project, as inaugurated by Hans Kurath in 1929. Collections to be moved to UGL at the time the faculty on-site editor assumes residence include:

1. Linguistic Atlas of the Middle and South Atlantic States [LAMSAS], and associated materials. c. 150,000 pp. Fieldrecords based upon a questionnaire of c. 105 pp. and informant sketches for 1216 informants from Ontario south to Florida in the region of American primary settlement. Associated materials include a) Southern England records by Guy Lowman (the only directly comparable evidence for the study of British and American English), b) Gullah records by Lorenzo Turner (the most extensive materials for the study of Sea Island speech), and c) Canadian Maritime records by Henry Alexander (evidence for eastern Canada directly comparable to American work).
2. Linguistic Atlas of the North-Central States [LANCS]. c. 50,000 pp. Fieldrecords based upon a questionnaire of c. 75 pp. and informant sketches for 564 informants from Ontario south to Kentucky and Ohio west to the Mississippi.

In addition to these two major collections, the ADS controls materials related to the Linguistic Atlas of New England [LANE] (fieldrecords, etc.) presently stored at the University of South Carolina; these materials will be located with the LAMSAS and LANCS materials.

Sometime after the establishment of the collections at UGL, possibly within a year, it will be possible to add the fieldrecords and informant sketches of the Linguistic Atlas of the Pacific Coast [LAPC], c. 50,000 pp. Copies of the taped fieldrecords (5200 hours) for the Linguistic Atlas of the Gulf States [LAGS] will also be made available by the Director of LAGS. These two collections should be located with the LAMSAS and LANCS collections. If other major research collections become available, the ADS will try to acquire them or copies of them to locate together with the existing archive at UGL. Official title for all collections and working materials thus acquired will be retained by ADS.

The condition of materials within the collections is variable: LAPC materials will generally be bound volumes; LAGS materials consist of reel-to-reel audio tapes; other materials exist as loose sheets of old, high-acid paper stored in file folders.

TITLE TO THE MATERIALS. ADS will retain title to any material transferred to UGL. Materials should be considered on indefinite loan to UGL as long as such loan is mutually agreeable to UGL and ADS. ADS could consider making a permanent gift of the materials only if permanent support (such as a separate endowment) were realized.

CHANGES IN LOCATION OF THE MATERIALS. Collections will be moved to UGL at times and under conditions mutually agreed upon by UGL and ADS. After the original transference of any collection to UGL, either UGL or ADS must provide one year's notice (unless a shorter period is mutually agreed upon) of intent to remove that collection from UGL.

MAINTENANCE OF COLLECTIONS BY UGL. Specific circumstances of storage and archiving by UGL will be mutually agreed upon by UGL and the faculty on-site editor, who will make himself available for whatever assistance he can offer for the cataloguing of collections. Generally speaking, the collections will be stored under conditions which will tend to prolong the life of fragile paper records, and in a manner which permits relatively rapid access by students and scholars wishing to use the collections (i.e. storage which would require significant advance notice for access would not be acceptable). ADS does not have the resources to provide continuing financial assistance for maintenance of the collections.

ACCESS TO THE COLLECTIONS. The collections will be available to students and scholars for use within the Special Collections Section (or other controlled, supervised working area) of UGL, under the usual terms and conditions for use of materials in Special Collections. Publication, reproduction, or photocopying of any materials from any collection will not be permitted except with the permission of the faculty on-site editor, this in order to protect the privacy of informants. Since the faculty on-site editor will be directing active research on portions of the materials in working space outside UGL, the editor will have access to remove relevant materials from UGL to that working space, at his discretion, for as long as the materials are required for active study. When materials are so removed, it is the editor's responsibility to control access to them by outside students and scholars, and to provide what security he can for the materials.

> Agreed and Signed [1986],
>
> David Bishop, Director, UGL
> On behalf of UGL
>
> William A. Kretzschmar, Jr., Faculty On-Site Editor,
> and Editor-in-Chief, LAMSAS and LANCS
> On behalf of ADS

NOTES

1. Pederson achieved, many times over through different innovative methods, the central goal of the American Atlases of full and fair presentation of the data, and that objectivity of description is what gives LAGS its enduring value. If Montgomery thought that potential users would find LAGS data to be inaccessible, one must wonder what he had in mind as an alternative to the most meticulously indexed, thoroughly described, and comprehensively presented body of data of which I am aware anywhere. It is a basic error to expect a descriptive atlas to be self-interpreting, because the act of interpretation might be thought to undercut the objectivity of the presentation of data. An atlas is simply not the same thing as a summary, and, as Pederson (1995) himself has noted, it is unfair for users to assume that dialects will emerge naturally from the data. Kurath created interpretive summaries separately from the LANE and his plans for LAMSAS (Kurath 1949; Atwood 1953; Kurath and McDavid 1961). Subsequent to Mongomery's review, Pederson (1993) has written an article which may serve as a guide for new users. Essays like Bailey, Wikle and Tillery (1997) and Bailey and Tillery (1999) provide a more objective assessment of how LAGS methods compare to some other possible data-collection practices.

2. This does not necessarily mean that American English is more homogenous now, though Johnson's results do demand interpretation, especially when sociolinguistics has become as popular as it has in the last two decades. The size and particular location of the study probably have much to do with the result, since other evidence (notably Labov's *Telsur Project* 2003) suggests that the earlier pattern of mountain, piedmont, and lowland varieties in the South may be in the process of radical change. Johnson says (pers. com., 2001) that her "most striking finding was fewer correlations [of lexical items] with regions OF THE SOUTH due, I believe, to the fact that what was once a transitional area, with upland and lowland features mixed, has now become the focal area."

REFERENCES

Atwood, E. Bagby. 1953. *A Survey of Verb Forms in the Eastern United States.* Ann Arbor: Univ. of Michigan Press.

Bailey, Guy, and Jan Tillery. 1999. "The Rutledge Effect: The Impact of Interviewers on Survey Results in Linguistics." *American Speech* 74: 389–402.

Bailey, Guy, Tom Wikle, and Jan Tillery. 1997. "The Effects of Methods on Results in Dialectology." *English World-Wide* 18: 35–63.

Burkette, Allison. 2001a. "An Examination of Language Variation in a Small Blue Ridge Community." Ph.D. diss., Univ. of Georgia.

———. 2001b. "The Story of Chester Drawers." *American Speech* 76: 139–57.

Chambers, J. K., and Peter Trudgill. 1998. *Dialectology*. 2d ed. Cambridge: Cambridge Univ. Press.

Dunlap, Howard G. 1977. *Social Aspects of a Verb Form: Native Atlanta Fifth-Grade Speech—The Present Tense of "to be."* Publication of the American Dialect Society 61–62. University: Univ. of Alabama Press.

Hoover, Sandra. 2001. "Lexical Change and Variation in Farming Words, 1970–2001." M.A. thesis, Univ. of Georgia.

Johnson, Ellen. 1996. *Lexical Change and Variation in the Southeastern United States, 1930–1990*. Tuscaloosa: Univ. of Alabama Press.

———. 1997. "Finding Aid for the Linguistic Atlas Archives." Unpublished MS. Hargrett Library, Univ. of Georgia. Updated as required (last major update by Betsy Barry).

Kirk, John, and William A. Kretzschmar, Jr. 1992. "Interactive Linguistic Mapping of Dialect Features." *Literary and Linguistic Computing* 7: 168–75.

Kretzschmar, William A., Jr. 1987. "From Manuscript to Print on a Budget." *Editors' Notes* 6.2: 11–19.

———. 1989. "Phonetic Display and Output." In Kretzschmar, Schneider, and Johnson, 47–53.

———. 1992. "Interactive Computer Mapping for the Linguistic Atlas of the Middle and South Atlantic States (LAMSAS)." In *Old English and New: Essays in Language and Linguistics in Honor of Frederic G. Cassidy*, ed. Joan H. Hall, Nick Doane, and Dick Ringler, 400–414. New York: Garland.

———. 1995. "Dialectology and Sociolinguistics: Same Coin, Different Currency." *Language Sciences* 17: 271–82.

———. 1996. "Quantitative Areal Analysis of Dialect Features." *Language Variation and Change* 8: 13–39.

———. 1998. "Analytical Procedure and Three Technical Types of Dialect." In *From the Gulf States and Beyond: The Legacy of Lee Pederson and*

LAGS, ed. Michael B. Montgomery and Thomas E. Nunnally, 167–85. Tuscaloosa: Univ. of Alabama Press.

———. 1999. "The Future of Dialectology." In *Dialectal Variation in English: Proceedings of the Harold Orton Centenary Conference 1998*, ed. Clive Upton and Katie Wales, 271–88. Leeds Studies in English 30. Leeds: School of English, Univ. of Leeds.

———. 2002. "Dialectology and the History of the English Language." In *Studies in the History of English: A Millennial Perspective*, ed. Donka Minkova and Robert Stockwell, 79–108. Berlin: de Gruyter.

Kretzschmar, William A., Jr., and Rafal Konopka. 1996. "Management of Linguistic Databases." *Journal of English Linguistics* 24: 61–70.

Kretzschmar, William A., Jr., and Edgar W. Schneider. 1996. *Introduction to Quantitative Analysis of Linguistic Survey Data: An Atlas by the Numbers*. Thousand Oaks, Calif.: Sage.

Kretzschmar, William A., Jr., Edgar W. Schneider, and Ellen Johnson, eds. 1989. *Computer Methods in Dialectology*. Special issue of *Journal of English Linguistics* 22.1.

Kretzschmar, William A., Jr., and Susan Tamasi. Forthcoming. "Distributional Foundations for a Theory of Language Change." *World Englishes*.

Kretzschmar, William A., Jr., et al. 1993. *Handbook of the Linguistic Atlas of the Middle and South Atlantic States*. Chicago: Univ. of Chicago Press.

Kurath, Hans. 1949. *A Word Geography of the Eastern United States*. Ann Arbor: Univ. of Michigan Press.

Kurath, Hans, and Raven I. McDavid, Jr. 1961. *The Pronunciation of English in the Atlantic States*. Ann Arbor: Univ. of Michigan Press.

Linguistic Atlas Projects (Web site). 1998. Available from http://us.english.uga.edu.

McDaniel, Susan L. 1989. "Databases of the LAGS Automatic Atlas." In Kretzschmar, Schneider, and Johnson, 63–68.

McDavid, Raven I., Jr. 1984. "Linguistic Geography." In *Needed Research in American English (1983)*, 4–31. Publication of the American Dialect Society 71. University: Univ. of Alabama Press.

McDavid, Raven I., Jr., and Raymond O'Cain, eds. 1980. *Linguistic Atlas of the Middle and South Atlantic States*. Fasc. 1, 2. Chicago: Univ. of Chicago Press.

McDavid, Raven I., Jr., et al. 1982–86. *Basic Materials: Linguistic Atlas of the Middle and South Atlantic States and Affiliated Projects*. Chicago Microfilm MSS on Cultural Anthropology, gen. ed. Norman McQuown. Series 68.360–64, 69.365–69, 71.375–80. Chicago: Joseph Regenstein Library, Univ. of Chicago.

Miller, Michael I. 1999. *Dynamics of a Sociolinguistic System: English Plural Formation in Augusta, Georgia.* Ed. Ronald R. Butters, William A. Kretzschmar, Jr., and Claiborne Rice. Special issue of *Journal of English Linguistics* 27.3.

Montgomery, Michael. 1993. "Review Article: The Linguistic Atlas of the Gulf States." *American Speech* 68: 263–318.

Pederson, Lee. 1981. *Linguistic Atlas of the Gulf States: Basic Materials.* Ann Arbor: UMI.

———. 1986. *Linguistic Atlas of the Gulf States: Concordance.* Ann Arbor: UMI.

———. 1993. "An Approach to Linguistic Geography." In *American Dialect Research,* ed. Dennis Preston, 31–92. Amsterdam: Benjamins.

———. 1995. "Elements of Word Geography." *Journal of English Linguistics* 23: 33–46.

——— 1996a. "LAMR/LAWS and the Main Chance." *Journal of English Linguistics* 24: 234–49.

——— 1996b. "LAWCU Project Worksheets." *Journal of English Linguistics* 24: 52–60.

———, ed. 1986–93. *Linguistic Atlas of the Gulf States.* 7 vols. Athens: Univ. of Georgia Press.

Pederson, Lee, and Michael Madsen. 1989. "Linguistic Geography in Wyoming." In Kretzschmar, Schneider, and Johnson, 17–24.

Telsur Project (Web site). 2003. Available from http://www.ling.upenn.edu/phono_atlas/home.html.

Thomas, Erik R. 2003. "Secrets Revealed by Southern Vowel Shifting." *American Speech* 78: 150–70.

3. REGIONAL LEXICON: *DARE* AND BEYOND

JOAN HOUSTON HALL

Dictionary of American Regional English

A RECURRING THREAD in the earlier American Dialect Society (ADS) reports of the status of work on regional speech (*Needed Research in American English* 1943, 1964, 1984) was disappointment at the failure of ADS to complete "major projects" identified and named as desiderata years before. A corollary theme was the recognition of the need for strong and continuing financial support to accomplish those endeavors.

Of the major projects mentioned, the primary one was the dictionary of regional and local speech that had been envisioned by the founders of ADS as a counterpart to Joseph Wright's *English Dialect Dictionary* (1898–1905). In the 1943 report (comp. Harry Morgan Ayres, Kemp Malone, and Allen Walker Read), George P. Wilson declared, "Systematic field work, with the use of well-planned question sheets, must be carried out; but for the present we must address ourselves to certain preliminary activities, largely bibliographical in nature" (42). By the time of the 1963 report, chaired by Albert H. Marckwardt, much preliminary work had been done at the University of Wisconsin by Professor of English Frederic G. Cassidy and his graduate assistant Audrey R. Duckert. The report did not say, however, that Cassidy had been appointed to head ADS's dictionary project, since the annual meeting at which that would occur was still several weeks away. The report did say that governmental support was about to be solicited for collecting materials for the dictionary. Forty years later, it is surprising to see the reluctance with which this step was taken: preferring foundation grants to federal support, the committee wrote, "The contractual nature of most government assistance is often inimical to the spirit and attitudes which underlie humanistic scholarship" (25). In very large part,[1] this attitude has proved to be unjustified, and

49

generous support by federal agencies[2] has been the foundation on which the Society's dictionary has been produced.

By 1983, the tone of the report on regional speech (Cassidy 1984) was significantly more upbeat. By then the project had received its name (*American Dialect Dictionary* had already been used for Harold Wentworth's slender volume in 1944, so Cassidy and Duckert settled on the acronymically auspicious *Dictionary of American Regional English* in 1965); Cassidy had expended the grant from the U.S. Office of Education to complete the nation-wide fieldwork and to compile a huge corpus of written citations; the project had had 13 years of support from the National Endowment for the Humanities, during which the field data had been computerized, *DARE*'s signature map outlining the states according to population density rather than geographic area had been developed, and most of the editing for the first volume (A–C) had been completed. A nagging concern, however, was still the uncertainty of adequate long-term funding. The need for the chief editor to spend large amounts of time beating the bush for financial support both stifled progress on the editing and dampened the morale of the staff.

Given such a long and problematical history for ADS's dictionary, it is a pleasure for me to be able to report, in 2003, on major milestones over the last 20 years and on what seems to be a promising future for *DARE*.

The first volume of the *Dictionary of American Regional English* (*DARE*), containing copious introductory materials and the letters A–C, was published by Harvard University Press in 1985 as Cassidy had predicted in his 1983 report. So enthusiastically was it received, both in lay and professional reviews, that it went through five printings within its first year. Although the speed of production of subsequent volumes fell short of Cassidy's characteristically optimistic projections (he had dreamed of a completed dictionary in 1989 in time for the ADS centennial), three more volumes were published at regular intervals: volume 2 (D–H, with Joan Houston Hall as associate editor) appeared in 1991; volume 3 (I–O, Cassidy and Hall) came out in 1996; and volume 4 (P–Sk, Hall) was published in 2002. Significant editorial work on Volume 5 (Sl–Z)

has also been done. Cassidy's dream of seeing the last volume come
off the press was not realized. But by his death at the age of 92 in
June 2000, he had made ADS's long-dreamed-of project a reality;
he had seen it more than halfway through the alphabet; he had
become the nation's best-known and most widely admired spokes-
person for dialect diversity; and he had trained a skilled and
devoted staff ready to carry the project to conclusion.

Over the last 20 years, in addition to the four volumes of text,
two ancillary volumes have appeared as numbers 77 and 82 of the
Publication of the American Dialect Society series (von
Schneidemesser and Metcalf 1993; von Schneidemesser 1999).
These volumes make it easy for readers to use the text of *DARE* to
answer questions about which words characterize which regions or
social groups and what languages and linguistic processes have
contributed to the regional vocabulary of our country. The corresponding index to volume 4 is scheduled to be published on
DARE's Web site in 2003, where it will also be available for downloading and printing.

An additional project carried out during the last 20-year reporting period was the remastering of all of the audiotape recordings made by the *DARE* field-workers between 1965 and 1970.
Many of the 1,843 recordings had been made not on standard
audiotape, but on computer tape that had been cut down to size
(the computer tape was free, but the decision proved to be penny
wise and pound foolish). The computer tapes were not entirely
uniform in width, which sometimes caused jamming in the recorders; and over time, all of the tapes became worn and brittle. In
1991 *DARE* was awarded a grant from NEH to make preservation
masters, duplication masters, and cassette copies so that we could
assure an archival copy while still using the tapes ourselves and
making copies for other scholars. At that point, digital technology
had not yet stood the test of time, and NEH was not granting funds
to digitize audiotape collections. Had we known what lay ahead, we
would have waited the year or two for that technology to be
approved and then made digital copies from the start; as it stands,
we now need (and have begun) to investigate funding sources to
make that conversion.

Despite the limitations on the tape recordings caused by sometimes noisy field conditions, the occasional inexperienced field-
worker, the overwide tape, and recording machines that were not
always as reliable as expected, the audiotapes have been extremely
useful not only for *DARE* itself, but also for other kinds of research
and teaching: they have been requested for phonological analysis
by Timothy Frazer, Terry Lynn Irons, Dennis Preston, Natalie
Schilling-Estes, David Shores, Beth Lee Simon, Erik Thomas, and
Walt Wolfram, for example; they have been used for sociolinguistic
investigations of gender and style-shifting by Beth Lee Simon;
sample tapes have been used by teachers in secondary schools and
universities across the country to demonstrate regional and social
diversity; they have also provided unique resources for oral historians and folklorists. In addition, the *DARE* audiotapes have proved
to be an invaluable archive for actors and dialect coaches both in
the United States and England. A letter from The Juilliard School's
dialect coach Kate Wilson (pers. com., 1 Feb. 2002) attests to their
usefulness in her work on Broadway productions: "As a historical
reference your tapes are invaluable in preserving the authenticity
of classic American plays. In short, they are a link to the past."

Looking ahead to the next 20 years, we can expect that the
DARE audiotapes will continue to be valuable tools, especially
once they have been digitized. We can also expect that volume 5 of
DARE, containing the letters Sl through Z, will be published in
about 2008; volume 6, which will include the data summary (all
the responses gathered in the fieldwork), contrastive maps, cumu-
lative indexes, and the bibliography (if it cannot be fit into volume
5), should appear within a couple of years thereafter. As soon as
possible after volume 5 is completed, an electronic edition of the
DARE text will be published, which will invite many kinds of
investigations and studies not possible to users of *DARE* before and
will make the text of the dictionary much more widely available.

In anticipation of the production of the electronic version, we
have recently initiated a major technological upgrade of our equipment and procedures. This not only will automate the typographic
coding and structural tagging of the text, but also should simplify
some editorial procedures and both improve and incorporate into

a new editing platform our existing programs that retrieve responses from the fieldwork database, analyze social distributions, and make the *DARE* maps. (It is essential to remark, however, that no technical tinkering can ever eliminate the most time-consuming part of the editorial process, the careful analysis of the evidence and thoughtful crafting of definitions.)

Because a dictionary is inevitably out of date by the time even a single volume is published, we have always maintained a file of supplementary materials with the expectation that supplements would someday be prepared. With an electronic edition, such supplementation as well as emendation will be a much simpler process than with a print edition.

The profusion of information—both historical and contemporary—now available on the Internet makes it both possible and essential to contemplate substantial revisions to the early volumes of *DARE*. Our experience with volume 4, in which we first started using the World Wide Web as a resource, was that the earliest quotes from our other sources could frequently be antedated, often by a hundred years or more, by quotations found in such extensive digital libraries as *The Making of America* (http://moa.umdl.umich.edu and http://cdl.library.cornell.edu) and the Library of Congress's *American Memory* site (http://memory.loc .gov/ammem). There are many other valuable collections as well, with more becoming available all the time. And there are also individual scholars (notably Fred Shapiro, Barry Popik, and George A. Thompson) who eagerly devote time to the discovery of earliest citations for specified terms and who share the results on the ADS discussion list (ads-l@uga.cc.uga.edu). *DARE* has benefited significantly from their research.

While it is extremely unlikely that face-to-face fieldwork of the kind employed by *DARE* will ever be done on a nationwide basis again, innovative work based on telephone surveys—such as the Phonological Survey of Texas (Bailey and Bernstein 1989), the Survey of Oklahoma Dialects (Bailey et al. 1993), and the *Atlas of North American English* (Labov, Ash, and Boberg forthcoming)— suggests that such methods can provide reliable results, particularly for determining phonological patterns. Electronic surveys of lexical use (e.g., Vaux 2002) present methodological challenges (such as the not uncommon clash between speakers' reports of their use and their actual, unself-conscious use), but methods will doubtless be refined as problems are discovered and addressed. The advantages of such projects in terms of their relative speed and affordability make them very attractive both to researchers and to funding agencies. *DARE*'s archival materials and published volumes can both contribute to and benefit from these kinds of projects.

In addition to utilizing the proliferation of electronic resources, future efforts to supplement and enhance *DARE* will need to make fuller use of Linguistic Atlas projects such as the Linguistic Atlas of the Gulf States (which became available to *DARE* only midway through volume 2), the Linguistic Atlas of the Middle and South Atlantic States (parts of which are available electronically, and all of which may ultimately be), as well as the Linguistic Atlas of the Rocky Mountain States and the Linguistic Atlas of the Western States, now in progress (see chapter 2 for details of the Linguistic Atlas projects).

Another area of research that will be important to mine in a revised edition of *DARE* will be that of the influence of immigrant groups on American English. American demographics have changed so dramatically since the 1960 census (on which the *DARE* fieldwork was based) that many numerically significant ethnic groups in our society today are either seriously underrepresented or totally unrepresented in the informant pool of 1965–70.

The projected work on volumes 5 and 6 of *DARE* as well as the electronic edition and supplements is, of course, contingent on the strong and continuing financial support recognized as a necessity in every previous ADS report. In 2003 I can report that although the need to spend a large amount of time soliciting support has not changed, the burden is no longer solely on the shoulders of the *DARE* editor. In 1998, after an enthusiastic review of the project by internal and external evaluators (commissioned by Dean Phillip R. Certain of the College of Letters and Science at the University of Wisconsin–Madison), Dean Certain agreed to provide the position of a fund-raiser for *DARE* for three years. If, in that period of time, we could not only stay afloat but find the financial momentum to reach the end of the alphabet, he would be glad; if not, he could help no further. With the significant help of Development Director David Simon, we have been able to build a base of individuals who have contributed gifts both small and large, and we have attracted new private foundations to our cause. We are hopeful that, with the continuing assistance of Simon (now working through the University of Wisconsin Foundation), we can maintain the coalition of federal, state, and private donors that has worked so effectively over the last few years, and can sustain the ADS's dictionary to Z and beyond.

NOTES

1. The one instance of unwarranted federal intervention of which I am aware occurred when the Office of Education, which was supporting the fieldwork, reviewed the text of the questionnaire. The reviewing officer did not approve of the question asking for other names for a woman's breasts and was even more unhappy that possible responses were actually listed in the questionnaire (so that the field-worker could simply circle a response rather than take the time to write it out). This objection was an ethical problem for Cassidy because it obstructed legitimate scholarly enquiry, and it was a procedural problem because all of the questionnaires had already been printed. The compromise that was struck obligated Cassidy to use a black marking pen to cross out all of the offending synonyms in each copy of the questionnaire. (Any inquisitive person could simply hold the page to the light and read the suggested responses through the black slash, but the letter of the law had been met.)
2. Continuing and generous support has been provided by the National Endowment for the Humanities (an independent federal agency) since 1970 and by the National Science Foundation for all but two years since 1980.

REFERENCES

Bailey, Guy, and Cynthia Bernstein. 1989. "Methodology for a Phonological Survey of Texas." *Journal of English Linguistics* 22: 6–16.

Bailey, Guy, Tom Wikle, Jan Tillery, and Lori Sand. 1993. "Some Patterns of Linguistic Diffusion." *Language Variation and Change* 5: 359–90.

Cassidy, Frederic G. 1984. "Regional Speech and Localisms." Part 3 of *Needed Research* (1983), 32–35.

DARE. Dictionary of American Regional English. 1985–. Vol. 1 (A–C), ed. Frederic G. Cassidy. Vols. 2 (D–H) and 3 (I–O), ed. Frederic G. Cassidy and Joan Houston Hall. Vol. 4 (P–Sk), ed. Joan Houston Hall. 4 vols. to date. Cambridge, Mass.: Belknap Press of Harvard Univ. Press.

Labov, William, Sharon Ash, and Charles Boberg, eds. Forthcoming. *Atlas of North American English: Phonetics, Phonology, and Sound Change.* Berlin: de Gruyter.

Needed Research in American English. 1943. Comp. Henry Morgan Ayres, Kemp Malone, and Allen Walker Read. Chicago: American Dialect Society. Repr. in *Publication of the American Dialect Society* 41 (1964): 42–54.

Needed Research in American English (1963). 1964. *Publication of the American Dialect Society* 41: 22–41.

Needed Research in American English (1983). 1984. Publication of the American Dialect Society 71. University: Univ. of Alabama Press.

Vaux, Bert. 2002. *Dialect Survey* (Web site). Available from http://www.hcs.harvard.edu/~golder/dialect/.

von Schneidemesser, Luanne, ed. 1999. *An Index by Region, Usage, and Etymology to the "Dictionary of American Regional English," Volume III.* Publication of the American Dialect Society 82. Durham, N.C.: Duke Univ. Press.

von Schneidemesser, Luanne, and Allan Metcalf, eds. 1993. *An Index by Region, Usage, and Etymology to the "Dictionary of American Regional English," Volumes I and II.* Publication of the American Dialect Society 77. Tuscaloosa: Univ. of Alabama Press.

Wentworth, Harold. 1944. *American Dialect Dictionary.* New York: Crowell.

Wilson, George P. 1943. "Regional Speech and Localisms." Part 1 of *Needed Research*, 42–44.

Wright, Joseph, ed. 1898–1905. *English Dialect Dictionary: Being the Complete Vocabulary of All Dialectal Words Still in Use, or Known to Have Been in Use during the Last Two Hundred Years.* 6 vols. London: Frowde.

4. A NATIONAL SURVEY OF NORTH AMERICAN DIALECTS

SHARON ASH

University of Pennsylvania

In February 1992, this author connected a Nagra open-reel tape recorder to a telephone and dialed a phone number in Sioux Falls, South Dakota. I reached a man known (by pseudonym) as Gerald P., who agreed to be interviewed and tape-recorded, whereupon I started the Nagra running. This interview was carried out as the first of a pilot project for a telephone survey of North American English. Over the next several years, the project grew to encompass first the entire Midwest, and then all of English-speaking North America, to produce the *Atlas of North American English: Phonetics, Phonology, and Sound Change* (*ANAE*; Labov, Ash, and Boberg forthcoming).

The Linguistic Atlas of the United States and Canada had been conceived in 1929 and had produced numerous substantial reports on the phonetics and phonology of American English, but there had been no national survey. Furthermore, the fieldwork of the Linguistic Atlas projects had been conducted over a period of time long enough that no one sample of American dialects could be claimed. The goal of *ANAE* was to sample the entire population of North American urban speakers of English within a short time, so as to obtain a snapshot of all of North American English.

Over the years, the interview schedule was revised, and variants were developed to target the variables of interest in different regions: the Midwest, the Northeast, the East, the South, the West, and Canada. Recording techniques were updated to digital tape recorders rather than open-reel. About 850 speakers were recorded in all, and acoustic analysis of the vowel systems was carried out for 439 speakers. The last speaker was interviewed in November 2001, less than a decade after the first interview.

For the pilot project, the sample was stratified by population of the town, from those of more than a million down to those of 2,000 to 10,000. As the project expanded, however, the target was limited to urban dialects: those places defined by the Census Bureau as Urbanized Areas, with a population over 50,000. For all but the largest cities, the experimental design was to interview at least two speakers in each place, at least one of whom was a woman between the ages of 20 and 40. Interviewees had to be local: they had to have lived in the place from at least the ages of 5 to 18, preferably longer. In places where the known variables included ones for which word class assignment was an issue, they had to have at least one parent who grew up in the town, and this condition was preferred for all speakers.

The *ANAE* interviews collected three types of speech. First, there was casual conversation of the type that occurs routinely between strangers speaking on the telephone. Speakers were asked for a detailed residence history and information about their parents. Next they were asked about their town: Is it a nice place to live? How is the economy? Are people moving in or moving out? There followed a formal elicitation section, and then speakers were asked for more personal information, about their jobs and essential demographic information: age, national ancestry, education, the racial composition of the speaker's high school, and other personal information. The formal elicitation consisted of semantic differentials (such as "What is the difference between a *pond* and a *pool?*") and explicit elicitation of minimal pairs, with queries about whether the elicited words (such as *Don* and *dawn*) sounded the same or different. The interviews range in length from about 20 minutes to more than an hour. The very last question is a request for the speaker to agree to being sent a word list by mail (or e-mail) and then reading the list back to the interviewer over the phone at a later date. This provided a fourth register of speech for most speakers.

This work leads to the surprising finding that regional dialects are becoming increasingly differentiated from each other. But within regional boundaries, linguistic changes in progress have the effect of solidifying and developing the regional pattern, and it appears that local dialects may indeed disappear. The initial aim of this research is to develop a classification of North American dialects. The features that characterize each dialect are to be discovered, and the bundles of features that differentiate each dialect from all others are to be identified. The ultimate end of this work is to discover and elucidate the causes of linguistic change.

Within a phonological system, there are two types of systemic changes: those that alter the phonemic inventory, by splits and mergers; and those that may wreak dramatic phonetic changes but do not alter the inventory, by chain shifts and parallel shifts.

Long before the *ANAE* work was begun, Labov (1991) proposed two pivot points in the vowel system as critical in defining the (originally two, later three) dialects of English. As a core, there is a relatively stable system of six short vowels:

i	(*pit*)	u	(*put*)
e	(*pet*)	ʌ	(*putt*)
æ	(*pat*)	o	(*pot*)

Of these, the two lowest members bear a variable relationship to a long and ingliding alternant: *æ* alternates with the tense variant *æh*, and short *o* is intimately bound up with the highly irregular and skewed class of /oh/. The phonemic split of short *a*, where it occurs—in the Mid-Atlantic region—produces a skewed /æh/ class, in marginal contrast with /æ/. Tense /æh/ occurs primarily before voiceless fricatives and nasals, but it is subject to tremendous dialect variation and shows highly irregular lexical distribution. Similarly, the migration of /o/ words into the /oh/ class is also favored by voiceless fricatives, and it too shows fine-grained dialect variation and irregular lexical distribution. Labov proposed that three dialects resulted from the resolution of the tension between these two pairs, whether they were merged or separate.

The merger of /o/ (as in *cot*) and /oh/ (as in *caught*) is a widespread and expanding feature of North American English. As is characteristic of mergers, it proceeds below the level of public notice and social evaluation. To begin a thumbnail sketch of the North American dialects, we consider the regions where there is resistance to this merger from structural factors.

The Inland North, the large, industrial, urbanized region on the Great Lakes, from Rochester, New York, to Chicago, Illinois, is home to more than 80 million people. This is the domain of the Northern Cities Chain Shift, the dramatic rotation of six vowels in acoustic space. Short /o/ is fronted as a part of this process, keeping its distance from /oh/ (which is lowered and fronted behind /o/), and the margin of security between the two vowels is maintained. The trigger for this chain shift is the wholesale raising of /æ/, the second of the two crucial elements in the configuration of North American dialects today.

In the Mid-Atlantic region, /oh/ is raised as part of a chain shift, thereby removing the possibility of merger with /o/. Short *a* exhibits a phonemic split, as mentioned above, into a tense *æh* and lax *æ*. This split has been the subject of extensive and ongoing investigation (e.g., Labov 1989; Ash 2002, among others).

The third region where the distinction of /o/ and /oh/ is maintained by structural factors is the South. Here, the nucleus of /oh/ may approximate the nucleus of /o/, but /oh/ develops a back upglide, as in [kaot] for *caught*, effectively maintaining its separateness. However, the more salient feature of the Southern region is the Southern Shift, which is precipitated by the removal of (ay) from low central position. This is accomplished by the monophthongization of (ay), a stereotype of Southern speech. Indeed, the occurrence of monophthongal (ay) before voiceless segments is a well-known social marker in the South. There are systemic consequences of the social divide, too: chain shifting is facilitated where a phoneme as a whole vacates its position, rather than just certain allophones. Thus, the Southern Shift is most advanced where monophthongization is most advanced.

We consider now the dialects that do exhibit the low back merger, which include Canada, Eastern New England, Western Pennsylvania, the West, and the Midland.

Canada is a solid exponent of the low back merger, but it shares this feature with many of the contiguous regions of the United States. It is, however, distinguished from its southern neighbor by the Canadian Shift, first described by Clarke, Elms, and Youssef (1995). In this chain shift, short *a* is backed into the low central space that short *o* occupies in the Inland North, as short *o* moves toward the back to merge with long open *oh*. Additionally, short *i* and short *e* are lowered and backed, trailing short *a*. A third feature of Canadian English is Canadian raising, the centralization of the nuclei of (ay) and (aw) before voiceless obstruents (Joos 1942; Chambers 1973). This well-known feature is found throughout Canada, whereas the Canadian Shift is not found in the Atlantic Provinces (New Brunswick, Nova Scotia, Prince Edward Island, and Newfoundland). However, the raising of the nucleus of (ay) before voiceless obstruents is found in much of the North of the United States as well.

New England is dialectally differentiated into East and West. Eastern New England is distinguished as being one of the regions where *r*-vocalization is found in North America. Western New England is a transitional area, where short *e* is somewhat backed and short *o* is somewhat fronted. Proximity in the front-back dimension of short *e* and short *o* is diagnostic of the Inland North's Northern Cities Shift, and much of the original settlement of the Inland North was made by migration from Western New England. The coincidence of these two facts leads to the inference that Western New England is the "staging ground" of the Northern Cities Shift.

Western Pennsylvania, centered around Pittsburgh, is a third locus of solid low back merger territory. It is also unique among North American dialects in that it exhibits the monophthongization of (aw).

The West is an additional large region in which the low back merger holds sway. The configuration of the upgliding back vowels makes an important contribution to the definition of this dialect, as well as others. Here, /uw/ is strongly fronted—as it is fronted in much of North America—but /ow/ is not, a feature that it shares with Canada and the rest of the North.

The Midland is a region of transition and internal differentiation, with nearly every city representing a local variant. The low back merger is in transition: speakers are inconsistent in both production and perception of *cot* and *caught*, *tock* and *talk*, and *Don* and *dawn*. Of the back upgliding vowels, however, /uw/ and /ow/ are both consistently fronted, as in the South. The fronting of /ow/ sets the Midland apart from the West, and the absence of (ay) monophthongization (except before resonants) sets it apart from the South.

The above is a brief outline of the primary features of dialect regions that have been established by the work of the *ANAE*. Figure 1 maps the geographical extent of these areas.

It must be emphasized that *ANAE* describes urban areas. A follow-up project on the diffusion of linguistic change in the Mid-Atlantic region highlighted the limitations of this sample for a complete picture of dialect differentiation. For this study, we conducted relatively short, anonymous, face-to-face interviews with speakers in towns dotting the Mid-Atlantic region, with the goal of locating the isoglosses for the conditioning of the phonemic split of short *a*. Since the tensing environments in Philadelphia are a subset of the tensing environments in New York City, we hypothesized that we would find a gradual shift from the New York City conditions to the Philadelphia conditions as we traversed the distance between them. We were mistaken. Instead, we found that the towns closest to Philadelphia exhibited the Philadelphia system, and so did the towns that had historically close links to Philadelphia, such as those on the banks of the Delaware River. In addition, the largest urban centers, Wilmington and Baltimore, followed the Philadelphia conditions for short *a* tensing. However, the towns just outside the Philadelphia orbit abruptly abandoned the Philadelphia system in favor of a much simpler system, by which short *a* is tensed and raised only before nasals.

NEEDED RESEARCH

As a purely linguistic feature, vowel trajectories, glides, and length need attention. The acoustical analysis that has been carried out centers on the nuclear peaks of vowels, partly for the practical reason that it is far clearer to represent a vowel by a single point than to muddy the picture by plotting two or more points. For purposes of statistical analysis, too, it is conceptually and computationally simple to work with one pair of numbers, but working with arrays is much more demanding. However, as noted above, glides

FIGURE 1

Dialect Areas of North American English
(each dot represents one *ANAE* speaker)

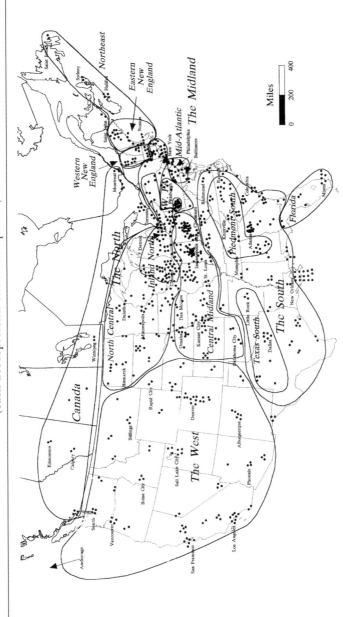

are important in distinguishing vowels with overlapping nuclei; and gliding, glide reduction, and monophthongization are highly salient aspects of Southern (ay).

Most of the work on dialect differences focuses on the vowel systems. To be sure, the consonantal systems of North American dialects do not exhibit the degree of variability of the vowels, but there are some dialectal differences. The liquids, in particular, are subject to variation. /l/-vocalization has received increasing attention in recent years, and /r/-vocalization continues to be an important area of investigation. Both /r/ and /l/ have strong effects on the adjacent vowels as well, and this subject merits closer study.

Perhaps the greatest gap in our understanding of North American dialects is in the paucity of data on ethnic minorities. *ANAE* conducted a modest set of interviews of African Americans, but these data are not included in the published atlas; they would fill a supplementary volume on their own. Erik Thomas (2001) has published the most extensive collection of vowel charts of African American, Mexican American, and Native American speakers to date, but otherwise the description of the phonology of these groups, and other Hispanic speakers too, is negligible. African American Vernacular English (AAVE) is clearly differentiated from Anglo varieties, and the differences are not diminishing. Thus, it must be studied as a separate dialect, and no project has as yet been devoted to defining the phonological system or systems of the African American community as a whole. It is generally understood that AAVE is relatively uniform across the North—at least in morphology and syntax—but this has yet to be conclusively demonstrated for phonology, although Jones (2003) is a thorough acoustic investigation of the phonological system of African Americans in Lansing, Michigan, and includes middle- and working-class speakers. What is clear is that AAVE is little influenced by the Anglo community. As for the South, it is evident that there are significant differences between Southern and Northern AAVE, but the description of Southern AAVE phonology by acoustical analysis has barely begun. The same can be said of the acoustical description of varieties of speech of Hispanics and other minorities.

The successor to the Atlas project, on diffusion in the Mid-Atlantic region, demonstrates the importance of looking at the urban/suburban/nonurban dimension in the study of phonological variation and change. As far back as 1975, Callary's study of short *a* tensing by college students in Illinois illustrated the importance of community size in influencing the realization of a linguistic variable; Bailey et al. (1993) showed that the influence of urbanity was a major feature of a selection of lexical and phonological variables. Our recent work in the Mid-Atlantic region adds the finding that what happens in a geographically interstitial community may not be at all linguistically intermediate. Although most work on linguistic variation and change is conducted as site studies, these observations indicate the need for a national survey of small communities to complement the work that is done in large urban centers.

Along with the social dimension of ethnicity (or national ancestry), other social parameters need to be included as American dialectology continues to move forward. This is nothing new: the careful fieldwork conducted under the direction of Hans Kurath targeted a speaker sample stratified by age, social class, and urbanity. This practice must be continued and developed, with the inclusion of stylistic variation as a parameter to be examined. It is found repeatedly that consideration of these variables greatly enhances the opportunity to discover the nature and direction of linguistic change within a community. As the study of dialectology reveals the structure and pattern of everyday communication among speakers, so is it also a means of illuminating the causes, mechanisms, and processes of diffusion of sound change and other types of linguistic change.

APPENDIX

What follows is a partial bibliography of works on phonology in American dialectology published during the last twenty years, with emphasis on the last five to ten years. It is by no means intended to be exhaustive; rather, it should serve as a starting point for further investigation and illustrate the variety of topics that researchers have recently undertaken to study.

Anderson, Bridget L. 1997. "Adaptive Sociophonetic Strategies and Dialect Accommodation: /ay/ Monophthongization in Cherokee English." In *A Selection of Papers from NWAVE 25*, ed. Charles Boberg, Miriam Meyerhoff, and Stephanie Strassel, 185–202. Special issue of *University of Pennsylvania Working Papers in Linguistics* 4.1.

Ash, Sharon. 1996. "Freedom of Movement: /uw/-Fronting in the Midwest." In *Sociolinguistic Variation: Data, Theory, and Analysis; Selected Papers from NWAV 23 at Stanford*, ed. Jennifer Arnold, Renée Blake, Brad Davidson, Scott Schwenter, and Julie Solomon, 3–25. Stanford, Calif.: Center for the Study of Language and Information, Stanford Univ.

Bailey, Guy. 1997. "When Did Southern American English Begin?" In *Englishes around the World: Studies in Honour of Manfred Görlach*, ed. Edgar W. Schneider, 255–75. Amsterdam: Benjamins.

Bailey, Guy, and Erik Thomas. 1998. "Some Aspects of African-American Vernacular English Phonology." In *African-American English: Structure, History, and Use*, ed. Salikoko S. Mufwene, John R. Rickford, John Baugh, and Guy Bailey, 85–109. London: Routledge.

Bailey, Guy, and Jan Tillery. 1996. "The Persistence of Southern American English." *Journal of English Linguistics* 24: 308–21.

Bailey, Guy, Thomas Wikle, and Lori Sand. 1991. "The Focus of Linguistic Innovation." *English World-Wide* 12: 195–214.

Baranowski, Maciej. 2000. "Changes in the Vowel System of Charleston, S.C." M.A. thesis, Univ. of Pennsylvania.

Benor, Sarah Bunin. 2001. "The Learned /t/: Phonological Variation in Orthodox Jewish English." In *Papers from NWAV 29*, ed. Tara Sanchez and Daniel Ezra Johnson, 1–16. Special issue of *University of Pennsylvania Working Papers in Linguistics* 7.3.

Boberg, Charles, and Stephanie M. Strassel. 1995. "Phonological Change in Cincinnati." In *Proceedings of the 19th Annual Penn Linguistics Colloquium*, ed. Rajesh Bhatt, Susan Garrett, Chung-Hye Han, and Roumyana Izvorski, 247–56. Special issue of *University of Pennsylvania Working Papers in Linguistics* 2.2.

Bowie, David. 1997. "Voah mei daett sei deitsh: Developments in the Vowel System of Pennsylvania German." In *Proceedings of the 21st Annual Penn Linguistics Colloquium*, ed. Alexis Dimitriadis, Laura Siegel, Clarissa Surek-Clark, and Alexander Williams, 35–49. Special issue of *University of Pennsylvania Working Papers in Linguistics* 4.2.

―――. 2001. "Dialect Contact and Dialect Change: The Effect of Near-Mergers." In *Papers from NWAV 29*, ed. Tara Sanchez and Daniel Ezra

Johnson, 17–26. Special issue of *University of Pennsylvania Working Papers in Linguistics* 7.3.

———. 2001. "The Diphthongization of /ay/." *Journal of English Linguistics* 29: 329–45.

Conn, Jeff, and Uri Horesh. 2002. "Assessing the Acquisition of Dialect Variables by Migrant Adults in Philadelphia: A Case Study." In *Papers from NWAV 30*, ed. Daniel Ezra Johnson and Tara Sanchez, 47–57. Special issue of *University of Pennsylvania Working Papers in Linguistics* 8.3.

Dorrill, George. 1986. "A Comparison of Stressed Vowels of Black and White Speakers in the South." In *Language Variety in the South: Perspectives in Black and White*, ed. Michael B. Montgomery and Guy Bailey, 149–57. Tuscaloosa: Univ. of Alabama Press.

DuBois, Sylvie, and Barbara M. Hovath. 2001. "Do Cajuns Speak Southern English? Morphosyntactic Evidence." In *Papers from NWAV 29*, ed. Tara Sanchez and Daniel Ezra Johnson, 27–41. Special issue of *University of Pennsylvania Working Papers in Linguistics* 7.3.

Edwards, Walter. 1996. "Sex-Based Differences in Language Choice in an African-American Neighborhood in Detroit." In Schneider, 183–94.

Feagin, Crawford. 1985. "Competing Norms in the White Speech of Anniston, Alabama." In *Language Variety in the South: Perspectives in Black and White*, ed. Michael B. Montgomery and Guy Bailey, 216–34. Tuscaloosa: Univ. of Alabama Press.

———. 1986. "More Evidence for Major Vowel Change in the South." In *Diversity and Diachrony*, ed. David Sankoff, 83–95. Amsterdam: Benjamins.

———. 1986. "Southern White in the English Language Community." In *Dialect and Language Variation*, ed. Harold B. Allen and Michael D. Linn, 259–83. Orlando, Fla.: Academic.

———. 1987. "A Closer Look at the Southern Drawl: Variation Taken to Extremes." In *Variation in Language: NWAV-XV at Stanford; Proceedings of the Fifteenth Annual Conference on New Ways of Analyzing Variation*, ed. Keith Denning, Sharon Inkelas, John R. Rickford, and Faye McNair-Knox, 137–50. Stanford, Calif.: Dept. of Linguistics.

———. 1990. "The Dynamics of a Sound Change in Southern States English: From *r*-less to *r*-ful in Three Generations." In *Development and Diversity: Linguistic Variation across Time and Space; A Festschrift for Charles-James N. Bailey*, ed. Jerold A. Edmondson, Crawford Feagin, and Peter Mühlhäusler, 129–46. Arlington: Summer Institute of Linguistics, Univ. of Texas at Arlington; Austin: Univ. of Texas.

————. 1990. "Two Vowel Shifts in Southern States English: An Acoustic Study of Change in Progress." In *Proceedings of the 14th International Congress of Linguists, Berlin/GDR, August 10–August 15, 1987*, ed. Werner Bahner, Joachim Schildt, and Dieter Viehweger, 1357–60. Berlin: Akademie-Verlag.

————. 1996. "Peaks and Glides in Southern States Short-A." In *Towards a Social Science of Language: Variation and Change in Language and Society*, ed. Gregory R. Guy, Crawford Feagin, Deborah Schiffrin, and John Baugh, 135–60. Amsterdam: Benjamins.

————. 1997. "The African Contribution to Southern States English." In *Language Variety in the South Revisited*, ed. Cynthia Bernstein, Thomas Nunnally, and Robin Sabino, 123–39. Tuscaloosa: Univ. of Alabama Press.

————. 1998. "Representing Southern States English: Pitfalls and Solutions." In *Conference Papers on American English and the International Phonetic Alphabet*, ed. Arthur J. Bronstein, 78–95. Publication of the American Dialect Society 80. Tuscaloosa: Univ. of Alabama Press.

————. 2003. "Vowel Shifting in the Southern States." In *English in the Southern United States*, ed. Stephen J. Nagle and Sara L. Sanders, 126–40. Cambridge: Cambridge Univ. Press.

Fought, Carmen. 1997. "A Majority Sound Change in a Minority Community: /u/-Fronting in Chicano English." *Journal of Sociolinguistics* 3: 5–23.

Frazer, Timothy C. 1987. "Attitudes towards Regional Pronunciation." *Journal of English Linguistics* 20: 89–100.

————. 1996. "The Dialects of the Middle West." In Schneider, 81–102.

————. 2000. "Are Rural Dialects Endangered Like Island Dialects?" *American Speech* 75: 347–49.

Fridland, Valerie. 1998. "The Southern Vowel Shift: Linguistic and Social Factors." Ph.D. diss., Michigan State Univ.

————. 1999. "The Southern Shift in Memphis, Tennessee." *Language Variation and Change* 11: 267–85.

————. 2001. "The Social Dimension of the Southern Vowel Shift: Gender, Age, and Class." *Journal of Sociolinguistics* 5: 233–53.

Gick, Bryan. 2002. "The American Intrusive *L*." *American Speech* 77: 167–83.

Gordon, Matthew J. 1997. "Urban Sound Change beyond the Cities: The Spread of the Northern Cities Chain Shift." In *A Selection of Papers from NWAVE 25*, ed. Charles Boberg, Miriam Meyerhoff, and Stephanie

Strassel, 125–40. Special issue of *University of Pennsylvania Working Papers in Linguistics* 4.1.

———. 1997. "Urban Sound Change beyond City Limits: The Spread of the Northern Cities Shift in Michigan." Ph.D. diss., Univ. of Michigan.

———. 2000. "Phonological Correlates of Ethnic Identity: Evidence of Divergence?" *American Speech* 75: 115–36.

———. 2000. "Tales of the Northern Cities." *American Speech* 75: 412–14.

———. 2001. *Small-Town Values and Big-City Vowels: A Study of the Northern Cities Shift in Michigan.* Publication of the American Dialect Society 84. Durham, N.C.: Duke Univ. Press.

Habick, Timothy. 1993. "Farmer City, Illinois: Sound Systems Shifting South." In *"Heartland" English: Variation and Transition in the American Midwest,* ed. Timothy C. Frazer, 97–124. Tuscaloosa: Univ. of Alabama Press.

Henderson, Anita. 1996. "The Short 'a' Pattern of Philadelphia among African-American Speakers." In *(N)WAVES and MEANS: A Selection of Papers from NWAVE 24,* ed. Miriam Meyerhoff, 127–40. Special issue of *University of Pennsylvania Working Papers in Linguistics* 3.1.

Herndobler, Robin. 1993. "Sound Change and Gender in a Working-Class Community." In *"Heartland" English: Variation and Transition in the American Midwest,* ed. Timothy C. Frazer, 137–56. Tuscaloosa: Univ. of Alabama Press.

Ito, Rika. 2001. "Belief, Attitudes, and Linguistic Accommodation: A Case of Urban Sound Change in Rural Michigan." In *Papers from NWAV 29,* ed. Tara Sanchez and Daniel Ezra Johnson, 129–43. Special issue of *University of Pennsylvania Working Papers in Linguistics* 7.3.

Jacobs-Huey, Lanita. 1997. "Is There an Authentic African American Speech Community: Carla Revisited." In *A Selection of Papers from NWAVE 25,* ed. Charles Boberg, Miriam Meyerhoff, and Stephanie Strassel, 331–70. Special issue of *University of Pennsylvania Working Papers in Linguistics* 4.1.

Johnstone, Barbara, Neeta Bhasin, and Denise Wittkofski. 2002. "'Dahntahn' Pittsburgh: Monophthongal /aw/ and Representations of Localness in Southwestern Pennsylvania." *American Speech* 77: 148–66.

Kretzschmar, William A., Jr., Virginia McDavid, Theodore Lerud, and Ellen Johnson, eds. 1994. *Handbook of the Linguistic Atlas of the Middle and South Atlantic States.* Chicago: Univ. of Chicago Press.

Labov, William. 1992. "Regular Sound Change in English Dialect Geography." In *History of Englishes: New Methods and Interpretations in Historical Linguistics*, ed. Matti Rissanen, Ossi Ihalainen, Terttu Nevalainen, and Irma Taavitsainen, 42–71. Berlin: de Gruyter.

Labov, William, and Sharon Ash. 1997. "Understanding Birmingham." In *Language Variety in the South Revisited*, ed. Cynthia Bernstein, Thomas Nunnally, and Robin Sabino, 508–73. Tuscaloosa: Univ. of Alabama Press.

Labov, William, and Wendell Harris. 1986. "DeFacto Segregation of Black and White Vernaculars." In *Diversity and Diachrony*, ed. David Sankoff, 1–24. Philadelphia: Benjamins.

Lance, Donald M. 1993. "Some Dialect Features in the Speech of Missouri Germans." In *"Heartland" English: Variation and Transition in the American Midwest*, ed. Timothy C. Frazer, 187–97. Tuscaloosa: Univ. of Alabama Press.

Larmouth, Donald, and Marjorie Remsing. 1993. "'Kentuck' English in Wisconsin's Cutover Region." In *"Heartland" English: Variation and Transition in the American Midwest*, ed. Timothy C. Frazer, 215–28. Tuscaloosa: Univ. of Alabama Press.

Myhill, John. 1988. "Postvocalic /r/ as an Index of Integration into the BEV Speech Community." *American Speech* 63: 203–13.

Niedzielski, Nancy. 1996. "Acoustic Analysis and Language Attitudes in Detroit." In *(N)WAVES and MEANS: A Selection of Papers from NWAVE 24*, ed. Miriam Meyerhoff, 73–85. Special issue of *University of Pennsylvania Working Papers in Linguistics* 3.1.

————. 1997. "The Effect of Social Information on the Phonetic Perception of Sociolinguistic Variables (American Dialects)." Ph.D. diss., Univ. of California, Santa Barbara.

Roberts, Julie. 1997. "Hitting a Moving Target: Acquisition of Sound Change in Progress by Philadelphia Children." *Language Variation and Change* 9: 249–66.

Roberts, Julie, and William Labov. 1995. "Learning to Talk Philadelphian: Acquisition of Short *a* by Preschool Children." *Language Variation and Change* 7: 101–12.

Schilling-Estes, Natalie. 1995. "Production, Perception, and Patterning: 'Performance' Speech in an Endangered Dialect Variety." In *Proceedings of the 19th Annual Penn Linguistics Colloquium*, ed. Rajesh Bhatt, Susan Garrett, Chung-Hye Han, and Roumyana Izvorski, 117–31. Special issue of *University of Pennsylvania Working Papers in Linguistics* 2.2.

———. 1997. "Accommodation versus Concentration: Dialect Death in Two Post-insular Island Communities." *American Speech* 72: 12–32.

———. 1997. "The Linguistic and Sociolinguistic Status of /ay/ in Outer Banks English." Ph.D. diss., Univ. of North Carolina at Chapel Hill.

———. 2000. "Investigating Intra-ethnic Differentiation: /ay/ in Lumbee Native American English." *Language Variation and Change* 12: 141–74.

Schilling-Estes, Natalie, and Walt Wolfram. 1997. "Symbolic Identity and Language Change: A Comparative Analysis of Post-insular /ay/ and /aw/." In *A Selection of Papers from NWAVE 25,* ed. Charles Boberg, Miriam Meyerhoff, and Stephanie Strassel, 83–109. Special issue of *University of Pennsylvania Working Papers in Linguistics* 4.1.

———. 1999. "Alternative Models of Dialect Death: Dissipation versus Concentration." *Language* 75: 486–521.

Schneider, Edgar W., ed. 1996. *Focus on the U.S.A.* Varieties of English around the World 16. Amsterdam: Benjamins.

Strassel, Stephanie M., and Charles Boberg. 1996. "The Reversal of a Sound Change in Cincinnati." In *(N)WAVES and MEANS: A Selection of Papers from NWAVE 24,* ed. Miriam Meyerhoff, 247–56. Special issue of *University of Pennsylvania Working Papers in Linguistics* 3.1.

Thomas, Erik R. 1996. "A Comparison of Variation Patterns of Variables among Sixth-Graders in an Ohio Community." In Schneider, 149–68.

———. 1997. "A Rural/Metropolitan Split in the Speech of Texas Anglos." *Language Variation and Change* 9: 309–32.

Thomas, Erik R., and Guy Bailey. 1992. "A Case of Competing Mergers and Their Resolution." *SECOL Review* 16: 179–200.

———. 1998. "Parallels between Vowel Subsystems of African American Vernacular English and Caribbean Anglophone Creoles." *Journal of Pidgin and Creole Languages* 13: 267–96.

Vance, Timothy J. 1987. "'Canadian Raising' in Some Dialects of the Northern United States." *American Speech* 62: 195–210.

Wolfram, Walt. 2000. "Issues in Reconstructing Earlier African-American English." *World Englishes* 19: 39–58.

Wolfram, Walt, Adrianne Cheek, and Hal Hammond. 1996. "Competing Norms and Selective Assimilation: Mixing Outer Banks and Southern /ɔ/." In *Sociolinguistic Variation: Data, Theory, and Analysis; Selected Papers from NWAV 23 at Stanford,* ed. Jennifer Arnold, Renée Blake, Brad Davidson, Scott Schwenter, and Julie Solomon, 41–67. Stanford, Calif.: Center for the Study of Language and Information, Stanford Univ.

Wolfram, Walt, Becky Childs, and Benjamin Torbert. 2000. "Tracing Language History through Consonant Cluster Reduction: Comparative Evidence from Isolated Dialects." *Southern Journal of Linguistics* 24: 17–40.

Wolfram, Walt, and Kirk Hazen. 1996. "Isolation with Isolation: The Invisible Outer Banks Dialect." In *(N)WAVES and MEANS: A Selection of Papers from NWAVE 24*, ed. Miriam Meyerhoff, 141–57. Special issue of *University of Pennsylvania Working Papers in Linguistics* 3.1.

Wolfram, Walt, and Natalie Schilling-Estes. 1995. "Moribund Dialects and the Endangerment Canon: The Case of the Ocracoke Brogue." *Language* 71: 696–721.

———. 1996. "Dialect Change and Maintenance in a Post-insular Island Community." In Schneider, 103–48.

———. 1996. "On the Social Basis of Phonetic Resistance: The Shifting Status of Outer Banks /ay/." In *Sociolinguistic Variation: Data, Theory, and Analysis; Selected Papers from NWAV 23 at Stanford*, ed. Jennifer Arnold, Renée Blake, Brad Davidson, Scott Schwenter, and Julie Solomon, 69–82. Stanford, Calif.: Center for the Study of Language and Information, Stanford Univ.

———. 1997. *Hoi Toide on the Outer Banks: The Story of the Ocracoke Brogue.* Chapel Hill: Univ. of North Carolina Press.

———. 1998. *American English: Dialects and Variation.* Malden, Mass.: Blackwell.

Wolfram, Walt, Erik R. Thomas, and Elaine W. Green. 2000. "The Regional Context of Earlier African American Speech: Evidence for Reconstructing the Development of AAVE." *Language in Society* 29: 315–55.

REFERENCES

Ash, Sharon. 2002. "The Distribution of a Phonemic Split in the Mid-Atlantic Region: Yet More on Short *a*." In *Papers from NWAV 30*, ed. Daniel Ezra Johnson and Tara Sanchez, 1–15. Special issue of *University of Pennsylvania Working Papers in Linguistics* 8.3.

Bailey, Guy, Tom Wikle, Jan Tillery, and Lori Sand. 1993. "Some Patterns of Linguistic Diffusion." *Language Variation and Change* 5: 359–90.

Callary, Robert E. 1975. "Phonological Change and the Development of an Urban Dialect in Illinois." *Language and Society* 4: 155–69.

Chambers, J. K. 1973. "Canadian Raising." *Canadian Journal of Linguistics/ La revue canadienne de linguistique* 18: 113–35.

Clark, Sandra, Ford Elms, and Amani Youssef. 1995. "The Third Dialect of English: Some Canadian Evidence." *Language Variation and Change* 7: 209–28.

Jones, Jamila. 2003. "African Americans in Lansing and the Northern Cities Vowel Shift: Language Contact and Accommodation." Ph.D. diss., Michigan State Univ.

Joos, Martin. 1942. "A Phonological Dilemma in Canadian English." *Language* 18: 141–44.

Labov, William. 1989. "Exact Description of the Speech Community: Short a in Philadelphia." In *Language Change and Variation*, ed. Ralph W. Fasold and Deborah Schiffrin, 1–57. Amsterdam: Benjamins.

———. 1991. "The Three Dialects of English." In *New Ways of Analyzing Sound Change*, ed. Penelope Eckert, 1–44. New York: Academic.

Labov, William, Sharon Ash, and Charles Boberg, eds. Forthcoming. *Atlas of North American English: Phonetics, Phonology, and Sound Change.* Berlin: de Gruyter.

Thomas, Erik R. 2001. *An Acoustic Analysis of Vowel Variation in New World English.* Publication of the American Dialect Society 85. Durham, N.C.: Duke Univ. Press.

5. CONVERSATION, TEXT, AND DISCOURSE

BARBARA JOHNSTONE

Carnegie Mellon University

IN HIS 2001 PRESIDENTIAL ADDRESS to the American Dialect Society, Ronald Butters used a narrative of personal experience he had elicited in the course of a sociolinguistic interview to illustrate how a close reading modeled on literary analysis could uncover reasons for a storyteller's linguistic choices that would be missed in a large-scale correlational study with prechosen demographic categories as its primary explanatory variables. Butters (2001, 228) expressed the hope that his address would "suggest to the editors of the next volume of *Needed Research* that we turn ourselves to issues of discourse as well as the more traditional areas." This chapter takes Butters up on the suggestion.

Indeed, the 1984 edition of *Needed Research in American English* did not mention work on discourse, text, or conversation. Nor was work in this vein represented, 12 years later, in a book-length overview of research on U.S. English (Schneider 1996). However, research about American English discourse structures, styles, genres, and speech acts, as well as work linking phonetic and grammatical variability with facts about conversation and text, predates even the former of these. The editors of *American Speech* have commissioned reviews of books about text and talk at least since the mid-1980s; *American Speech* has been publishing articles about discourse analysis since the late 1980s, and such work had started appearing in other venues long before that. Official recognition by the ADS of discourse analytic work on American English has thus been belated, and there is, in fact, much to report in this chapter.

The chapter proceeds as follows. I first attempt a sketch of work on American English discourse published during the past 20 years. Since this is the first time *Needed Research* has included this topic, this involves looking back somewhat further in some instances, in order to contextualize more recent work. This research review is divided into two parts. The first, more substantial section has to do with discourse IN American English: aspects of grammar "beyond the sentence" (or outside the sentence) in American English talk and writing. I explore research about American interactional styles, strategies for discourse management, and ways of referring to and acting in the world.

A shorter section will touch on several topics having to do with discourse AND American English: how "American English" can itself be seen as a product of talk and written discourse, how the distribution of features of American varieties is affected by their functions in discourse, and how regional and ethnic variability can function as a strategic resource in discourse. This section also highlights the increasing reflexivity of American dialectology about its methods, which invariably involve talk and/or writing, and about its objects of study. In the prospective part of the chapter, I raise some questions that might be addressed in the next 20 years.

There is an enormous amount of discourse analytic work that happens to be about American English, but which either makes universalizing claims, explicitly or implicitly, about speakers in general (or sometimes English-speakers in general or women or men in general) rather than about how Americans or particular groups of Americans are distinctive, or which simply does not address the issue of how the variety being described might compare with another. The present overview is limited to studies that in some way thematize the issue of regional or ethnic variation, so that they are about American speech not just because their data happen to have been collected in North America, but because their goal includes contrasting some more or less nameable variety of North American English with some other language or with some other variety of English. Even in this limited domain, I have not been able to describe or even mention everything that has been done. My strategy has been to concentrate on work of the sort that is published in *American Speech* and other journals and books whose purpose is to explore particular varieties of English, rather than providing a complete review of work about discourse in North America, and I have aimed for representativeness rather than comprehensiveness. To minimize overlap between this chapter and others, I focus on linguistic variation that has been linked with region and/or with ethnicity, touching on differences associated with such factors as gender and age only tangentially.

DISCOURSE IN AMERICAN ENGLISH

The term *discourse* means different things to different groups of scholars. Linguists have typically used the term in one of two ways. For some, discourse analysis is the study of aspects of linguistic competence that go "beyond the sentence." These discourse analysts are interested in describing what speakers have to know in order not just to generate grammatical, meaningful sentences, but to deploy sentences (and other kinds of utterances) in coherent paragraphs and conversations. Discourse analysts working in this mode tend to focus on describing relatively fixed connections between linguistic strategies and discursive goals. Their descriptions of "rules," "structures," "strategies," or "styles" are both generalizations about recurring ways interlocutors have done things in talk and text and also, often, claims about knowledge or skill interlocutors have to possess prior to engaging in successful interaction.

In order to arrive at generalizations about this layer of competence, these discourse analysts study recorded instances of text and talk—written documents or transcribed speech. This means that their approach inevitably overlaps with a different kind of discourse analysis, in which discourse is defined as "language in use" or "interaction," and the focus is on the processes by which people create coherence and meaningfulness as they interact, rather than on preexisting knowledge of patterns or tactics which they bring to interactions. Various terms have been used in various ways to label this distinction. In the United States, the latter approach is sometimes identified as Conversation Analysis (CA), even though not all its practitioners share the strict ethnomethodological view held by the core practitioners of CA that linguistic interaction can be understood without reference to any preexisting "cultural knowledge" at all.

INTERACTIONAL STYLE. Since the first of these two approaches lends itself more easily to making claims about variation among groups of speakers, much of the work to date on discourse in American English has asked questions about relatively stable, frequently made, conventionalized connections between linguistic strategies and interactional, textual, or semantic effects. Some of the earliest was that of Tannen (1984, 2000), whose research on "conversational style" drew on Gumperz's (1982a, 1982b) model of "discourse strategies." In her analysis of a dinner-table conversation involving people from California, Great Britain, and the U.S. East Coast, Tannen (1984) identified contrasting styles of interaction: the New Yorkers' faster paced, with more questions, overlapping talk, personal narratives, and humorous routines; the others' involving longer pauses, more distinct turns at talk, and fewer direct questions, personal stories, and repetitions of parts of others' utterances. These differences, she found, contributed to the feeling on the New Yorkers' part that the others were not doing their share of the conversational work, and to the feeling on the part of the British and Californians that the New Yorkers were dominating the conversation. Though not explicitly focused on regional differences, Tannen's analysis provides a powerful account of some of the reasons why Americans often characterize urban Northeasterners as "pushy" and Westerners as "laid back," attributing heavily evaluated psychological causes to what Tannen shows are at least in part just small differences in expectations about conversational timing and the signaling of cooperativeness.

Tannen's work influenced subsequent research that did explicitly attempt to tie regional differences in interactional style with other linguistic, cultural, and historical facts about regional differences in the United States. One such body of work has to do with how interpersonal relations are indexed and negotiated in Southern whites' discourse. Traditional Southern greetings have often been described as being more elaborate, and more often required, than greetings elsewhere; an early study of them was by Spears (1974). More recently, Coles (1997) found that people in New Orleans can use local-sounding greetings as a way of displaying their identification with people they talk to on the telephone, particularly when the speakers do not know each other, as when they call a radio talk show or speak to the receptionist at a clinic.

Coles also showed how the use of local-sounding forms of address like *babe*, *doll*, and *darling* can function as solidarity-building moves in New Orleans. Forms of address like these have often been described as having more and/or different significance in the Southern United States than elsewhere. For example, using *sir* or *ma'am* to one's parents, as a required adjunct to the answer to a yes/no question, is a particularly Southern usage. So is the use of *sir* or *ma'am* to peers or to younger people.

In a study based on observation, interviews, and questionnaires, Ching (1987) concluded that the expression of deference is the core function of *sir* and *ma'am* in the South. Other uses were found to include emphasis, and, in some contexts, the expression of friendly solidarity. Davies (1997) asked Southerners to comment on uses of *sir* and *ma'am* in the film *The Trip to Bountiful* (1985) while viewing clips from the movie. Like Ching, she found that a central function of the forms was to express deferential or "negative" (Brown and Levinson 1987) politeness, that is, to create and maintain appropriate social distance among speakers so as to avoid imposing on others' autonomy. In addition, Davies shows how shifts in intonation as one uses *sir* or *ma'am* can foreground other things about speakers' social relations. For example, shifting to flatter intonation can signal a shift to a less formal footing. She also explores other uses of the terms, including emphasis as well as sarcastic uses.

In a study of Harry Crews's novel *Body* (1990), working-class white rural Georgia characters were found to use a wide variety of address forms to signal and manipulate social relations, often in quite subtle and strategically ambiguous ways (Johnstone 1992, 1994). Many uses of address forms (which include *son*, *boy*, *bud*, *girl*, *old honey*, and others), particularly to the speaker's elders, display a sort of ritual deference, but other, less ritual, uses can help to defuse social tension by putting on display, at a key moment, the fact that the speaker's attitude is deferential. Address forms such as these may also appear in bids for dominance or threats of belligerence, as speakers use them to point up the need for deference on their audience's part.

Crews's characters also express deferential negative politeness by means of a range of strategies for linguistic indirectness, including the use of conditional grammar to hedge assertions and requests. Like address terms, conditional structures not only serve to mitigate potential impositions, but also, sometimes, to signal heightened awareness of the social distinctions that make such deference necessary, so they often occur at tense moments and can be an element of a threat, as in "There'll be trouble if you can't learn to keep a civil tongue about my family" (46). Furthermore, frequent markers of evidential uncertainty also serve to hedge speakers' utterances, making them more indirect. Evidentials in the novel are overwhelmingly in the negative (*I don't believe, I don't misdoubt, I don't guess, I can't say as, I don't know as*); when they are not, their meanings express insecurity (*reckon, think, believe, have the feeling,* and *seem* are examples). Evidentials can combine with conditional grammar in expressions like *I wouldn't know about X.* These evidential predicates protect speakers from the potential social embarrassment of having their claims turn out to be false; they are also deferential, since hedging assertions is one way of avoiding imposing one's version of the world on others.

The use of question intonation in assertions, which McLemore (1991) calls "uptalk," has also been identified as Southern, and particularly characteristic of the discourse style of young women (Ching 1982; McLemore 1991), although it appears to have spread rapidly in the United States since these studies in Tennessee and Texas were done. Mitigating the directness of an assertion is among the functions of this feature, too.

Research on American conversational styles has also explored interactional practices associated with ethnic identification. Tannen's (1984) observations about New Yorkers were about Jewish New Yorkers, and that aspect of her study is discussed in greater depth in her article on "New York Jewish Conversational Style" (1981). In a similar vein, Schiffrin (1984) shows that arguments, in the conversations she studied among working-class Jews in Philadelphia, could build "sociability" in an interaction. Scollon and

Scollon's (1981) research with Athabaskans in Canada and Alaska explored an interactional style much more attuned to face-saving negative politeness than to the rapport-building, more "in-your-face" positive politeness described by Tannen and Schiffrin. (Similar findings are described by Basso 1970.) Silence is appropriate until Athabaskans are comfortable together, for example, and it is the responsibility of the higher-status person in an interaction rather than the lower-status one to initiate conversation. Scollon and Scollon describe some of the cross-cultural difficulties such expectations can cause: Athabaskans applying for jobs are reluctant to volunteer how their backgrounds qualify them for the positions, for example, and may come across to Anglo interviewers as apathetic.

There is an extensive body of scholarship about the African American practices of discourse, much of which touches on features of interactional style such as politeness, forms of address, indirectness, and conversational pacing, beginning with work by Abrahams (1962, 1976), Kochman (1972), and Mitchell-Kernan (1972) on such speech events as "signifying," "hoorawing," and "styling out." Kochman (1981) described African Americans' speech styles in aggressive talk, boasting, flirting, and dealing with accusations and personal information. In a recent overview of research on African American discourse styles, Morgan (1998, 251) "locates various [African American] speech genres within a system of social face that is partially constructed through directed and indirect discourse." Interactional practices and styles such as "signifying" or "sounding," "instigating," and "reading" test and reinforce speakers' "cool face," the ability to respond to challenging situations with eloquence, skill, wit, patience, and precise timing. Morgan traces these speech genres, which have in common indirectness and the use of intermediaries, to a set of strategies adapted from African slaves' practices in the face of whites' control over public talk.

DISCOURSE STRUCTURE. In addition to managing their social relations with their interlocutors, communicatively competent speakers must also be able to manage the textual relations among parts of the conversations, monologues, and written texts they produce. One important body of work on discourse structure has to do with cohesion, the strategies by which speakers and writers show how sentences are semantically linked to other sentences in a text, thus differentiating conversations or paragraphs from lists of random utterances. Work on textual cohesion (Halliday and Hasan 1976), at least in the United States, has tended not to be comparative. Differences in strategies for linking conversational utterances and sentences in text—such as the use of pronouns and other forms of substitution, ellipsis, and repetition on various levels—do not appear to index socially significant differences as often as do differences in linguistic strategies for negotiating social relations. As a result, while particular pronouns and other items which are used for cohesive purposes may be identified with particular regional or ethnic dialects (an obvious example in American English being the second person plural pronoun), general strategies of cohesion are typically associated with languages rather than dialects (as problematic as those categories are). For example, Fellegy (1995) reports on a study of "minimal responses" (forms such as *mmhmm*, *yeah*, and *right*) in American conversations, showing how these forms help structure a conversation by marking boundaries. While the particular forms used for this function clearly can vary across varieties of English (*yeah* might sound American, at least to some speakers, whereas *righto* or *brilliant* might sound British), Fellegy does not focus on this aspect of the topic, nor does she suggest that the functions served by such forms might be different in other varieties.

One body of research that does bear, at least indirectly, on ethnic differences in patterns of cohesion has to do with what are sometimes called "rhetorical strategies," particularly those involving the use of syntactic parallelism and other forms of repetition as cohesive devices. For example, Erickson (1984) describes the "rhapsodic" structure of African American boys' conversations, and Gumperz (1982a, 187–203) analyzes African American political oratory, touching both on patterns of repetition and on stylistic shifts among distinct oratorical voices that signal moves from one part of the speech to another.

Another influential research tradition bearing on variation in discourse structure has to do with narrative. Labov's (Labov and Waletzky 1967; Labov 1972) analysis of the structure of oral narratives of personal experience showed how narrators guide their audiences through stories by means of grammatical choices that signal the functional status of each clause as part of the narrative core or as introductory "abstract," scene-setting "orientation," "evaluation" of the events' significance, and concluding "coda." This analysis was not explicitly comparative; in fact, it was described with reference to narratives by speakers whose dialects were otherwise quite different

The fact that Labov was able to describe personal-experience stories by white New Englanders and African American boys in New York in the same way raises the issue of variability in narrative structure. If the structure of narrative is dictated by semantic and interactional function (such that, for example, orientation is necessary so that people can understand subsequent references to place and characters, and evaluation is necessary so that people will keep listening), might interactions differ across groups in ways that would affect the structure of narrative? On the other hand, might it be the case that the kinds of linguistic differences that construct and index social differences do not occur on the level of discourse structure, but on other levels, such as phonology and lexis? The point has frequently been made that not all situations require the kind of "fully developed" narratives Labov's sociolinguistic interviewing elicited. But while anthropologists and linguists have paid considerable attention to variability in how narratives function for different groups of North Americans (see below), there has been relatively little work exploring correlations between formal variation in narrative structure and ethnicity and region. (One exception is McLeod-Porter 1991.)

A series of studies published in *American Speech* (Blyth, Rechtenwald, and Wang 1990; Romaine and Lange 1991; Ferrara and Bell 1995) has traced the development and spread of new ways of performing one of the many "discourse marking" functions (Schiffrin 1987) that are required in narrative: signaling when clauses in narrative are to be taken as the words of others. These discourse markers, called "quotatives," include the older *say* and *go* (along with a large number of more semantically loaded verbs such as *yell, whisper, aver,* and so on) and newer forms such as *be like.*

REFERRING AND ACTING. The strategies a speaker chooses for making a story, a conversation, or a paragraph cohesive may reflect the speaker's ideas about how language works and how the world works in general. They may also reflect his or her particular goals for the utterance or conversation at hand. In other words, cohesive strategies may be related to referential strategies (what world is to be evoked, created, and/or portrayed) and to purposive strategies (what particular speech acts and more global communicative actions are to be accomplished). For example, African American orators' reliance on repetition as a primary cohesive device can be related to the way preaching and other forms of public address are conceived of in the African American tradition. When meaning is thought to be created interactively, and when persuasion is thought to be accomplished through poetic allusion and aesthetic resonance as well as through logic, then repetition within and across speakers and the signaling of structure via shifts in style make particularly good sense.

This way of imagining what oratory is for and how persuasion works has been traced to oral genres from West Africa (Pitts 1989) and the African diaspora (Edwards 1989). Labov (1972, 201–40) compares the expository styles of a lower- and a middle-class African American, showing (among other things) that the middle-class speaker makes less effective use of on-the-spot strategies for stitching oral discourse together than the lower-class speaker does, with the result that his response to the question both speakers were asked is both less cohesive and less persuasive, even by formal, syllogistic standards for persuasive discourse. In research on the history of Virginia and North Carolina tobacco auctioneers' chants, Kuiper (Kuiper and Tillis 1985; Kuiper 1992) traces prosodic aspects of this oral genre to the African American oratorical tradition; other aspects of the genre are traced to traditions from England.

Characteristics of Native Americans' expository styles have also been related to world and purpose. Bartelt (1993) explores how a number of features of Apacheans' oral discourse (in English), such as repetition and the use of categorizations such as "Europeans" and "Americans" and other terms such as "Indian" and "north" and "south" that retain special cultural meaning, may come together to signal, create, and reinforce a new kind of intertribal consciousness among Native Americans at contemporary urban festivals called powwows. Echoing Scollon and Scollon (1981) and others who have studied unwritten traditional discourse practices among many groups, Bartelt also suggests a link between "redundancy" as a cohesive and stylistic device and "orality" as a characteristic of the speakers' epistemological world. (Tannen 1988 and others suggest, on the other hand, that characteristics of oral discourse may at least sometimes be more a result of functional demands imposed by face-to-face, real-time interaction than a result of "oral" culture or epistemology.)

Contrasting narrative styles are also linked to contrasting worlds evoked and created in narrative and contrasting purposes for narrating. Polanyi's (1981, 1985) analysis of American personal experience stories draws on Labov's structural/functional analysis of oral narrative in identifying recurring features of American narrative plots. Polanyi shows how constructing "adequate paraphrases" of conversational stories by Americans can be a way of arriving at the basic propositions that express their beliefs about the world. Linde (1993) also uses structural analysis of recorded and transcribed stories as a basis for generalizing about the underlying plots of Americans' stories. Like Polanyi's, Linde's work does not focus explicitly on one or another group of Americans or variety of American English, though both base their analysis on stories told mainly by middle-class white Americans.

Other work on narrative has tried to link aspects of form with observations about the ideas and purposes of subsets of Americans. Among the earliest work by ethnographers of communication were studies of the functions of narrative and speech events in which narrative was central (Darnell 1974), and ethnographers have continued to explore the uses of narrative in various parts of North America (see, e.g., Scollon and Scollon 1981 and Patrick and Payne-Jackson 1996). Scollon and Scollon (1981) claim, for example, that for Athabaskans, experiences and stories about them are the primary source of knowledge, as reality is socially constructed through narrative. (This claim has been made more generally about "oral" cultures by scholars such as Goody and Watt 1968 and Ong 1982).

In a study of the forms and functions of personal storytelling in Indiana (Johnstone 1990a, 1990b), I suggested that these Midwesterners' characteristically monologic, nonparticipatory, highly detailed narratives could be seen to reflect (and help construct) regional ideas about what language is for (in essence, to reflect reality) and who is responsible for meaning (generally, the speaker). In the city I studied, as in others, sharing stories and ways of telling stories is one way in which community and a common sense of place are evoked and constructed in discourse. Etter-Lewis (1993) discusses life stories of professional African American women with an eye to connecting their referential goals (what they want to say about themselves and about life) with the structure of their stories. Bauman (1986) discusses stories and storytelling events as they serve to negotiate social relations in Texas. Shuman (1986) examines the uses of stories by urban adolescents. Riessman (1988) compares narratives by an Anglo American woman and a Puerto Rican, pointing out that social class and ethnicity both help account for the women's different experiences and different ways of recounting them.

Learning to narrate means learning to evoke, create, and share physical, social, and moral environments in talk. Thus describing how children learn to tell stories in different cultural and discursive traditions is a way of seeing how and why variation in discourse structure and style comes to be linked to variation in how people fundamentally imagine the world. Heath (1983) contrasts language socialization practices in a working-class African American neighborhood in the Appalachian piedmont with those in a similar white neighborhood, describing differences in such things as how children are encouraged to construct and perform narratives. For the literalist white parents, narratives were thought to be factual recountings of events in the service of moral lessons; in the African American community, children were rewarded for compelling, entertaining fantasy based only loosely on personal experience. These differences in what stories were expected to be about and accomplish in interaction had ramifications for their tellers' linguistic choices on all levels.

Another research tradition that connects variation in discourse with variation in speakers' purposes is the quantitative study of genre associated with Biber and his colleagues. In an article in *American Speech* called "A Textual Comparison of British and American Writing," Biber (1987) shows that British and American writers in a variety of genres differ systematically with respect to linguistic features that suggest interactivity and contextual situatedness versus editing and contextual abstractness. American writing is, on the whole, more colloquial, more interactive, and more tolerant of nominal style and technical jargon than is British writing in the same genres. (For a historical study of genre and language use in early American English, see Devitt 1989.)

Finally, research on the performance and function of particular speech acts has also explored or at least touched on peculiarities of American varieties. A great deal of research in the tradition of "contrastive pragmatics" (Wolfson 1981; Blum-Kulka, House, and Kasper 1989) has explored how Americans (usually college students) do, or report that they would do, such things as responding to compliments (Herbert 1986), often comparing this group with people from other countries. Studies situated in applied linguistics and second-language acquisition often identify competence in performing speech acts like complimenting, requesting, and apologizing as more or less parallel to the kinds of competence that are involved in producing grammatical utterances: in other words, as skills that could (and should) be taught in ESL classes. As more ethnographically minded work shows, however, differences in the linguistic details of questions, requests, and so on can arise from differences in social and linguistic ideologies: in other words, differences in how people imagine the social world and the workings of language. For example, Heath (1983) contrasted the kinds of questions working-class white and African American parents asked their children in the communities she studied. In many ways, she found, white parents' questions were oriented toward teaching children to participate in conversational interactions and to categorize things correctly, whereas African American parents' questions reflected their belief that children learn language on their own and need only to be encouraged to be creative, flexible contributors to interactions. In her study of an Appalachian coalfield community, Puckett (2000) showed how control of land and labor are negotiated via ways of ordering, requesting, and responding. For example, she explores why these Appalachians often seem, to outsiders, unwilling to ask for things, linking this reticence with their sense of social and material rights and obligations.

DISCOURSE AND AMERICAN ENGLISH

The work summarized in the preceding section describes patterns of discourse in American English. Current work is supplementing this with a move toward linking facts about American English on all levels with facts about discourse. This corresponds with a general tendency away from seeing "discourse" simply as another level of linguistic structure and/or another set of linguistic habits or strategies, toward seeing "discourse" as the process in which the repeatable patterns and strategies that are portrayed in descriptions of "languages" and "dialects" emerge and exploring how this process works. This trend can be seen in several overlapping areas of endeavor, which I will very briefly describe and exemplify in what follows.

INCREASED ATTENTION TO PRAGMATIC CORRELATES OF VARIATION. Studies of phonological, lexical, and morphosyntactic features that differ among American dialects are increasingly likely to explore their distribution not just by asking who uses them (men or women, older people or younger, whites or African Americans, and so on) and in what regions, but also by asking what functions these features serve in conversations and texts. For example, Mishoe and Montgomery (1994) show that the lack of historical evidence about multiple modal constructions (*might could* and other such combinations) in North and South Carolina probably has to do with the fact that multiple modals tend to occur in situations where face-saving is particularly important: face-to-face encounters in which indirectness and negotiation are at a premium. These are often family and service encounters and thus tend not to be the sorts of conversations that get preserved in historical records. In an analysis of a judge's uses of more standard-sounding *you* versus more regionally marked *ya'll*, Ching (2001) finds that the use of one or the other pronoun depends in part on the genre of the speech and on more particular features of the context. For example, *ya'll* (this is Ching's spelling of the form) can be used to establish plurality, then be followed by *you*, and sometimes the use of *ya'll* can serve as a politeness strategy.

INCREASED ATTENTION TO STRATEGIC USES OF REGIONAL AND SO-CIAL VARIATION. American dialectology was traditionally oriented to the description and documentation of older forms of folk speech, and the people who were most likely to be studied in projects like the dialect atlas surveys were likely to live in fairly homogeneous communities and to be relatively immobile socially and geographically. This meant that speaking in a particular dialect could easily be seen as a more or less automatic consequence of being from a certain place and being born into a certain ethnic group. Now, in the context of increasingly visible social and geographical mobility and economic and cultural homogenization, dialectologists and sociolinguists are becoming more and more attuned to the ways in which ways of speaking associated with region and ethnicity can function as strategic, rhetorical resources for constructing and expressing relationships and identities.

For example, Eckert's (1996, 2000) work in suburban Detroit shows that high-school students who raise the nucleus in the diphthong /ay/ more are more likely than others to orient to a local identity rather than to the larger world represented by official school activities. This association between raised /ay/ and local identity arises and is reinforced when members of the "burnout" group use this variant in particular communicative situations, such as talk about getting in trouble. Schilling-Estes (2000) explores how shifting degrees of *r*-lessness in a conversation between an

African American and a Lumbee (a North Carolina Native American) track their negotiation and renegotiation of ethnic boundaries. In Texas, Bailey and his colleagues (Bailey 1991; Bailey et al. 1993) show that monophthongization of /ay/ can be correlated with the strength of a person's affiliation with the region, and in several case studies I have explored how ways of talking and writing that sound rural, Southern, and/or feminine can function strategically for Texas women (Johnstone 1995, 1998, 1999; Johnstone and Bean 1997).

INCREASED ATTENTION TO THE FUNCTIONS OF DISCOURSE ABOUT VARIATION. For critical theorists, "discourses" are repeated ways of talking, linked to ways of imagining the world, which circulate in society via networks of power, causing people to think that the familiar way to describe, explain, and otherwise think about things is the "true" or "natural" way. Research on folk-linguistic attitudes and beliefs about regional and ethnic variation (see Preston's chapter in this volume) has extensively described popular discourses about variation in the United States. Lippi-Green's (1997) work on imitations of and discourse about nonstandard English and foreign accents in the media, the workplace, and the school shows how sociolinguistic "realism" may mask a variety of political and educational agendas. Others have explored how Anglo Americans use "junk" or "mock" Spanish expressions like *numero uno* or *hasta la vista* (Hill 1993, 1995) and how white supremacists promulgate racism through written representations of African American English on the Internet (Ronkin and Karn 1999). In addition to serving such ideological purposes in public life and the expression of personal and communal identity, representations of speech may play a role in language change, as part of the discursive process through which certain forms come to have heightened perceptual saliency and clearly elaborated, focused symbolic connections to place, ethnicity, and other elements of social meaning (Johnstone 2000a; 2000b).

INCREASED ATTENTION TO THE IMPLICATIONS OF METHOD. American dialectologists and sociolinguists have become more and more reflexive about our own discourse, about our objects of study, and in our research methods. We have begun to wonder to what extent we create categories such as "American English," "AAVE," or "Southern speech" in the process of drawing boundaries around our research sites and populations, and we have become more self-conscious about how our data-collection techniques (which almost always involve conversation) may affect our data. For example, Rickford and McNair-Knox (1994) and Cukor-Avila (2000) have shown that characteristics of interviewers can influence the speech of interviewees in ways that have not always been acknowledged. In addition to Cukor-Avila's, two other essays in the Diamond Anniversary volume of *American Speech* (Fuller 2000; Simon and Murray 2000) also urge us to consider the ways in which people act out and negotiate identities in the course of sociolinguistic interviews and underline the importance of considering the features in which we are interested in their particular, situated discursive contexts.

THE NEXT TWENTY YEARS

These summaries of past and current work suggest many directions for future research on discourse in American English and discourses about American English. The traditional focus of the American Dialect Society on region, enriched by sociolinguists' insights about the linguistic importance of ethnicity, class, age, and gender, will no doubt continue to structure many important inquiries into variation in conversation and text. But the significance of place in Americans' lives continues to evolve. Being located in the same physical place is less and less a prerequisite for mutual influence, as virtual places supplement geographical ones as sites for linguistic interaction. A person's regional identity is more and more a matter of choice, and, as cities and regions race to attract both global industry and local tourism, North Americans are required to think about, talk about, and orient to places in multiple competing ways. The significance of ethnicity, gender, and other resources for identity is also evolving. For various historical and theoretical reasons, it is no longer as easy as it once was to categorize people as "white," "Asian," or "African American," "male" or "female," or to predict how such categorizations will be reflected in their speech and writing.

New contexts for discourse in American English are also likely to encourage new lines of research. Emerging genres in new media are raising new questions: How do Americans talk in e-mail? in synchronous electronic chat? to artificially intelligent interlocutors such as talking robots? Along what lines do Americans differentiate themselves from other Americans, and how do individuals vary their discourse from situation to situation, as they do such things? American dialectologists and sociolinguists are paying increasing attention to the fact that style, however defined, plays a key role in accounting for variation. Individuals use language differently on different occasions, this be because their purposes are different, because their audiences are different, because they are projecting different identities, or some combination of these factors and others (Biber and Finegan 1994; Eckert and Rickford 2001).

These developments mean that research about American discourse will need to evolve, too. Some U.S. regions, such as the South or Appalachia, continue to have strong identities, and it will continue to be interesting and important to see how features of discourse and discourses about language and place are implicated in these identities. Likewise, some kinds of ethnic and other social differentiation continue to be pervasive and very likely to be correlated with variation in discourse structure and style, and describing those patterns of variation continues to be crucial both descriptively, to enlarge our understanding of the things North Americans do with language, and, practically, to reduce misunderstanding of one group by another.

It will also be important, however, to do newer kinds of analysis that start with particular speakers, conversations, or texts rather than with predefined groups of speakers, regions in North America, or genres of discourse, working outward to see how features of interactional style, discourse structure, and ways of referring and acting get associated with places, ethnic categories, genders, or age groups, and with situations and purposes, and how such features work as resources for individual "acts of identity" (Le Page and

Tabouret-Keller 1985; Johnstone 1996) in particular instances. In this sort of work, discourse analysis—the close, systematic unpacking of particular texts and transcripts—is increasingly likely to be the analytical method of choice.

REFERENCES

Abrahams, Roger D. 1962. "Playing the Dozens." *Journal of American Folklore* 75: 209–18.

————. 1976. *Talking Black*. Rowley, Mass.: Newbury.

Bailey, Guy. 1991. "Directions of Change in Texas English." *Journal of American Culture* 14: 125–34.

Bailey, Guy, Tom Wikle, Jan Tillery, and Lori Sand. 1993. "Some Patterns of Linguistic Diffusion." *Language Variation and Change* 5: 359–90.

Bartelt, Guillermo. 1993. "Urban American Indian Intertribal Discourse." *English World-Wide* 14: 57–70.

Basso, Keith H. 1970. "'To Give Up on Words': Silence in Western Apache Culture." *Southwestern Journal of Anthropology* 26: 213–30.

Bauman, Richard. 1986. *Story, Performance, and Event: Contextual Studies of Oral Narrative*. Cambridge: Cambridge Univ. Press.

Biber, Douglas. 1987. "A Textual Comparison of British and American Writing." *American Speech* 62: 99–119.

Biber, Douglas, and Edward Finegan, eds. 1994. *Sociolinguistic Perspectives on Register*. New York: Oxford Univ. Press.

Blum-Kulka, Shoshana, Juliane House, and Gabriele Kasper, eds. 1989. *Cross-Cultural Pragmatics: Requests and Apologies*. Norwood, N.J.: Ablex.

Blyth, Carl, Jr., Sigrid Rechtenwald, and Jenny Wang. 1990. "I'm Like, 'Say What?!' A New Quotative in American Oral Narrative." *American Speech* 65: 215–27.

Brown, Penelope, and Stephen C. Levinson. 1987. *Politeness: Some Universals in Language Usage*. Cambridge: Cambridge Univ. Press.

Butters, Ronald R. 2001. "Presidential Address: Literary Qualities in Sociolinguistic Narratives of Personal Experience." *American Speech* 76: 227–35.

Ching, Marvin. 1982. "The Question Intonation in Assertions." *American Speech* 57: 95–107.

————. 1987. "'Ma'am' and 'Sir': Modes of Mitigation and Politeness in the Southern United States" (abstract). *Newsletter of the American Dialect Society* 19.2: 10.

————. 2001. "Plural *you/ya'll* Variation by a Court Judge: Situational Use." *American Speech* 76: 115–27.

Coles, Felice Anne. 1997. "Solidarity Cues in New Orleans English." In *Language Variety in the South Revisited*, ed. Cynthia Bernstein, Thomas Nunnally, and Robin Sabino, 219–24. Tuscaloosa: Univ. of Alabama Press.

Crews, Harry. 1990. *Body*. New York: Poseidon.

Cukor-Avila, Patricia. 2000. "Revisiting the Observer's Paradox." *American Speech* 75: 253–54.

Darnell, Regna. 1974. "Correlates of Cree Narrative Performance." In *Explorations in the Ethnography of Speaking*, ed. Richard Bauman and Joel Sherzer, 315–36. New York: Cambridge Univ. Press.

Davies, Catherine. 1997. "Social Meaning in Southern Speech from an Interactional Sociolinguistic Perspective: An Integrative Discourse Analysis of Terms of Address." In *Language Variety in the South Revisited*, ed. Cynthia Bernstein, Thomas Nunnally, and Robin Sabino, 225–41. Tuscaloosa: Univ. of Alabama Press.

Devitt, Amy J. 1989. "Genre as a Textual Variable: Some Historical Evidence from Scots and American English." *American Speech* 64: 291–303.

Eckert, Penelope. 1996. "(ay) Goes to the City: Exploring the Expressive Use of Variation." In *Towards a Social Science of Language: Papers in Honor of William Labov*, vol. 1, *Variation and Change in Language and Society*, ed. Gregory R. Guy, Crawford Feagin, Deborah Schiffrin, and John Baugh, 47–68. Amsterdam: Benjamins.

————. 2000. *Linguistic Variation as Social Practice: The Linguistic Construction of Identity in Belten High*. Oxford: Blackwell.

Eckert, Penelope, and John R. Rickford, eds. 2001. *Style and Sociolinguistic Variation*. Cambridge: Cambridge Univ. Press.

Edwards, Walter. 1989. "*Suurin, koocharin*, and *grannin* in Guyana: Masked Intentions and Communications Theory." *American Speech* 64: 225–32.

Erickson, Frederick. 1984. "Rhetoric, Anecdote, and Rhapsody: Coherence Strategies in a Conversation among Black American Adolescents." In *Coherence in Spoken and Written Discourse*, ed. Deborah Tannen, 81–154. Norwood, N.J.: Ablex.

Etter-Lewis, Gwendolyn. 1993. *My Soul Is My Own: Oral Narratives of African American Women in the Professions*. New York: Routledge.

Fellegy, Anna M. 1995. "Patterns and Functions of Minimal Response." *American Speech* 70: 186–99.

Ferrara, Kathleen, and Barbara Bell. 1995. "Sociolinguistic Variation and Discourse Function of Constructed Dialogue Introducers: The Case of *be + like.*" *American Speech* 70: 265–90.

Fuller, Janet M. 2000. "Changing Perspectives on Data: Interviews as Situated Speech." *American Speech* 75: 388–90.

Goody, Jack, and Ian Watt. 1968. "The Consequences of Literacy." In *Literacy in Traditional Societies*, ed. Jack Goody, 27–84. Cambridge: Cambridge Univ. Press.

Gumperz, John J. 1982a. *Discourse Strategies.* Cambridge: Cambridge Univ. Press.

———, ed. 1982b. *Language and Social Identity.* Cambridge: Cambridge Univ. Press.

Halliday, M. A. K., and Ruqaiya Hasan. 1976. *Cohesion in English.* London: Longman.

Heath, Shirley Brice. 1983. *Ways with Words: Language, Life, and Work in Communities and Classrooms.* Cambridge: Cambridge Univ. Press.

Herbert, Robert K. 1986. "Say 'Thank You'—or Something." *American Speech* 61: 76–88.

Hill, Jane H. 1993. "Is It Really 'No Problemo'? Junk Spanish and Anglo Racism." In *Salsa I: Proceedings of the First Annual Symposium about Language and Society—Austin*, ed. Robin Queen and Rusty Barrett, 1–12. Austin: Dept. of Linguistics, Univ. of Texas.

———. 1995. "Junk Spanish, Covert Racism, and the (Leaky) Boundary between Public and Private Spheres." *Pragmatics* 5: 197–212.

Johnstone, Barbara. 1990a. *Stories, Community, and Place: Narratives from Middle America.* Bloomington: Indiana Univ. Press.

———. 1990b. "Variation in Discourse: Midwestern Narrative Style." *American Speech* 65: 195–214.

———. 1992. "Violence and Civility in Discourse: Uses of Mitigation by Rural Southern White Men." *SECOL Review* 16: 1–19.

———. 1994. "'You Gone Have to Learn to Talk Right': Linguistic Deference and Regional Dialect in Harry Crews's *Body.*" In *The Text and Beyond: Essays in Literary Linguistics*, ed. Cynthia Goldin Bernstein, 278–95. Tuscaloosa: Univ. of Alabama Press.

———. 1995. "Sociolinguistic Resources, Individual Identities, and the Public Speech Styles of Texas Women." *Journal of Linguistic Anthropology* 5: 1–20.

———. 1996. *The Linguistic Individual: Self-Expression in Language and Linguistics.* New York: Oxford Univ. Press.

————. 1998. "'Sounding Country' in Urbanizing Texas: Private Speech in Public Discourse." *Michigan Discussions in Anthropology* 13: 153–64.

————. 1999. "Uses of Southern Speech by Contemporary Texas Women." In *Styling the Other*, ed. Ben Rampton, 505–22. Special issue of *Journal of Sociolinguistics* 3.4.

————. 2000a. "How to Speak Like a Pittsburgher: Representations of Speech and the Study of Linguistic Variation." Plenary address presented at the Sociedad Argentina de Lingüística, Mar del Plata, Argentina, Sept.

————. 2000b. "Representing American Speech." *American Speech* 75: 390–92.

Johnstone, Barbara, and Judith Mattson Bean. 1997. "Self-Expression and Linguistic Variation." *Language in Society* 26: 221–46.

Kochman, Thomas. 1972. *Rappin' and Stylin' Out*. Urbana: Univ. of Illinois Press.

————. 1981. *Black and White Styles in Conflict*. Chicago: Univ. of Chicago Press.

Kuiper, Koenraad. 1992. "The Oral Tradition in Auction Speech." *American Speech* 67: 279–89.

Kuiper, Koenraad, and Frederick Tillis. 1985. "The Chant of the Tobacco Auctioneer." *American Speech* 60: 141–49.

Labov, William. 1972. *Language in the Inner City: Studies in the Black English Vernacular*. Philadelphia: Univ. of Pennsylvania Press.

Labov, William, and Joshua Waletzky. 1967. "Narrative Analysis: Oral Versions of Personal Experience." In *Essays on the Verbal and Virtual Arts*, ed. June Helm, 12–44. Seattle: Univ. of Washington Press. Repr. in *Oral Versions of Personal Experience: Three Decades of Narrative Analysis*, ed. Michael G. W. Bamberg, 3–38. Special issue of *Journal of Narrative and Life History* 7.1–4 (1997).

Le Page, R. B., and Andrée Tabouret-Keller. 1985. *Acts of Identity: Creole-Based Approaches to Language and Ethnicity*. Cambridge: Cambridge Univ. Press.

Linde, Charlotte. 1993. *Life Stories: The Creation of Coherence*. Oxford: Oxford Univ. Press.

Lippi-Green, Rosina. 1997. *English with an Accent: Language, Ideology, and Discrimination in the United States*. London: Routledge.

McLemore, Cynthia Ann. 1991. "The Pragmatic Interpretation of English Intonation: Sorority Speech." Ph.D. diss., Univ. of Texas at Austin.

McLeod-Porter, Delma. 1991. "Gender, Ethnicity, and Narrative: A Linguistic and Rhetorical Analysis of Adolescents' Personal Experience Stories." Ph.D. diss., Texas A&M Univ.

Mishoe, Margaret, and Michael Montgomery. 1994. "The Pragmatics of Multiple Modal Variation in North and South Carolina." *American Speech* 69: 3–29.

Mitchell-Kernan, Claudia. 1972. "Signifying and Marking: Two Afro-American Speech Acts." In *Directions in Sociolinguistics: The Ethnography of Communication*, ed. John J. Gumperz and Dell Hymes, 161–79. New York: Holt, Rinehart and Winston.

Morgan, Marcyliena. 1998. "More than a Mood or an Attitude: Discourse and Verbal Genres in African-American Culture." In *African-American English: Structure, History, and Use*, ed. Salikoko S. Mufwene, John R. Rickford, Guy Bailey, and John Baugh, 251–81. London: Routledge.

Needed Research in American English (1983). 1984. Publication of the American Dialect Society 71. University: Univ. of Alabama Press.

Ong, Walter J. 1982. *Orality and Literacy: The Technologizing of the Word*. London: Methuen.

Patrick, Peter L., and Arvilla Payne-Jackson. 1996. "Functions of Rasta Talk in a Jamaican Creole Healing Narrative: 'A bigfoot dem i' mi.'" *Journal of Linguistic Anthropology* 6: 47–84.

Pitts, Walter. 1989. "West African Poetics in the Black Preaching Style." *American Speech* 64: 137–49.

Polanyi, Livia. 1981. "What Stories Can Tell Us about Their Tellers' World." *Poetics Today* 2: 97–112.

———. 1985. *Telling the American Story: A Structural and Cultural Analysis of Conversational Storytelling*. Norwood, N.J.: Abex.

Puckett, Anita. 2000. *Seldom Ask, Never Tell: Labor and Discourse in Appalachia*. New York: Oxford Univ. Press.

Rickford, John R., and Faye McNair-Knox. 1994. "Addressee- and Topic-Influenced Style Shift: A Quantitative Sociolinguistic Study." In *Sociolinguistic Perspectives on Register*, ed. Douglas Biber and Edward Finegan, 235–76. Oxford: Oxford Univ. Press.

Riessman, Catherine Kohler. 1988. "Worlds of Difference: Contrasting Experience in Marriage and Narrative Style." In *Gender and Discourse: The Power of Talk*, ed. Alexandra Dundas Todd and Sue Fisher, 151–73. Norwood, N.J.: Ablex.

Romaine, Suzanne, and Deborah Lange. 1991. "The Use of *like* as a Marker of Reported Speech and Thought: A Case of Grammaticalization in Progress." *American Speech* 66: 227–79.

Ronkin, Maggie, and Helen E. Karn. 1999. "Mock Ebonics: Linguistic Racism in Parodies of Ebonics on the Internet." *Journal of Sociolinguistics* 3: 360–80.

Schiffrin, Deborah. 1984. "Jewish Argument as Sociability." *Language in Society* 13: 311–35.

———. 1987. *Discourse Markers*. Cambridge: Cambridge Univ. Press.

Schilling-Estes, Natalie. 2000. "Redrawing Ethnic Dividing Lines through Linguistic Creativity." *American Speech* 75: 357–59.

Schneider, Edgar W., ed. 1996. *Focus on the USA*. Varieties of English around the World 16. Amsterdam: Benjamins.

Scollon, Ron, and Suzanne B. K. Scollon. 1981. *Narrative, Literacy, and Face in Interethnic Communication*. Norwood, N.J.: Ablex.

Shuman, Amy. 1986. *Storytelling Rights: Uses of Oral and Written Texts by Urban Adolescents*. New York: Cambridge Univ. Press.

Simon, Beth Lee, and Thomas E. Murray. 2000. "Richly Qualitative and Rigorously Quantitative." *American Speech* 75: 401–5.

Spears, James E. 1974. "Southern Folk Greetings and Responses." *Mississippi Folklore Register* 8: 218–20.

Tannen, Deborah. 1981. "New York Jewish Conversational Style." *International Journal of the Sociology of Language* 30: 133–49.

———. 1984. *Conversational Style: Analyzing Talk among Friends*. Norwood, N.J.: Ablex.

———. 1988. "The Commingling of Orality and Literacy: Giving a Paper at a Scholarly Conference." *American Speech* 63: 34–43.

———. 2000. "'Don't Just Sit There—Interrupt!' Pacing and Pausing in Conversational Style." *American Speech* 75: 393–95.

The Trip to Bountiful. 1985. Directed by Peter Masterson. Screenplay by Horton Foote. 105 min. Dallas, Tex.: Film Dallas Pictures; New York: Bountiful Film Partners.

Wolfson, Nessa. 1981. "Compliments in Cross-Cultural Perspective." *TESOL Quarterly* 15: 117–24.

6. SOCIAL VARIATION
IN AMERICA

PENELOPE ECKERT

Stanford University

1. FOUNDATIONS FOR THE EIGHTIES

THE PAST 20 YEARS of study of social variation have built on the solid foundation set out by the early community studies of class stratification and of ethnic dialects that began in the 1960s. These were the years that introduced quantitative methods to the study of variation and that developed an overview of dialect diversity across large urban populations. A series of urban survey studies in the late 1960s and the 1970s (Labov 1966; Wolfram 1969; Trudgill 1974; Macaulay 1977) laid out the systematic structure of class diversity, showing a regular stratification of regional and ethnic differentiation in speech across the socioeconomic hierarchy, with the most differentiated language at the lower end of the hierarchy and the least differentiated at the upper. The relatively undifferentiated upper-middle-class variety is commonly referred to as the *standard*, and the locally differentiated working-class variety is commonly referred to as the *vernacular*. The vernacular identifies the speaker's local origins and signals local membership and loyalty. The standard, on the other hand, is associated with the institutions of education, culture, government, and business that set global prestige standards for society at large. These institutions and networks have been theorized as the sites of a standard language market (Bourdieu and Boltanski 1975; Sankoff and Laberge 1978). The relative ethnic and geographic uniformity of the standard is symbolic of the global networks that constitute these institutions, and downplaying difference amounts to a rejection of the local (and its interests) in favor of global and institutional interests.

The notion of the vernacular underlies most of the theory construction during the early period and has been extremely powerful in laying down a coherent foundation for understanding variation and change. To some extent, work in the past 20 years has begun to reexamine the status of the vernacular, and this reexamination has been increasingly powerful as we move into the second millennium. For this reason, I will begin with a somewhat lengthy discussion of the vernacular-standard opposition and its significance for the study of social variation. I will then move on to discuss the work of the 1980s and 1990s, and the questions this work has raised for the future.

1.1. THE VERNACULAR. Labov (1972c) redefined and placed the vernacular at the center of linguistic study by locating each speaker's "natural" language in his or her most unmonitored speech:

The style which is most regular in its structure and in its relation to the evolution of the language is the vernacular, in which the minimum attention is paid to speech. [112]

Labov's vernacular is a cognitive object—almost presocial—learned early in life and systematic by virtue of its direct relation to the language faculty. By the same relation, it is the source of natural, regular linguistic change. By contrast, the standard is a social invention, the result of the conscious retention of conservative patterns—the embodiment of the rejection of natural change. With this definition, Labov departed from the popular use of *vernacular* to refer to the language of "the people," and placed the vernacular at the spontaneous, casual end of every speaker's repertoire. However, class is central to the speaker's use of this repertoire as the social meanings of standard and vernacular derive from the class hierarchy and are embedded in each speaker's language development and lifelong usage strategies. Social meaning is located in the socioeconomic continuum by virtue of the global prestige of the standard and the networks and institutions in which it is located. By contrast, the vernacular is stigmatized. Speakers first learn their vernacular, and as they come into increasing contact with the standard and the situations of its use, they internalize standard norms and the social evaluation of the opposition between standard and vernacular. The avoidance of stigma, or even the search for prestige (in the case of hypercorrection; Labov 1972b), is presented as what drives stylistic variation, locating social agency in language use to conservative correction. (Needless to say, the higher one is in the socioeconomic hierarchy, the less adjustment this will involve.) This yields a personal stylistic continuum from more vernacular to more standard—and from more natural to less.

Labov (2001a), in describing this intraspeaker stylistic continuum, emphasizes the role of attention to speech, providing a cognitive mechanism for the social impact on language use. The subtle association between the class hierarchy and attention to speech has emerged in a variety of ways. If the individual's stylistic continuum has been seen as a continuum of decreasing naturalness from the speaker's most vernacular to the speaker's most standard style, some (Kroch 1978; Kroch and Small 1978) have viewed the socioeconomic continuum itself as a continuum of naturalness, arguing that those engaged in the standard language market, whether by virtue of education, occupation, or social networks, are more inclined to monitor their speech.

My emphasis on the vernacular here stems from the fact that it has created an underlying metaphor of naturalness that has touched every aspect of the study of variation. While this metaphor has been fundamental to modern linguistic science since the Neogrammarians (Eckert 2003), it does not account for all variation, and most particularly, it precludes exploration of some of the most interesting social dynamics of language use. As I will discuss in section 3, work in recent decades has probed the limits of attention paid to speech and has expanded the range of study of variation—most particularly the use of variation to construct social meaning.

1.2. THE ASYMMETRIC TREATMENT OF ETHNIC DIALECTS. Simultaneously with the studies of the social stratification of variation in urban communities, there was considerable work done on ethnic variability. While the socioeconomic hierarchy was treated as a continuum, however, analytic practice constructed strict boundaries between ethnic dialects and the speech of the white Anglo population. This was particularly true of work on the African American Vernacular in the 1960s and 1970s (Shuy, Wolfram, and Riley 1967; Labov et al. 1968; Wolfram 1969; Labov 1972a), stemming from the social and educational motivations for this work. The concern with African American Vernacular English (AAVE) arose from the importance of legitimating the dialect of poor kids in school in the eyes of educators and was part of a liberatory project. And since grammar was the focus of stigmatization of AAVE, this work primarily examined syntax and morphology rather than phonology. The establishment of AAVE (then referred to as *Non-Standard Negro English*, later as *Black English*) as a fully systematic variety separate from (hence not to be evaluated from the perspective of) white dialects—both standard and vernacular—led to a very different focus in the study of African American speech than of white speech. The focus on the vernacular effectively erased diversity within the African American community and left fairly unexplored the nature of the borders between white and black dialects. Aside from Wolfram's (1969) study, there has been no systematic treatment of the socioeconomic continuum within African American communities. Thus while white dialects are seen as a continuum from standard to vernacular, African American dialects have been defined as vernacular, despite the protests of a number of African American scholars (Taylor 1971; Hoover 1978). This leaves a tacit assumption that African American English exists only in the vernacular and that the standard is not only uniform across ethnic groups, but defined by white speakers. It ignores the long-standing African American bourgeoisie with its own African American standard that differs phonologically but not grammatically from the white standard, and it views any differences in African American speakers' standard speech as nonstandard by virtue of missing an external target.

Further, while African American vernaculars have been studied in a variety of locations in the United States, the emphasis has been on the similarity of the dialect across the United States, and there has been little attention to regional differences. These differences no doubt reside primarily in phonology—differences that have been attested by a variety of African American linguists (Rickford 1977). This erasure of regional difference renders AAVE a kind of deterritorialized dialect, while the regional dialects are defined by white speech. While there has been some attention to African Americans' adoption or nonadoption of certain regional phonological features of white regional dialects (Ash and Myhill 1986; Jones 2003), the lack of attention to African American phonology has precluded attention to phonological regionalisms that are purely African American.

Scholarship on Latino English began with early studies of Puerto Rican English in New York City and vicinity (Wolfram 1971; Fishman et al. 1973) and years of work at the Centro de Estudios Puertorriqueños in New York, much of which has focused on code-switching. While the study of code-switching is beyond the purview of this chapter, a good many dialect resources in English come from coterritorial languages and emerge in the dynamics and linguistic practices of bilingual communities. Studies of these dynamics and ideologies about language choice and language mixing are fundamental to our understanding of the meanings of the variables once they enter English. I will return to this in section 3.

1.3. UNFINISHED BUSINESS. Moving into the final two decades of the twentieth century, the study of social variation was ready to build on a solid foundation in what one might call the "big picture"—the ethnic, socioeconomic, and stylistic stratification of variables and its relation to the spread of change. There remain, though, some serious gaps in this picture.

The asymmetric treatment of ethnic dialects continues to this day, and there is a clear need for the study of diversity within the speech of African Americans. The study of the phonology of African American English in its full range of variability—by class and region—is clearly called for. The picture of the social stratification of white dialects is not complete either. There are actually few large systematic survey studies of the social stratification of English in U.S. cities, and the findings in one city are likely to have an inordinately large impact on theories of class stratification. Labov's (1966) New York City study serves as the touchstone for variation theory, but it is not clear how typical New York is of U.S. cities, especially in other regions. It is not clear, for example, that local phonological features are as strongly evaluated in cities of the Midwest and the West, and the social significance of regional features in Southern cities is no doubt complex. Furthermore, the lower-middle-class crossover that Labov (1966) found in New York

City endures for many as a regular pattern, and one that indicates a change in progress. In actual fact, this pattern has not been widely replicated, and it is not at all clear whether it is specific to the Labov study. More generally, work since the 1980s has shown considerable interaction among social variables (e.g., gender, age, and class), yet most community studies do not separate these variables out in a very clean way (with the exception of Wolfram 1969). Another large gap in our "big picture" is the nature of the continuum between urban and rural dialects. If traditional dialectology focused on rural speakers, the study of sociolinguistic variation has neglected them almost entirely (but see Ito 1999).

2. RETHINKING CATEGORIES:
THE MOVE INTO THE EIGHTIES

As the survey method provided an invaluable outline of societal variation, it raised a variety of questions that became central preoccupations in the ensuing 20 years. One set of questions centered on the nature of demographic constraints and possible interactions among them. The early emphasis on class dominated thought about variation in such a way that it subordinated other demographic categories. For example, gender was viewed in terms of its relation to class, so that women were viewed as more class-conscious than men or as having less access to mobility through occupation, hence opting for symbolic means to achieve status (Trudgill 1972). More textured consideration of gender, race, and even age followed in the 1980s as variationists examined social categories more closely and as they became more engaged with current social theory. The stratified model of class that these studies embodied also raised questions about whether some situations might call more for other models. Rickford (1986), for example, pointed out that a conflict model may be more appropriate in some situations, and Frazer (1983) pointed out that the study of rural communities requires a reconsideration of class as well.

2.1. INSIDE THE DEMOGRAPHIC VARIABLES. Perhaps most far-reaching was the recognition that social variables are not necessarily independent. This became particularly clear in the study of gender. People have generally sought evidence of, and explanations for, gendered patterns of language variation in across-the-board differences between male and female speakers. However, the original belief that women are more conservative than men (Trudgill 1972) became untenable as it became clear that women were leading in sound change. Further, Labov (1991) noted a common crossover pattern in which the gendered use of variables switches altogether across the socioeconomic hierarchy. Thus, working-class women often lead in the use of vernacular variables, while upper-middle-class women lead in the use of standard variables. If work on gender in the early days of variation was inhibited by a lack of a good gender theory, the explosion of research in the field of language and gender and the construction of theories of language and gender have had significant implications for variation. The crossover pattern that Labov found is an illustration of a more general fact that women use variation more than men to signal social differences among themselves. Thus, the importance of gender is not simply an opposition between male and female across the board, but the structuring of differences among women and among men (Eckert 2000; Eckert and McConnell-Ginet 2003). At the same time, it would not do to discount the importance of male-female distinction, but the gender hierarchy makes this distinction asymmetric. It is quite probable that the construction of hegemonic masculinity constrains men to be concerned with differentiating themselves from women (Meyerhoff 1996), while women are not similarly constrained. This may well explain why male sociolinguists tend to focus on the male-female opposition in their analyses.

If early work on gender suffered from a lack of good gender theory, a similar problem has plagued the study of rural dialects. The general view of rural dialects as conservative appeared to be supported by Callary's (1975) finding that the height of /æ/ in Illinois was a function of the size of the speaker's community, suggesting that change spreads down the urban hierarchy. However, Schilling-Estes (2002), using Smith Island, Maryland, as an example, argues that tight-knit isolated communities are not necessarily linguistically conservative, but may (as in the Smith Island case) show significant linguistic differentiation both from outside dialects and among groups within. Frazer (1983) found that raising of the nucleus in /aw/ in rural Illinois was spreading not from town to the rural area, but vice versa, and emphasized the importance of social changes in rural America in considering rural dialects. He also pointed out the importance of cultural meanings that transcend across-the-board categorizations like urban and rural, as the opposition between North and South is a very live social issue in the community he studied. For that matter, the phenomenon of "country" speech and its relation to ideology across the United States is worth exploring (see section 3.1).

The importance of examining a variety of variables in any given community cannot be overemphasized. Bailey et al. (1993) have shown a variety of geographic patterns of spread of innovations in Oklahoma and have argued that the pattern of spread of innovation depends on the social meaning of the innovation. For example, external norms tend to enter through, and spread from, urban areas (hierarchical diffusion), whereas innovations that represent the revitalization of traditional norms tend to spread counter-hierarchically. Understanding these movements requires both a broad survey picture and an ethnographic study of the social dynamics of rural areas and the interfaces among city, town, and country. Above all, we need a coherent account of rural social structure and practice to inform linguistic analysis.

Age is another social parameter that has required a good deal of work. It has generally been treated as a continuum and plays a central role in the study of change in progress. However, this role depends on the critical period—on the assumption that the speaker's system does not change significantly after a fairly early age, and the daunting task of establishing the extent to which this is actually true still lies before us (Eckert 1997). Meanwhile, it is clear that age enters into the social order in important ways, and its social construction is diverse from community to community. Aging certainly has different consequences for people in different social locations—for example, for women and men, and for middle class and working class people. One life passage that has received some attention in the past 20 years is adolescence. Given the intensity of identity work in adolescence, it is not surprising that adolescents have emerged as leaders in the use of vernacular features (Chambers 1995), hence as leaders in change. Thus, the earlier attention to the relation between variation and adult class has expanded to include the study of adolescent social and linguistic practice, with a variety of ethnographic studies of adolescent variation. Adolescent identity work in the United States emerges as part of the construction of a peer-based social order and involves the ordering of diversity within the cohort and the negotiation of the terms of insertion in the wider society. Roberts (1999) has convincingly argued that the creolization of Hawaiian Pidgin English was accomplished in the early part of the nineteenth century by multiethnic groups of preadolescents and adolescents as they worked together to constitute a joint local identity.

If the 1980s brought about a reconsideration of categories, they also brought about a shift in perspective—not necessarily a new perspective, but a shift back to considerations that had been around in the early years but were backgrounded during the survey era. One might call the past 20 years of the study of social variation the "ethnographic era." Although the earliest quantitative studies of variation by Fisher (1958) and Labov (1972b) focused on local groups, the survey era that followed eclipsed ethnographic work and the local identities found in such work. Studies of local "native" categories have brought back the insights of the Martha's Vineyard study, making it clear that broad categories such as class and gender both structure, and emerge from, local dynamics.

2.2. THE ETHNOGRAPHIC TURN: EXPLORING "THE LOCAL." Milroy's (1980) study of Belfast reintroduced the use of ethnographic methods into community studies, examining the significance of social network structure in the speech of the working class. This move from categories to configurations was an important shift to a focus on speakers' direct social engagement as a force in language use. It emphasized an aspect of class difference—that is, that working-class networks tend to be dense, multiplex, and locally based, while middle-class people tend to have more separate networks for different domains of activity and to be not as locally based. The expansion of this view to ethnic communities (e.g., African American, Edwards 1992; Jewish, Knack 1991; Cajun, Dubois and Horvath 1998; and Polish, Edwards and Krakow 1985) emphasizes that engagement in distinctive communities yields linguistic distinctiveness (Gal and Irvine 1995). It has been clear that the vernacular is associated with local communities and with the positive values associated with those communities. Woolard (1985) has emphasized the force of alternative linguistic markets, and variationists have always recognized the fundamental force of the local vernacular market. Thus, although the pull of the vernacular market has been theorized as the pull of the unconscious, the strategic use of the vernaculars of juxtaposed diverse urban groups competing to define the local is no doubt a key force in the development of linguistic innovation and diversity.

The nature of localness is key to the understanding of the spread of change and the social meaning of variation. Localness can be established only in distinction with some extralocal, and that extralocal can be salient only if it participates in some way in the life of the local. Labov's (1972b) study of Martha's Vineyard showed a reversal of the lowering of the nucleus of /ay/ and /aw/ among people who embraced the traditional local fishing culture in response to the threat of incursion from the mainland tourist economy. While the material for this pattern came from the contrast between the local raised nucleus and the mainland lowered nucleus, its social salience was established locally between groups with opposing orientations. My own work with adolescents in Detroit suburban schools (Eckert 2000) found a hegemonic opposition between class-based social categories—the middle-class-based jocks, who centered their lives in the school institution, and the working-class-based burnouts, who centered their lives in the local area. The terms of this opposition were based in the opposition between the local and the institutional—but the local is defined not in terms of neighborhood or town, but more broadly as participation in the wider conurbation. Milroy and Milroy (1985) argued that the strong ties of the local network enforce local conformity, while casual extralocal contact through weak ties is the vehicle for the spread of change. This implies a fairly strict opposition between the local and the extralocal. However, the burnouts focus jointly on building lives and expanding their networks to take in more urban opportunities, hence the relation between strong and weak ties is far more organic than suggested by Milroy and Milroy's work. The very exploration of weak ties is part of the practice of these dense and multiplex network clusters, and the constant exposure to urban speech is integral to their local practice. Similarly, Labov's (2001b) neighborhood studies in Philadelphia have traced the adult leaders in sound change to people who have both dense and multiplex ties within the neighborhood and extensive ties outside. In this work, Labov hints at a tie between network structure and specific kinds of life histories and personalities—a link that is crucial to our understanding of variation but that has not yet become part of our analytic practice. I will return to this in section 3.

The study of variation has traditionally involved the circumscription of a speech community, and the use of variation has been interpreted with respect to the boundaries of the community. Thus, Labov's (1972a) lames were defined as peripheral to the gang under study, and while the burnouts' networks extended well beyond the school that served as the locus of my own study, the study focused on speakers in school. The result is an idealization of the community as centered, with little attention to its borders. But these communities are ideological objects and often the construction of the analysts themselves, and our focus on centers leaves us only to speculate about the human movement that locates people both geographically and socially. Pratt (1987) has argued for a focus on borders in the study of language, and a study of language and social networks that does not take speech community as its object of study could be a crucial part of this focus. The borders, for example, between the urban, the suburban, and particularly the rural remain surprisingly unexplored. And even more unexplored are the borders between groups that have been until now treated as separate (Sweetland 2002).

3. THE COMPLEXITY OF IDENTITY

As the focus turns from the macrostructure of language use to linguistic practice in local communities, it becomes more difficult to think of speakers as coincidences of multiple categories and to think of their language use as unfolding passively from their social address. The social order, the identities that make it up, and speakers' identities from moment to moment are not simple or stationary, and stylistic practice is an integral part of social movement. Le Page and Tabouret-Keller (1985) have emphasized that speakers construct selves as they navigate a diverse social and linguistic landscape. This view has been taken up by a variety of researchers in recent years, leading us away from the view of style as purely a function of attention to speech, and into the relatively intentional construction of distinctiveness.

3.1. AGENCY. Acts of identity are not simply acts of affiliation with categories, but interpretive acts. The spread beyond the group of origin is a complex process of identification, interpretation, and reinterpretation, and understanding this process requires not simply the analyst's understanding of the group of origin, but the adopters' understanding of that group and of the meaning of the variable. Speakers look out on a social landscape, identifying social types and interpreting their significance in that landscape, and assessing their own relation and orientation to those types. In the process, they note aspects of speech styles and imbue them with meaning based on this social interpretation. The meaning of variables, thus, changes as the variable spreads beyond its point of origin. Understanding this process is central to the study of the social meaning of variation and requires that we pay more attention to the process of iconization (Gal and Irvine 1995; Irvine 2001)—the imbuing of linguistic varieties and/or features with stereotypic qualities associated with the speakers who employ them. Work on language ideology (Hill 1993; Lippi-Green 1997) and perceptual dialectology (Preston 1989) is crucial, in this case, to understand the potential meanings of material borrowed from other varieties. Future research should be pairing studies of stylistic resources with experimental methods and other measures for assessing the interpretation of these resources.

Some work on bilingual communities has focused on the nativization of features of coterritorial languages in English, examining substrate effect directly in the emergence of a local native English vernacular. Nativization, like creolization, occurs when a locally born generation coconstructs a local identity based in English. In this process, second-language features that are particularly identified with desirable aspects of group culture may be deployed as first-language variables. Several researchers have found evidence of this process in bilingual communities in which the younger generation, functioning in a primarily English environment, use substratal variants at rates similar to their grandparents', who have functioned primarily in the coterritorial language. The in-between generation—the first fluent English speakers—have had a significantly lower use of these variants. Santa Ana (1992) and Bayley (1994) found this pattern for *t/d* deletion in Mexican American Spanish, and Dubois and Horvath (1998) found it for the fortition of /th/ and /dh/ in Cajun English.

This latter variable seems to have emerged in ethnic communities across the country—as variable features that are not regional, but that seem to take on meaning locally—most likely by virtue of their association with immigrant languages. The lack of interdental fricatives in most of the immigrant languages of the United States makes the substitution of stops or other fricatives for /th/ and /dh/ a common feature of the accents of nonnative speakers. The stop variants are common variables in urban dialects—they have been found in the Polish community of Hamtramck in Detroit (Edwards and Krakow 1985), Chicano gangs in California (Mendoza-Denton 1997), Italians in Chicago (Eckert unpublished), and German farmers in Wisconsin (Rose 2003). Labov (1966) found them socially stratified in New York City, and while he did not emphasize their ethnic significance, it is notable that his working- and lower-middle-class samples were made up primarily of Italians. This is not to say that this feature is limited to second-language groups, but this may well be their origin.

Coupland (1985, 2001) has demonstrated how speakers use a wide range of dialect resources in constructing personae—resources that one would not argue were part of one's "native" dialect, but resources that are both spontaneously and meaningfully employed. By reaching out to employ speech characteristics of well-known types, Coupland's (2001) disc jockey, for example, evokes and invokes social associations to position himself with respect to his radio audience. Bucholtz's (1999) and Cutler's (1999) studies of white kids using resources from AAVE have moved farther from the native dialect. In doing so, they emphasize that it is not an appropriation of racial identity but of qualities that the white speakers find admirable in their view of this racial group. These studies emphasize the performative nature of social identity and move the focus from the reflection of identity to the construction of identity. In the process, the focus shifts from local change in progress and ingrained patterns, seriously expanding the repertoire of variables to study. The popular press has been systematically excited about the role of the media in the spread of linguistic change, particularly among the adolescent population, but linguists—in their eagerness to emphasize the complexity of linguistic change—have not taken these observations seriously. Nonetheless, it is clear that there are features that can spread via very weak ties. It is important to consider the ways in which speakers interact with media—for example, the ways in which people interact over popular television shows, assuming the identities of characters in long discussion of plots and developments. And since linguistic style may be an integral part of certain musical genres (e.g., country music, blues, hiphop), any individual can quasi-legitimately adopt a style not their own while singing. And inasmuch as music is part of social situations, this style can bleed into conversational style—possibly via other spoken genres specific to the same kinds of situations in which one might expect to hear the music.

As we expand our study to consider social agency in variation and variables that do not behave like changes from below, we need to explicitly examine the nature of the relations among these variables. This is not an argument for discarding the theory of the vernacular, but for studying both agency and the limits of attention paid to speech.

3.2. STYLE AND THE MEANING OF VARIABLES. The traditional view of variation focuses on variation as reflecting categories that people belong or aspire to. But people also use variation to tell lies about who they are—for instance, graduate students who adopt hyperfeminine styles to support themselves by doing phone sex (Hall 1992). And they use variation to move themselves around a complex landscape of communities and to push the envelope in that landscape. This means that variation is not a consequence, but an integral part, of social change. Zhang's (2001) examination of the central use of linguistic style in the construction of a new financial ("yuppy") elite in Beijing is a case in point. This means that the social meaning of variation cannot be understood through a focus on existing types, but through consideration of the construction of types—of personae. The attention-paid-to-speech model of style assumes a static identity, and that stylistic variation amounts to a muting of that style. If we accept that variation is a resource for the construction of complex identities, then we need to focus on the variety of personae that an individual may want to assume from one time to the next. Podesva (2003) has begun to examine this in his study of a gay medical student as he moves from a professional setting with patients, through a phone conversation with his father, to a barbecue with his friends. The "gay diva" and the medical professional are quite different personae, and one cannot be said to be more "natural" than the other, and certainly one cannot be said to be a casual or formal version of the other. Hopefully, the future will bring more studies of individuals as they move from situation to situation and from community of practice to community of practice (Eckert and McConnell-Ginet 1992), deploying different personae or emphasizing different aspects of the same persona.

The early assumption in the study of variation was that phonological variables have no meaning independent of their social correlates—that they mark the categories of speakers who use them most frequently and may take on meanings based on qualities associated with those categories. The emphasis has been on the role of variables in reflecting category membership and not on the nature of association and the manipulation of meanings. However, it is clear that many variables index such things as qualities and stances, which in turn construct the categories that they have been believed to index (Silverstein 1976; Ochs 1991; Eckert 2000).

A particularly clear case in point is the reduction of *-ing*—a variable that is found across the English-speaking world and that is class stratified (Labov 1966; Trudgill 1974). The greater use of reduction by working-class speakers has led many to consider the reduced variant to be stigmatized. Unlike negative concord or *r*-absence in New York City, however, the reduction of *-ing* does not carry stigma. Rather, it signals "casual"—a style that may be stigmatized or inappropriate in certain situations, but not in others. A CEO who uses a lot of the reduced variant in a meeting may be seen as condescending, but not as working class or "ignorant." It is in fact possible that the greater reduction among working-class speakers indicates a working-class persona signaled by a class-based attention to casualness.[1] This interpretation is not based on the variable itself, but on its role in a larger style. For example, the fortition of /th/ in Italian communities in New Jersey (this is my own, admittedly informal, observation) is part of a more general pattern of fortition, so that /t/ is pronounced particularly fortis as well, yielding a particular emphatic style. Mendoza-Denton (1997) has linked this fortition in Northern California Chicano English to the raising of /ɪ/ before [ŋ] so that words such as *nothing* carry particularly symbolic value. This calls for a radical change in the conception of, and approach to, style in the study of variation, which has been based in the unidimensional casual-formal, vernacular-standard axis, and limited to intraspeaker variation. The kind of style that is at issue here is the distinctive style that is directly related to identity in a complex social landscape. We can talk about middle-class Los Angeles dialect, or we can talk about Surfer Dudes, Valley Girls, and Korean American clubbers. While all three of these "types" may use the same Southern California dialect resources, they embed these resources in very different linguistic milieus. These milieus, however, cannot be described simply in terms of the regional dialect features but include a wide range of stylistic resources that are not the usual fare of variation studies.

If the meaning of variation depends on its embedding in a style, then the study of variation needs to radically expand its view of style. So far, style has been a means for studying variables selected for their interest to the study of linguistic structure and change. If we move our focus to style itself, we need to include a variety of variables that do not fit into these categories, such as prosody, voice quality, and segmental features that have so far gone largely unnoticed. For example, the release of word-final /t/ has turned out to be an extremely interesting variable. Bucholtz's (1996) study of /t/ release among self-styled geek girls in California, Benor's (forthcoming) study of Orthodox Jews, and Podesva, Roberts, and Campbell-Kibler's (2002) study of a gay lawyer indicate that this variant is associated with conciseness and articulateness across English-speaking communities in the United States. Not a change in progress, this variable no doubt derives its meaning from the contrast between North American and British speech, carrying the U.S. stereotype of British speakers as intelligent and precise. This fairly abstract meaning (similar to the abstract meaning of reduced -*ing*) is vivified differently within the more general linguistic style of each group—a style that in some way involves articulateness.

The focus of variation studies on sound change in progress has also encouraged a view of variation as one-dimensional, based on the assumption that a change follows a unidirectional path. So the focus may be on one aspect of a variable such as the raising of the nucleus of /æ/, ignoring other stylistically salient aspects of the variable such as the offglide. Podesva (2003) has shown that all kinds of variables may have an analog quality similar to a gradual vowel change, but not as part of a trajectory of change. Thus, in his study of a gay doctor moving from situation to situation, not only the occurrence, but the duration, of both word final stop release and falsetto voice had clear stylistic significance.

The study of the semiotic potential of variation is just beginning. The link between variables, styles, and personae leads to the abandonment of the view of variation as simply reflecting social categories in favor of a view of variation as being part of what constructs these categories. It also leads away from the treatment of variables as functioning separately and similarly, to a view of variables as heterogeneous resources for the construction of styles.

4. WHERE DO WE GO NEXT?

My recommendations for needed research in the study of social variation are rather sweeping, ranging from filling out the big picture to rooting around in day-to-day interactions. Survey studies can give us a general map of the linguistic landscape, but they cannot provide us with the meanings that inhabit that landscape or the linguistic practices that constitute it. At the same time, ethnographic studies cannot transcend the local unless they have a broader structure to orient to. It is important, therefore, that we focus on developing an integrated model of variation. By the same token, the study of the ingrained patterns that have largely preoccupied variationists is fundamental to our understanding of the language faculty. However, we cannot afford to draw lines around naturalness without exploring the limits of agency. There is clearly a continuum from the most automatic patterns to our most intentional acts of identity, and from the kinds of linguistic patterns that can only be learned at an early age or with considerable exposure to patterns that can be picked up from the television. And finally, the study of variation has opened up a tremendously interesting window on social meaning. In our focus on linguistic change, we have limited our vision of social meanings and of the role of style in constructing that meaning. This, I would argue, is the hugely unexplored future of the study of variation.

This expansion of the study of variation requires textured analysis of the situational and discourse deployment of resources and the construction of personae, which can only come from detailed ethnographic study and case studies of individuals. This calls for bringing the ethnography of speaking to central stage, once again narrowing the gap between sociolinguistics and linguistic anthropology. Up until now, there has not been much of an interpretive component to the study of variation, and many variationists are in fact either hostile to, or afraid of, such a component. This can only hold us back as the use of variation is itself an interpretive enterprise, and it is our task to maximize empirical methods for verifying our interpretations.

NOTE

1. This is an issue that Lavandera (1978) raised in relation to syntactic variation.

REFERENCES

Ash, Sharon, and John Myhill. 1986. "Linguistic Correlates of Inter-ethnic Contact." In *Diversity and Diachrony*, ed. David Sankoff, 33–44. Amsterdam: Benjamins.

Bailey, Guy, Tom Wikle, Jan Tillery, and Lori Sand. 1993. "Some Patterns of Linguistic Diffusion." *Language Variation and Change* 5: 359–90.

Bayley, Robert. 1994. "Consonant Cluster Reduction in Tejano English." *Language Variation and Change* 6: 303–26.

Benor, Sarah Bunin. Forthcoming. "Sounding Learned: The Gendered Use of /t/ in Orthodox Jewish English." In *Selected Papers from NWAV 2000*. Special issue of *University of Pennsylvania Working Papers in Linguistics*.

Bourdieu, Pierre, and Luc Boltanski. 1975. "Le fétichisme de la langue." *Actes de la recherche en sciences sociales* 4: 2–32.

Bucholtz, Mary. 1996. "Geek the Girl: Language, Femininity, and Female Nerds." In *Gender and Belief Systems: Proceedings of the Fourth Berkeley Women and Language Conference, April 19, 20, and 21, 1996*, ed. Natasha Warner, Jocelyn Ahlers, Leela Bilmes, Monica Oliver, Suzanne Wertheim, and Melinda Chen, 119–31. Berkeley: Berkeley Women and Language Group, Univ. of California.

———. 1999. "You da Man: Narrating the Racial Other in the Production of White Masculinity." *Journal of Sociolinguistics* 3: 443–60.

Callary, Robert E. 1975. "Phonological Change and the Development of an Urban Dialect in Illinois." *Language in Society* 4: 155–69.

Chambers, J. K. 1995. *Sociolinguistic Theory: Linguistic Variation and Its Social Significance*. Oxford: Blackwell.

Coupland, Nikolas. 1985. "'Hark, Hark, the Lark': Social Motivations for Phonological Style-Shifting." *Language and Communication* 5: 153–71.

———. 2001. "Language, Situation, and the Relational Self: Theorizing Dialect-Style in Sociolinguistics." In Eckert and Rickford, 185–210.

Cutler, Cecilia A. 1999. "Yorkville Crossing: White Teens, Hip Hop, and African American English." *Journal of Sociolinguistics* 3: 428–42.

Dubois, Sylvie, and Barbara M. Horvath. 1998. "Let's Tink about Dat: Interdental Fricatives in Cajun English." *Language Variation and Change* 10: 245–62.

Eckert, Penelope. 1997. "Age as a Sociolinguistic Variable." In *Handbook of Sociolinguistics*, ed. Florian Coulmas, 151–67. Oxford: Blackwell.

———. 2000. *Linguistic Variation as Social Practice: The Linguistic Construction of Identity in Belten High*. Malden, Mass.: Blackwell.

———. 2003. "Elephants in the Room." *Journal of Sociolinguistics* 7: 392–97.

Eckert, Penelope, and Sally McConnell-Ginet. 1992. "Communities of Practice: Where Language, Gender, and Power All Live." In *Locating Power: Proceedings of the Second Berkeley Women and Language Conference*, ed. Kira Hall, Mary Bucholtz, and Birch Moonwomon, 89–99. Berkeley: Berkeley Women and Language Group, Univ. of California.

———. 2003. *Language and Gender*. Cambridge: Cambridge Univ. Press.

Edwards, Walter F. 1992. "Sociolinguistic Behavior in a Detroit Inner-City Black Neighborhood." *Language in Society* 21: 93–115.

Edwards, Walter F., and Cheryl Krakow. 1985. "Polish-American English in Hamtramck: A Sociolinguistic Study." Paper presented at the 14th annual conference on New Ways of Analyzing Variation in English (NWAVE 14), Washington, D.C., 25–27 Oct.

Fisher, J. L. 1958. "Social Influences on the Choice of a Linguistic Variant." *Word* 14: 47–56.

Fishman, Joshua A., Robert L. Cooper, Roxana Ma, et al. 1973. *Bilingualism in the Barrio*. The Hague: Mouton.

Frazer, Timothy C. 1983. "Sound Change and Social Structure in a Rural Community." *Language in Society* 12: 313–28.

Gal, Susan, and Judith T. Irvine. 1995. "Disciplinary Boundaries and Language Ideology: The Semiotics of Differentiation." *Social Research* 62: 967–1001.

Hall, Kira. 1992. "Women's Language for Sale on the Fantasy Lines." In *Locating Power: Proceedings of the Second Berkeley Women and Language Conference*, ed. Kira Hall, Mary Bucholtz, and Birch Moonwomon, 207–22. Berkeley: Berkeley Women and Language Group, Univ. of California.

Hill, Jane H. 1993. "Hasta la Vista, Baby: Anglo Spanish in the American Southwest." *Critique of Anthropology* 13: 145–76.

Hoover, Mary Rhodes. 1978. "Community Attitudes toward Black English." *Language in Society* 7: 65–87.

Irvine, Judith T. 2001. "'Style' as Distinctiveness: The Culture and Ideology of Linguistic Differentiation." In Eckert and Rickford, 21–43.

Ito, Rika. 1999. "Diffusion of Urban Sound Change in Rural Michigan: A Case of the Northern Cities Shift." Ph.D. diss., Michigan State Univ.

Jones, Jamila. 2003. "African Americans in Lansing and the Northern Cities Vowel Shift: Language Contact and Accommodation." Ph.D. diss., Michigan State Univ.

Knack, Rebecca. 1991. "Ethnic Boundaries in Linguistic Variation." In *New Ways of Analyzing Sound Change*, ed. Penelope Eckert, 252–72. New York: Academic.

Kroch, Anthony. 1978. "Toward a Theory of Social Dialect Variaton." *Language in Society* 7: 17–36.

Kroch, Anthony, and Cathy Small. 1978. "Grammatical Ideology and Its Effect on Speech." In *Linguistic Variation: Models and Methods*, ed. David Sankoff, 45–56. New York: Academic.

Labov, William. 1966. *The Social Stratification of English in New York City.* Washington, D.C.: Center for Applied Linguistics.

———. 1972a. *Language in the Inner City: Studies in the Black English Vernacular.* Philadelphia: Univ. of Pennsylvania Press.

———. 1972b. *Sociolinguistic Patterns.* Philadelphia: Univ. of Pennsylvania Press.

———. 1972c. "Some Principles of Linguistic Methodology." *Language in Society* 1: 97–120.

———. 1991. "The Intersection of Sex and Social Class in the Course of Linguistic Change." *Language Variation and Change* 2: 205–51.

———. 2001a. "The Anatomy of Style-Shifting." In Eckert and Rickford, 85–108.

———. 2001b. *Principles of Linguistic Change.* Vol. 2, *Social Factors.* Oxford: Blackwell.

Labov, William, Paul Cohen, Clarence Robins, and John Lewis. 1968. *A Study of the Non-standard English of Negro and Puerto Rican Speakers in New York City.* Final Report. 2 vols. New York: Columbia Univ. Supported by the Cooperative Research Program of the Office of Education, U.S. Department of Health, Education and Welfare, project 3288.

Lavandera, Beatriz R. 1978. "Where Does the Sociolinguistic Variable Stop?" *Language in Society* 7: 171–82.

Le Page, R. B., and Andrée Tabouret-Keller. 1985. *Acts of Identity: Creole-Based Approaches to Language and Ethnicity.* Cambridge: Cambridge Univ. Press.

Lippi-Green, Rosina. 1997. *English with an Accent: Language, Ideology, and Discrimination in the United States.* London: Routledge.

Macaulay, R. K. S. 1977. *Language, Social Class, and Education: A Glasgow Study*. Edinburgh: Univ. of Edinburgh Press.

Mendoza-Denton, Norma. 1997. "Chicana/Mexicana Identity and Linguistic Variation: An Ethnographic and Sociolinguistic Study of Gang Affiliation in an Urban High School." Ph.D. diss., Stanford Univ.

Meyerhoff, Miriam. 1996. "Dealing with Gender Identity as a Sociolinguistic Variable." In *Rethinking Language and Gender Research: Theory and Practice*, ed. Victoria L. Bergvall, Janet M. Bing, and Alice F. Freed, 202–27. London: Longman.

Milroy, James, and Lesley Milroy. 1985. "Linguistic Change, Social Network, and Speaker Innovation." *Journal of Linguistics* 21: 339–84.

Milroy, Lesley. 1980. *Language and Social Networks*. Oxford: Blackwell.

Ochs, Elinor. 1991. "Indexing Gender." In *Rethinking Context: Language as an Interactive Phenomenon*, ed. Alessandro Duranti and Charles Goodwin, 335–58. Cambridge: Cambridge Univ. Press.

Podesva, Robert J. 2003. "The Stylistic Use of Phonation Type: Falsetto, Fundamental Frequency, and the Linguistic Construction of Personae." Unpublished MS.

Podesva, Robert J., Sarah J. Roberts, and Kathryn Campbell-Kibler. 2002. "Sharing Resources and Indexing Meanings in the Production of Gay Styles." In *Language and Sexuality: Contesting Meaning in Theory and Practice*, ed. Kathryn Campbell-Kibler, Robert J. Podesva, Sarah J. Roberts, and Andrew Wong, 175–90. Stanford, Calif.: Center for the Study of Language and Information.

Pratt, Mary Louise. 1987. "Linguistic Utopias." In *The Linguistics of Writing: Arguments between Language and Literature*, ed. Nigel Fabb, Derek Attridge, Alan Durant, and Colin MacCabe, 48–66. New York: Methuen.

Preston, Dennis R. 1989. *Perceptual Dialectology: Nonlinguists' Views of Areal Linguistics*. Dordrecht: Foris.

Rickford, John R. 1977. "The Question of Prior Creolization in Black English." In *Pidgin and Creole Linguistics*, ed. Albert Valdman, John Reinecke, and Ian F. Hancock, 190–221. Bloomington: Indiana Univ. Press.

———. 1986. "The Need for New Approaches to Class Analysis in Sociolinguistics." *Language and Communication* 6: 215–21.

Roberts, Sarah Julianne. 1999. "Nativization and the Genesis of Hawaiian Creole." In *Language Change and Language Contact in Pidgins and Creoles*, ed. J. H. McWhorter, 257–300. Amsterdam: Benjamins.

Rose, Mary. 2003. "'On de Farm': Sociolinguistic Meaning in Town and Country." Paper delivered at the 32d annual conference on New Ways of Analyzing Variation in English (NWAVE 32), Philadelphia, 9–12 Oct.

Sankoff, David, and Suzanne Laberge. 1978. "The Linguistic Market and the Statistical Explanation of Variability." In *Linguistic Variation: Models and Methods*, ed. David Sankoff, 239–50. New York: Academic.

Santa Ana A., Otto. 1992. "Chicano English Evidence for the Exponential Hypothesis: A Variable Rule Pervades Lexical Phonology." *Language Variation and Change* 4: 275–88.

Schilling-Estes, Natalie. 2002. "On the Nature of Isolated and Post-Isolated Dialects: Innovation, Variation, and Differentiation." *Journal of Sociolinguistics* 6: 64–85.

Shuy, Roger W., Walter A. Wolfram, and William K. Riley. 1967. *Linguistic Correlates of Social Stratification in Detroit Speech.* Final Report. East Lansing: Michigan State Univ. Supported by the National Institute of Mental Health, project MH 15048-01.

Silverstein, Michael. 1976. "Shifters, Linguistic Categories, and Cultural Description." In *Meaning in Anthropology*, ed. Keith H. Basso and Henry A. Selby, 11–55. Albuquerque: Univ. of New Mexico Press.

Sweetland, Julie. 2002. "Unexpected but Authentic Use of an Ethnically-Marked Dialect." *Journal of Sociolinguistics* 6: 514–36.

Taylor, O. 1971. "Response to Social Dialects and the Field of Speech." *Sociolinguistics: A Crossdisciplinary Perspective*, 13–20. Washington, D.C.: Center for Applied Linguistics.

Trudgill, Peter. 1972. "Sex, Covert Prestige, and Linguistic Change in the Urban British English of Norwich." *Language in Society* 1: 179–95.

———. 1974. *The Social Differentiation of English in Norwich.* Cambridge: Cambridge Univ. Press.

Wolfram, Walter A. 1969. *A Sociolinguistic Description of Detroit Negro Speech.* Washington, D.C.: Center for Applied Linguistics.

———. 1971. *Sociolinguistic Aspects of Assimilation: Puerto Rican English in New York City.* Arlington, Va.: Center for Applied Linguistics.

Woolard, Kathryn A. 1985. "Language Variation and Cultural Hegemony: Toward an Integration of Sociolinguistic and Social Theory." *American Ethnologist* 12: 738–48.

Zhang, Qing. 2001. "Changing Economics, Changing Markets: A Sociolinguistic Study of Chinese Yuppies." Paper presented at the Stanford Linguistics Colloquium, Stanford, Calif., 19 Jan. Abstract available from http://www-linguistics.stanford.edu/colloq/20010119.html.

7. IDEOLOGIES, ATTITUDES, AND PERCEPTIONS

RICHARD W. BAILEY

University of Michigan

CONTRIBUTORS TO PAST COLLECTIONS of *Needed Research* essays have regularly urged others to connect the dots, and, in particular, to undertake or complete what the late Donald M. Lance used to call "LALS: The Linguistic Atlas of the Left-out States." In other words, somebody ought to get busy working out the dialect boundaries (and their underlying usages) in Missouri and other states that had not been assigned when Hans Kurath proposed the enormously ambitious Linguistic Atlas of the United States and Canada in the late 1920s.

In his 1983 *Needed Research* essay, Thomas L. Clark (1984, 1) made just this point and quoted Albert H. Marckwardt's 1963 essay in which he lamented: "What is disappointing is the failure to complete, or in some instances even to embark upon, major projects which were recognized and named as desiderata some twenty years ago, and in some cases long before that" (1964, 24). Writing in the 1983 volume, Raven I. McDavid, Jr. (1984, 5), recalled the fate of the materials gathered for the Society's proposed American dialect dictionary in the decades after its founding in 1889. When someone wished to consult them at Harvard in 1941, it was discovered that they had disappeared. McDavid was also obliged to admit that the entire collection of materials from Pennsylvania for the Linguistic Atlas had vanished in the summer of 1983 while in his custody at the University of Chicago.

Being of a more hopeful frame of mind, I believe that we should celebrate—as others in this volume have done—the remarkable progress we have made, or that has been made on our behalf by energetic and dedicated colleagues, particularly Frederic G. Cassidy and Joan Houston Hall in the nearly complete *Dictionary of American Regional English* (1985–), Lee Pederson (1986–92) in the *Linguistic Atlas of the Gulf States*, William A. Krezschmar, Jr.

(1998), in the interactive Web site for portions of the Linguistic Atlas Project, and William Labov, Sharon Ash, and Charles Boberg for the TELSUR Project (2003) and the *Atlas of North American English* (forthcoming). Completing and extending the lines of research identified as "needed" by the early members of the American Dialect Society is a worthy and excellent goal.

Given that these projects have been so ambitious and have required so much effort on a national scale, it is a wonder that we have so much to celebrate. And it is also quite reasonable that the principles and methods of these founders needed to be sustained so that the same questions could be asked in the "left-out states" as were asked in the others and that the end of the work would resemble the beginning. Nonetheless, it is a reasonable criticism to point to the fact that these multigenerational projects do not leave much room for innovation, and field-workers in dialectology are expected to ask the names of parts of harness or calls to animals when these have vanished from the experience of most Americans.

At the celebration to mark the completion of the *Middle English Dictionary* (1952–2001), Eric Stanley of Oxford recalled a conference held in 1969 to consider a new *Dictionary of Old English.* Someone asked the associate editor of the *Middle English Dictionary* what editorial decisions had been made at the beginning of the project that he would wish had been decided differently. After a moment's pause, the editor replied: "Almost all of them." (Though the proceedings of this conference contain quite detailed transcripts of discussion, this memorable exchange was omitted. See Cameron, Frank, and Leyerle 1970). Of course this answer roused laughter, but the underlying point is clear: long-term philological enterprise has a distinctly, and necessary, conservative character.

In considering "usage" in the 1983 *Needed Research* collection, John Algeo (1984) looked more to the future than to the past, and he reported results of a survey of Dialect Society members in which he asked what topics should be investigated and what priorities should be given to them. In the study of "opinions and attitudes," he argued, "the casual approach of past studies ... should be avoided" (41–42). One of his respondents mentioned methods of measurement; another noted that surveys should be designed to allow statistical significance testing. Still another drew attention to individual rather than community facts: "the psychology of our reactions to usage variation is almost unknown, even to ourselves" (42).

What has been accomplished since?

Statements about language, and particularly the varieties of English, have been a focus of cultural history.

It was (and remains) possible to criticize an individual or a group by addressing linguistic issues rather than the matters of race, gender, or politics that are at the heart of the matter. Sometimes this criticism has been oblique. The segregationist governor of Alabama, George Wallace, recognized this technique and complained about it: "Yeah, they smooth, these newsboys—but they'll getcha. When they quote Wallace, it always comes out bad grammar. But Martin Luther King and [Ralph] Abernathy? They always come out speakin' the King's English" (Lesher 1972, 35). Here medium and message coalesced. The reporter demonstrated exactly the journalistic technique of which Wallace complained, and he left it explicit (and obvious) that in a similar story he would not have employed vernacular spellings in quoting African Americans like King or Abernathy and conventional ones for the white supremacist Wallace. The same linguistic bigotry that beset Wallace was turned back with redoubled viciousness in the "grammars" of African American English that festered on many recent Web sites, allowing users to create "translations" of ordinary edited English into some sort of minstrel stereotype with *brudda* substituted for *brother*, *mouf* for *mouth*, and *be* for almost any auxiliary verb. What needs to be noticed, however, is that these ideological specimens provide excellent evidence for the beliefs and attitudes that bear on the linguistic community.

Specimens like these, particularly ones from earlier times, have proved invaluable clues to larger issues. In his study of nineteenth-century America, for instance, Kenneth Cmiel (1990) used opinions about usage in dramatizing cultural turmoil, asserting that "the promiscuous usage of American speech was at odds with the refined self-control of the educated gentlemen and ladies" (126). A similar approach to history based on questions of usage appeared in books by Dennis Baron: *Grammar and Good Taste* (1982) and *Grammar and Gender* (1986). These investigations mined schoolbooks, usage manuals, and journalistic sources to approach the study of power, virtue, and gentility (and their opposites).

Yet much more historical work needs to be done. The history of American English is a sadly neglected field, and linguistic topics of great interest need more concerted effort and attention from people skilled in the ways of language variety. It is largely true, as Michael Kramer declared in 1992, that the history of American linguistic ideas has "until recently remained an all-but-neglected area of intellectual history, stomping grounds for a few antiquarians, folklorists, and intellectual historians of language or education" (ix). Fortunately, one may detect that there is more stamping on the stomping ground.

Literary scholars have renewed their interest in dialect fiction, partly as a result of opening the "canon" of literature to many more authors and partly because critics have recognized that issues surrounding language variety are important in even the most canonical of American writers—Emerson, Dickinson, Poe, and Melville (see Reynolds 1988). These new readings of literature are far more complex (and more interesting) than earlier inquiries which tended toward two foci: whether or not writers like Joel Chandler Harris, Mary Noilles Murfree, or Edward Eggleston were "authentic"; and whether or not the great profusion of dialect writing in nineteenth-century America was merely "a highbrow convention which employed exaggerated, humorous speech to camouflage a patronizing sentimentality and satire" (this is a paraphrase of the view of George Philip Krapp; Jones 1999, 8). Instead, talk about (and in) dialect can now be used to uncover all sorts of cultural anxieties, including the extent to which dialects have threatened the hegemony of the Anglo American descended elite. Scholars giving attention to the position of women, African Americans, and new immigrants have found in the ideological debates about dialect a rich source of interpretative material (see particularly Jones 1999).

These investigations into our national literature have raised important questions about American "exceptionalism," that is, the idea that the United States is a country unlike any other. Historical studies have clarified methodological problems and illustrated how even scanty surviving evidence can be used to reach useful conclusions. So, for instance, Paula Blank's *Broken English* (1996) shows how the English renaissance mediated competing ideas of "English" as part of the formation of nationhood in the British Isles. Studies of the first of the distinctive varieties of English in the Western Hemisphere have also offered useful correctives to national narrow-mindedness, whether British or American (see Chamberlin 1993). Early American English can usefully be considered as part of the dynamic of "colonizing" that would later animate its spread as a "world language" (see Talib 2002). It is certainly worth considering, both ideologically and factually, the ways in which American English is a "postcolonial" variety.

Historical inquiry into the debates about government regulation (and imposition) of language has also deepened understanding of linguistic issues in the past. So, for instance, a casebook on the "official English" dispute uncovered a report from the federal commissioner of Indian affairs written in 1887; the editor extracted words from the report for use as a title: "Barbarous Dialects Should Be Blotted Out." (The "dialects" needing "blotting" were Native American languages.) In this policy paper, the official declared: "This [English] language, which is good enough for a white man and a black man, ought to be good enough for the red man" (quoted in Crawford 1992, 51). English, and not foreign languages, was the sole source of civilization: "Every nation is jealous of its own language, and no nation ought to be more so than ours, which approaches nearer than any other nationality to the perfect protection of its people" (49).

Here is the idea of American "exceptionalism" in an unvarnished form. While America had always been multilingual, this routine social fact—common in most large nations then and now—suddenly appeared as an obstacle to the fulfillment of the national dream of democracy. First, as the official declared, languages other than English needed to be "blotted out"; then varieties declared to be "nonstandard" had to be put down and replaced by the variety favored by the elite. Far from a few cosmetic usages that needed to be "fixed" (for instance, the use of *ain't*), the program of these language reformers was profound and deeply connected to terrors about the future identity of America. Thomas Bonfiglio (2002) has pointed out that the liberation of the slaves and the influx of immigrants after 1863 produced, among the elite, a sense of alarm that drew English into the orbit of politics.

> The waxing anxiety of race that one sees in the later nineteenth century escalated to xenophobic proportions in the early twentieth century. Directed against immigration to the eastern seaboard and coupled with the fear of southern black migration to the northern industrial centers, this xenophobia acted to frame the general discussions of race, identity, and national language. [116]

The self-help industry in language courses and manuals flourished so people, hoping to better themselves in Horatio-Alger fashion, might emerge from the huddled masses. Dreiser caught just this aspect of urban life when he represented Carrie Meeber (in his novel *Sister Carrie* [1900]) as speaking "better" than the other young women with whom she worked (ever so briefly) in a Chicago shoe factory. Just as America became an "exceptional" country (not weighted down by the problems of other nations), so Carrie could be an "exception" to the thousands of young people migrating to the cities from farms and villages by employing an "elevated" speech.

Past and present, the powerful have enlisted the aid of laws to regulate the language of the powerless. In colonial New England, statutes were passed to ensure hierarchy and patriarchy would be respected. Beginning in the 1640s, several of the puritan colonies enacted laws forbidding a child (of any age) to fail to heed "the voyce of his Father, or the voyce of his Mother" (quoted by Kamensky 1997, 102), and "children" who failed to do so were seen as having committed a capital offense and thus to deserve hanging. All sorts of language was regulated in these laws, though "mocking and cursing" were the focal offenses. Drawing their justification on the commandment to honor father and mother, the laws put clergymen—as "perfected" fathers—first among those most deserving of respect; then male householders, then women, and finally servants and slaves. This outburst of "political correctness" made slander a tediously familiar offense brought before the courts, though it was seldom taken to the limit of the death sentence.[1] For instance, in October 1663, John Williams, a frequent litigant in Plymouth Colony who between 1648 and his death was involved in more than a hundred lawsuits, was sued by one John Bayley for having called his wife, Elizabeth Lothrop, John Bayley's "whore." Bayley brought two witnesses to affirm this affront, and the jury ruled in his behalf and fined Williams "ten pounds damage, and the cost of the suite" (Shurtleff 1857, 111). By imposing stiff fines of this sort, New Englanders regulated what was said and how it might be said.

The witchcraft trials in Salem constituted a culmination of the attempt to preserve dominance by regulating language, and the matter of dialect even penetrated here. On 11 April 1692, a woman was accused of sorcery and, to test her innocence, was obliged to say the Lord's Prayer. Asked to repeat some words that had seemed to the magistrates doubtful, she did not say "hallowed be thy name: "[S]he exprest it, *Hollowed be thy Name,* this was counted as depraving the words, as signifying to make void, and so a Curse rather then a Prayer" (Calef 1700, 347). Upon such a linguistic detail was a deadly accusation hung, and the woman whose dialect crossed the boundary from good to evil was sent to prison.

Time and again, linguistic ideas (and regulations) have entered influentially into larger cultural questions. The Salem trials were about witchcraft, not about language, but they certainly had a linguistic dimension when how a word was said (and by whom) could play so crucial a role. Seeing the language as central rather than peripheral to these cultural tumults provides abundant evidence of the importance of linguistic ideology. Later, in the eighteenth century, Britons became convinced that Americans must speak a foreign language or a barbarous dialect of English since they had set themselves at a distance from the prevailing cultural assumptions about monarchy and government. It became common wisdom that language was an effect (if not a cause) of rebellion. As Olivia Smith (1984) has pointed out in her important book on this history, eighteenth-century theorists had one idea clearly in mind as they formulated ideals of elocution, usage, and grammar: "the vulgar . . . demonstrate their unworthiness every time they employ language by the nature of the language that they speak" (25). No one understood this idea better than the American revolutionary Thomas Paine. He asserted that "changing the style of language is a means of political and moral reformation" (quoted in Smith 1984, 51). It is not an accident that the first articulation of the political revolt of 1776 began with a "declaration" of reasons for changing government, and the connection between "style of language" and politics has remained central to American ideology ever since.

As the ideology of a "standard" English emerged with great force in the second half of the eighteenth century, the myth was created that only a monolithic and unchanging English was worthy of respect. In earlier times, the notion of a "court" language spoken by those surrounding the monarch allowed for some variety within the court (and in fact this variety was noticed and treated as normal). But with the rise of a linguistically self-conscious middle class, the definition of "standard" hardened, and in the early nineteenth century it was thoroughly established. (The 19-year-old Queen Victoria asked an elderly courtier whether to pronounce *Rome* and *gold* with [u] as he did or to use the [o] she often heard around her. No earlier British ruler would have asked the question, let alone taken the advice she was given. See Bailey 1996, 84.) This cultural anxiety about language variety carried over to the United States, sometimes expressed among anglophiles as fear that English would wander from the immutable standard of London. Patriotic Americans accepted the idea that English ought to be uniform but allowed for its excellence (and uniformity) to arise on American soil. So, in 1774, an anonymous essayist, usually taken to be John Adams, eventually the second president of the United States, wrote: "As the people through this extensive country will speak English, their advantages for polishing their language will be great, and vastly superior to what the people in England ever enjoyed" (An American 1774, 6). The idea of a standard was here embraced; the only "revolutionary" idea in this formulation is that this "superior" English might arise in North America.

One reason for assigning the authorship of the letter by "An American" to Adams is that he wrote to Congress in 1780 urging the adoption of an "American academy for the refining, improving, and ascertaining the English language" (1852, 250). This idea was at once radical—asserting the value of an "American" language—and at the same time distinctly conservative. (Adams echoed the very words of Jonathan Swift, who, in 1712, urged famously an academy for "correcting, refining and ascertaining the English tongue" by giving custody of the "standard" to various aristocrats and Tory politicians.) Adams's main contribution to the debate was asserting that the language in America should be IMPROVED (rather than CORRECTED), a faint concession to revolutionary optimism when most who expressed themselves on the subject believed that English was rapidly declining from a prior period of excellence (see Bailey 2003). Views of English even played a small part in the conflict between Adams, during his presidency, and Thomas Jefferson, his successor, who made Adams's linguistic views part of the dispute. Writing to a friend in 1813, Jefferson declared himself "no friend . . . to what is called *Purism*, but a zealous one to *Neology*" (quoted by Kramer 1992, 120). Adams craved authority and stability in both language and government; Jefferson, at least theoretically, professed democracy and perpetual change.

Recognizing that there is a distinct connection between language and the perception of social instability, scholars have given renewed attention to linguistic attitudes. During the Civil War, for instance, A. S. Worrell, a Southern author, took the same line that Adams had articulated at the time of the conflict with England: that the center of linguistic authority had to be moved away from the corrupted domain of old government. So, in 1861, a grammar published in Nashville (and virtually identical to the schoolbooks then current everywhere in English-speaking countries), Worrell gave a patriotic justification for his efforts.

The Southerners, in their previous history, have been content to have their books furnished them by the North. This not only *discouraged Southern authorship*, and *cramped genius*, but it allowed the North the *chief means of shaping national bias*—THE PRESS. But now that the Southern people have separated from the North, and established an *independent nationality*, she will, of course hail with pleasure every industrious effort of *"her own sons"* to free her from *Abolition dependencies.* [1]

Once again, the ideology of a single approved kind of English shapes the discourse. Multilingualism and multidialectalism are not even considered and thus not dismissed. The "cramped genius" of a Southern writer simply shoves aside the hegemony of the great publishers of Boston, New York, and Cincinnati, and replaces the old linguistic authority with a new one more suited to an independent nation, the Confederate States of America.

At the end of the nineteenth century, immigration and internal migration gave a new urgency to the quest to find a source of authority. In his study of early twentieth-century culture, Thomas Bonfiglio (2002) has given particular attention to the institutionalization of language culture as it emerged as part of contemporary race theory, nativism, and anti-semitism. Yet there is clearly more to be unearthed in the history of this ideology. In a report to the National Council of Teachers of English in 1917, for instance, Claudia E. Crumpton, a teacher from Montevallo, Alabama, described her energetic efforts at "speech betterment."

Recently, with the aid of Mr. John M. Clapp, secretary of the American Speech League, we gained the hearty indorsement [*sic*] of the Alabama Federation of Women's Clubs. That body of over six thousand women, one of the most potent agencies in Alabama, will have a committee actively at work for promoting the cause. They will follow, so far as they can, Mr. Clapp's suggestions: that they make it fashionable for young people to speak correctly, distinctly, pleasantly; that they insist that teachers be selected with particular reference to habits of speech; that they urge the adoption of definite requirements in oral English for the elementary schools; that they undertake surveys with reference to speech conditions in Alabama. [99]

As is often the case, it is impossible to ascertain what might have happened to Alabama English had the forces of "speech betterment" not been loosed upon it. One can, however, note that the campaign sustained the idea that there was something called "standard English" and that those who approached it deserved rewards that others could not hope to gain.

The process of standardization has come to be a focal topic in English linguistics, particularly in scholarly discourse taking place outside north America. From a global perspective, the explosive growth of English threatens to make it (in whatever variety) an international "standard" as it supplants other languages and functional domains within languages. (Many publications in medicine and the natural sciences appear in English, even from communities and by authors where English is not the vernacular of everyday intellectual life in the laboratory.) These developments have been vigorously criticized by many writers, particularly Robert Phillipson (1992, 2003) and Tove Skutnabb-Kangas (2000). They have argued very fervently that English NOT become the lingua franca of the world, and they have made various proposals within the European Union to thwart its spread. Similarly, Arjuna Parakrama (1995) has pointed out that the community of English speakers need not adopt one of the metropolitan varieties—that of England or the United States—and that the dialectic between competing "standards" needs attention.

In Britain, where the facts of class and region have long been the subject of study, the selection, promotion, and enforcement of a "standard" has been seen both from the perspective of history (e.g., Crowley 1989) and of contemporary battles (e.g., Milroy and Milroy 1999). While there are occasional similarities in the debates (and the educational policies that flow from them), there are also great national differences, as Lesley Milroy (1999) has pointed out in surveying developments in the two countries. Among the best book-length treatments of the American scene is that by Rosina Lippi-Green (1997), who concludes that "ideology is most effective when its workings are least visible, and standard language ideology in the US functions like a silent but efficient machine" (242). There are, because of the stealthy application of these values, wonderful opportunities for study and interpretation of American linguistic ideologies.

Nowhere is the opportunity greater than in the documentation presented by the public debate over African American English. These issues need not be rehearsed here since they are very well surveyed in many popular books, particularly those by John

Baugh (2000), John Rickford (1999), and Russell Rickford (Rickford and Rickford 2000). In early-twenty-first-century America, African American English is widely seen as "subversive," by both those who flaunt it and those who view it with alarm. In most parts of the United States, popular culture celebrates vernacular culture founded on ideas of African American culture (though not necessarily invented or enacted by African Americans). The dialectic between "hip-hop" and "country," "soul" and "techno," contains a linguistic dimension of great interest. (One might imagine what historians of English might do with even fragments of a spirited debate between a *scop* and a *jongleur* from the twelfth century.)

Famous (and even "trade-marked") ways of speaking provide conversational fodder for the linguistically curious, but the meanings associated with varieties of English are far more subtle and draw upon deeply hidden tacit knowledge.

The fact, easily discerned both experientially and experimentally, is that listeners will immediately associate a recorded voice with an image of the speaker. Of course their decisions are based upon stereotypes, but they also show how quickly the sounds of voices yield decisions. Since the selection of voices for these experiments might include unanticipated cues to identity, various methods have been used to reduce unwanted influences. Matched guise techniques (in which the voices of a single speaker are manipulated by mimicry or otherwise to represent more than one stereotype) have revealed again and again how ideology and decision-making are connected. Research into this topic began in the 1960s—the study by Tucker and Lambert (1969) was influential in the growth of the field—and has regularly displayed differences based on ethnicity, gender, sexual orientation, and other demographic characteristics. In general, the findings have distinguished "them" from "us," and for speakers of stigmatized varieties of English, "them" are imagined to be educated, efficient, and cold, and "us" as experientially wise, relaxed, and intimate. Edwards's (1992) study of African Americans in Detroit affirmed just this dimension: the more the speakers were felt to express African American identity, the more they were considered friendly, warm, and attractive. Those with fewer linguistic expressions of this identity were seen as aloof, ambitious, and upwardly mobile.

One might easily presume from such studies that individuals express a single identity, and certainly the raters judging the speech samples made that presumption. In another study involving Detroiters, Niedzielski (1999) explained that a recorded female voice was "Canadian," and she asked respondents to identify the features that they believed to be distinctively "Canadian." People easily recognized and described the nonlowered onsets of diphthongs in words like *about* and *how*. When another set of evaluators were told that the voice was that of a speaker from Michigan, these distinctive diphthongs were not noticed, even though the recording was the same for both groups (and, in fact, the vowels had been "resynthesized" to make them unambiguous for "Canadian" and "Michigan" features). Results like these make it vividly clear that once a speaker has been "identified" (as, for instance, "Canadian"), the perception of judges is rapid and unequivocal.

Such a study reflects the remarkable development of "folk linguistics," a field that barely existed a quarter century ago. The intellectual foundation was laid by Dennis R. Preston, the editor of this volume, and a bibliography of international work in the field appears at the end of the *Handbook of Perceptual Dialectology*, a collection of papers edited by Preston (1999). One focus of this research has been to test the fit between the "folk" regions of American English and those defined by the dialectologists. Preston has examined this question using informants in various U.S. locations, and the match varies in ways that might be expected— Hawaiians, for instance, have rather indistinct ideas of the eastern parts of the United States beyond a North-South distinction (Preston 1989, 35). A national survey of the contiguous United States by Donald M. Lance (1999) revealed a widespread consensus among the students surveyed and a good fit with the traditionally recognized areas derived from careful surveys of usage. Preston's studies regularly show that unlike the "scholars," the "folk" are tempted to believe that political boundaries and linguistic boundaries generally match, as they do, in fact, in separating West Virginia from

Virginia and Pennsylvania. The "scholars" see intrastate complexity in Indiana, Illinois, and Missouri, for instance, but so do the "folk" best acquainted with these regions.[2]

Not only is there widespread agreement about just where to locate the distinctive English of "New England" or "the South," but Americans also have a remarkable consensus about the values to be associated with the regions they identify: some are "good," others "bad." But they do not agree about which is which. Michigan informants believe that their English is "good," but they are not very surprised when they discover that others do not have that opinion of them. However, they fall back on the claim that Michigan English is "correct." Students at Auburn University in Alabama do not regard Michigan English as unusually "correct," and they do not view it as especially "pleasant" either. While recognizing that outsiders view their Southern speech as not "correct," the Auburn students console themselves in the belief that the English of neighboring Mississippi, Louisiana, and Texas is less "correct" than theirs. The idea of "linguistic insecurity"—the belief that "good English" belongs to someone else—is here magnified on a national scale.

The agreement between the "folk" and the "scholars" in the matter of regions entirely evaporates when it comes to judgments about *correct, good,* or *pleasant* (see Preston 1998). As Preston says elsewhere, these beliefs about the merits of varieties of English "represent strongly held, influential beliefs in the linguistic life of large and small speech communities" (1993, 375; see also 2002). One of these is a paradox: dialects are "disappearing" while at the same time a distinctive regional English is flourishing. "Folk dialectology" is not an entirely new field—Leonard Bloomfield (1944) recognized that "tertiary responses" to language (the sort of metadiscourse that asserted that peasant English has a vocabulary of a few hundred words, young people fail to enunciate, and other such chestnuts) had a structure and a history. But only recently has it become a coherent field of study. Having discerned the pattern of these beliefs, scholars need now to turn attention to the actions that ensue. While the "job interview" is used to terrorize students—the idea that the slightest deviation from "correct" English will result in permanent unemployment—it is not clear just what uses are made of speech judgments in practical affairs. ("Scholars" may view the situation with far too much alarm. The threats are dire, the punishments less obviously so, although recent research with actual employer evaluations of regional standard voices suggests that even that variation may cause hiring difficulties; e.g., Cukor-Avila 2000; Markley 2000; Cukor-Avila and Markley 2002.)

Just as dialect boundaries in "folk" dialectology have sharp boundaries, so too the categories of speech types are stark and distinct: black English or white; guy or gal; proper or slang; aloof or downright. In judging the language of others, the assignment of expression to group is rapid, unequivocal, and resistant to change.

In real life, of course, people express multiple identities with their linguistic behavior. Languages are "socially constructed," and communities are "imagined" (see Anderson 1991 for the classic account of this view). All normal human beings belong to several such imaginary communities at the same time, and the task for research is to explain the minute (or manifest) adjustments that speakers make in expressing both the fact and the degree of affiliation with particular ones. Often these cues are very subtle, particularly when there is some peril of offering an identity that may be unwelcome. Precisely this approach to variation is persuasively argued by Robin M. Queen (1997) in her discussion of "zones of contact" (a term borrowed from Mary Louise Pratt 1984) involving lesbian English. The "indexical markers" in such communities show just how fluid the expression of this identity can be, allowing ambiguous signals to work toward eventual resolution in gay or straight (and many other nuanced social identities).

In these micronegotiations, speakers adjust their speech to "accommodate" others—or pointedly refuse such accommodation. (See the essays collected by Giles, Coupland, and Coupland (1991) for more details on "accommodation theory.") The directions of accommodation often pass unnoticed by the participants, but they are central to linguistic ideology. A study of the African American television interviewer Oprah Winfrey produced evidence of just this sort of accommodation. In Winfrey's speech, the vowel of words like *I* and *my* may be either a monophthong or a diphthong. In discussing African Americans or introducing them as guests on her program, Winfrey used the monophthongal pronunciation 38% of the time; in introducing guests who were not African American she used this pronunciation only 10% of the time (see Rickford and Rickford 2000, 106–7). This difference was almost certainly below the threshold of consciousness for nearly everyone, participant or audience, but this minute detail shows just one way in which accommodation works. Another dimension of it was discerned in a study of the white television personality Larry King. A study of 25 celebrity guests showed that King "accommodated" persons of higher social standing than himself; the guests of lower status accommodated to him (Gregory and Webster 1996). Yet all of this accommodation needs to be kept below the level of overt consciousness, and speakers who are too prone to accommodate risk the peril of being regarded as mimics (thus threatening the security of the person being mimicked) or as sycophants (thus undermining the presumption of equality and politeness).

Attitudinal and ideological studies like these offer promising insights, particularly for the study of language change. Social network theory argues essentially that people talk the way the other people they talk to most talk. Yet this is not a zero-sum game. At the end of it all, people who accommodate increase one usage and decrease another while people who do not accommodate remain relatively unchanged. Whatever features are perceived as "attractive" increase in use; those not so perceived do not. Another study—this one of U.S. presidential debates—located accommodation in "the fundamental frequency of phonation," sounds below 0.5 kHz. In ingenious studies by Stanford W. Gregory, Jr., and colleagues, that frequency band was eliminated in samples presented for the judgment by some raters and kept present for others. Judgments in the two groups were different, though the sound band is merely "a low-pitched and segmented hum absent of any clearly discernible verbal content" (Gregory and Gallagher 2002, 298). With the "hum" audible in the specimens, raters recognized "social dominance"; when it was omitted, they were not so clearly able to do so. The experiment demonstrated that this "low-pitched and segmented hum" was a crucial factor in "conveying a social dominance signal" (300). Furthermore, it was possible to determine which speech samples expressed more "dominance" and which less. Acoustic analysis of these extracts from presidential debates showed a strong correlation between this "hum" and the outcome of the popular vote in elections since 1960!

Clearly "social dominance" is a complex idea and one that needs greater scrutiny, but it provides a clue to the way in which language change evolves. Speakers who "attract" imitation through social dominance lead those systematic changes in language that Edward Sapir, among others, identified as "drift." Language change is clearly not random but motivated by various internal and external factors.

Now developments in the mathematical theory of networks offer promising directions for inquiry into American English. As studies of the World Wide Web have shown, networks are not systems of points randomly connected in a way described by the bell-curve of a normal distribution but something quite different. Networks of all sorts are connected by individuals called "hubs" (from the use of these ideas in designing airline schedules) with many links. As popular treatments of these ideas have shown, certain named individuals are more closely connected with huge numbers of others than would be predicted if the playing field were equal. Vernon Jordan, the Washington lawyer, was connected to more corporate and foundation leaders than any other person in the 1990s. A known flight attendant was revealed to be a "hub" in the spread of AIDS because of his many contacts with others in scattered places. As the physicist Albert-László Barabási (2002) has shown, these "hubs" are not necessarily innovators themselves; "with their numerous social contacts, they are among the first to notice and use the experience of the innovators" (129–30).

Barabási discusses properties of networks that are of special interest to those interested in language change: "real networks are governed by two laws: *growth* and *preferential attachments*" (86). The idea of *growth* is simple enough; networks must add new nodes to remain intact. American English is typical of a linguistic community that experiences growth with the arrival of each new immigrant and the birth of each infant. The second of these "laws" is more interesting: "given the choice between two nodes, one with twice as many links as the other, it is twice as likely that the new node will connect to the more connected node" (86). Here Gregory's idea of "social dominance" returns in an intriguing way, since the "socially dominant" speaker will attract more imitators and thus spread the linguistic change favored in her (or his) speech. These "hub" figures with many connections need not be themselves innovators in language (or anything else). To repeat Barabási's words: "they are among the first to notice and use the experience of the innovators."

One would like to identify the "hubs" fostering the Northern Cities Shift, for instance, and it may be that some of the frustration in finding its origin is based on a mistaken assumption: that innovation is the special province of persons of a particular social class, gender, region, or some other demographic. What is necessary is to identify the "hubs" of linguistic change and to follow the nodes by which they express their social dominance.

Let me conclude this essay with an example from the ideological realm (rather than attempting to explore the more mysterious regions of tacit linguistic knowledge).

A colleague of mine regards the use of *hopefully* as a sentence adverb with particular horror and says she corrects it whenever she can. She was disappointed to learn that I do not share her zeal. "You don't use English like that," she said. "You shouldn't let your students use it either." Learning that this usage has only recently become a shibboleth, she was not mollified. It might not be an antique horror, but it was horrible enough to tear at the fabric of her composure today.

Obviously it is not something intrinsic in the word. *Thankfully, certainly,* and many other such adverbs connected to a speaker's evaluation of what is being asserted appear without being criticized or even noticed. Further, *hopefully* is not an innovation, though not until the 1930s did it become common. (Allan Metcalf 2002, 148, offers the earliest example so far identified: from a discourse on the circumstances for dismissing a pastor, a work composed by Cotton Mather and published in 1702.) Here is a typical modern

example from a news conference given by President Dwight
Eisenhower in 1954:

> Now the quest for peace in this world is too important to let any particular
> political situation here stand in our way, and there is the one field,
> hopefully, and I really believe, is the one field where we ought to have the
> greatest possible chance to get ahead. [*New York Times*, 4 Nov. 1954, 24.]

Language critics were scornful of Eisenhower's English—*nuculur*
for *nuclear* was roundly criticized, though Eisenhower was not its
inventor nor exceptional in pronouncing the word in that way.
Had *hopefully* been the subject of horrified objection, this example
would have been among the most memorable. Instead, it went
entirely unremarked until Theodore M. Bernstein, an editor of the
New York Times, drew attention to it in a stylebook published in
1962.

Because innovative ideas about usage tend to appear early in
written form, it is quite easy to date the spasm of outrage over
hopefully.

> I can't remember Mrs. [Norma Krause] Hertzfeld's indictment precisely,
> although I know it left out my own No. 1 grievance—the prevalence of the
> dangling "hopefully" in *Commonweal* editorials (as in the sentence "hope-
> fully things will get better" Hopefully the English language will survive
> this aberration). [Wilfrid Sheed, *Commonweal*, 25 Sept. 1964, 17]

> The first time we heard the word "hopefully" used to mean something it
> doesn't mean was from the lips of a pretty woman whom we were wining
> and dining in a restaurant. [(E. B. White), *New Yorker*, 27 Mar. 1965, 35]

> And, "hopefully," as current jabberwocky has it, [he will] make the
> reader's task just a trifle easier. [Charles Poore, *New York Times*, 11 Dec.
> 1965, 31]

The authors of these views—Bernstein, Sheed, White, and Poore—
were all very influential journalists, but it is not likely that they were
the "hubs" of the spread of this belief. Almost certainly this distinction belongs to Jacques Barzun, who got the matter out of the
magazines and into the mainstream usage books. The editor of
Modern American Usage, Wilson Follett, had died in 1963 before the

bonfire around the feet of *hopefully* had been kindled, and the work was completed by Barzun and published in 1966. Barzun had already expressed himself as against "permissiveness" in language, particularly in the debate that surrounded the publication of the *Webster's Third New International Dictionary* in 1961, and he had written a scathing review of it in *The American Scholar* (Barzun 1963). He had even earlier made something of a specialty of lambasting the field of linguistics, particularly in a book lamenting the loss of old intellectual certainties, *The House of Intellect* (1959), and he would later declare: "Every defect in language is a defect in somebody" and "the anarchy is always with us" (1986, 29, 107). In his explanation of *hopefully* in *Modern American Usage*, he speculated that the usage had somehow arisen from the German *hoffentlich*, though he offered no evidence to substantiate the idea.

Barzun was very much a "hub" in the network of intellectuals who regarded themselves as qualified to rule on questions of English usage. Inserting a criticism of *hopefully* in Follett's book was only the first step. Following the criticism of the *Webster's Third*, James Parton first attempted to buy its publisher. When this failed, he entered into an agreement with Houghton Mifflin to prepare a new dictionary, and he hired the former actor William Morris to organize the work. In 1969, Parton's book was published as *The American Heritage Dictionary of the English Language*, and the advertising campaign made much of the fact that it provided unequivocal advice "in these permissive times." As part of this effort, a "usage panel" had been created to offer judgments; it consisted of 11 women and 94 men with an average age of 64. Some seem to have been selected because they had been publicly scornful of the *Webster's Third*, and reports of their views were presented in "notes" appended to 318 items. Here is the one for *hopefully*:

Usage: *Hopefully*, as used to mean it is to be hoped or let us hope, is still not accepted by a substantial number of authorities on grammar and usage. The following example of *hopefully* in this sense is acceptable to only 44 per cent of the Usage Panel: *Hopefully, we shall complete our work in June.*

Perhaps the most striking word in this report is *still*, since the identification of *hopefully* as a solecism had occurred only five years earlier. *Still* gives the impression that "the authorities" had long objected to it, though some had relaxed their strictures.

The "hub" of the *hopefully* network thus formed around the plan to develop the *American Heritage Dictionary*, and founder members of its Usage Panel were Jacques Barzun and Theodore M. Bernstein.

Various speculations arose concerning the origin of the expression, and many writers parading their learning followed Barzun in regarding it as of German (or even Yiddish) origin. This entirely unsubstantiated etymology would be offered again in a letter to the *London Times* (4 Sept. 1971, 11), inspiring an affirmation from another correspondent: "I first heard it [*hopefully*] in Los Angeles in 1965" (24 Sept. 1971, 13). Whatever one may think about this writer's view of "sloppy thinking" and "sloppy writing," her speculation about the time and the place seemed just right—California, the land of low culture and migrants who mangled the English language. Four years later, the editor of the *Times* published a promise under the headline: "Hopefully to be eliminated." He began by describing it as "an aborted mistranslation of the German word *hoffentlich*," and he asserted that it has been "introduced in the 1950s by sloppy American academics, who may be presumed to have spoken German better than English. In a synopsis of his reasons for keeping it out of his newspaper, he summarized: "*Hopefully* should be disqualified because it is obscure and ambiguous, as well as illiterate and ugly" (24 Oct. 1975, 16).

The former editor of *The American Scholar* and Barzun's intellectual kinsman, Joseph Epstein, kept the issue alive in a review of a usage book in *The Times Literary Supplement.* Writing in 1976, he declared his admiration for the novelist Jean Stafford, whom he regarded as "attractively crankish on the subject of usage." He reported that she had installed a sign placed over her "back door" declaring: "'Hopefully' must not be misused on these premises. Violators will be humiliated" (13 Feb. 1976, 162). (Presumably those entering by the back door were unworthy to be welcomed as guests in the front room.) Not surprisingly, Stafford accepted membership on the American Heritage Usage Panel; her sign must have made her especially qualified to offer "crankish" views on matters of English. Hence it is not surprising that the 1986 survey of the Panel showed that disapproval of sentence-adverbial *hopefully* increased from 56% in the 1960s to 73%. The diffusion of the idea that *hopefully* is a shibboleth was rapid and effective, reaching large numbers of opinion-makers and leaving as a residue the idea expressed by my colleague: that *hopefully* is a virulent usage she is obliged to suppress.[3]

This long example suggests new directions for research in American English. One is that it may well be possible to identify routes of diffusion of linguistic ideas (and of linguistic features) if we can uncover the "hubs" of the networks by which they are spread. It is likely that the introduction and diffusion of some kinds of changes are much more rapid than has usually been presumed by historical linguistics. (*Hopefully* was only noticed in 1962 as an expression of interest; by late 1964 and early 1965, the opinion about it had been formed and spread.) Second, it displays how "social dominance" predicts which persons are likely to act as "hubs" because they function as attractors (and diffusers) of innovation. (Barzun was the "hub" of *hopefully*, and the Usage Panel was the network.) Third, it shows that the "meaning" attached to expressions determines the success or failure of the innovation. (*Hopefully* was "marketed" as a shibboleth, and knowing that it was "wrong" became a small piece of cultural baggage. *Mercifully* escaped the same fate, mercifully.)

Political and ideological ideas about language need more of our attention. The concluding sentence of Niedzielski's (1999) investigation of "Canadian" and "Michigan" English summarized above seems to me to capture exactly this idea: "The results of this study suggest social information must be included in future research in phonetics, sociolinguistics, and social psychology, particularly in the areas of speech perception and language change" (84).

The era since the publication of the last volume of Needed Research has been an enormously productive one, more productive than any 20-year period in the life of the American Dialect Society. Substantial progress has been made in filling in the blanks on the dialect maps and moving the several dictionaries of American usage closer to completion. But it is not just the old program that drives the energy of scholars; it is also the array of new questions (and new methods of answering them) that has transformed the field. Still more research is "needed" because we have found new ways to answer our questions, both the old ones that activated the founders and the new ones that are now enlarging our understanding of language.

NOTE

1. In the Essex County Courts during 1630–92, 285 women were punished under the speech and silence regulations. The punishments meted out were: compulsory acknowledgement (138), voluntary confession or petition (122), pinned with paper (18), gagged with cleft stick (6), tongue mutilated (1). See Kamensky 1997, 199.

2. I once asked a student at Hanover College in far-southern Indiana where "the South" began. She unhesitatingly said: "Raymond Street" in Indianapolis. Another student from Indianapolis immediately affirmed her judgment.

3. Like true believers of many kinds, these objectors have sometimes recanted in very public ways. Rudolf Flesch, one of the early complainants in 1964, declared in 1983 that "the purists have been roundly defeated." Theodore Bernstein, in 1977, said that "additional thought about the matter has changed my mind." Philip Howard, the editor of the *Times* quoted above, declared in 1983: "I sweat with embarrassment to read the article that I wrote about 'hopefully' in 1975." A novelist lately arrived on the *hopefully* battlefield hoped, in the *New York Times* in 1993, that the word might "someday . . . claim its rightful place in the language" (Schine 1993). By then only the Barzun loyalists in their isolated outposts had much doubt that it had. (My discussion of *hopefully* draws much, including several of these quotations, from Gilman 1989, 512–13.)

REFERENCES

Adams, John. 1852. Letter to the president of Congress, Amsterdam, 5 Sept. 1780. In *The Works of John Adams*, ed. Charles Francis Adams, 7: 249–51. Boston: Little, Brown.

Algeo, John. 1984. "Usage." In *Needed Research in American English (1983)*, 36–53. Publication of the American Dialect Society 71. University: Univ. of Alabama Press.

An American [John Adams?]. 1774. "To the Literati of America." *Royal American Magazine* 1: 6–7.

The American Heritage Dictionary of the English Language. 1969. Ed. William Morris. New York: American Heritage.

Anderson, Benedict. 1991. *Imagined Communities: Reflections on the Origin and Spread of Nationalism*. Rev. and expanded ed. London: Verso.

Bailey, Richard W. 1996. *Nineteenth-Century English*. Ann Arbor: Univ. of Michigan Press.

———. 2003. "The Ideology of English in the Long Eighteenth Century." In *Insights into Late Modern English*, ed. Marina Dossena and Charles Jones, 22–44. Bern: Lang.

Barabási, Albert-László. 2002. *Linked: The New Science of Networks*. Cambridge, Mass.: Perseus.

Baron, Dennis E. 1982. *Grammar and Good Taste: Reforming the American Language*. New Haven, Conn.: Yale Univ. Press.

———. 1986. *Grammar and Gender*. New Haven, Conn.: Yale Univ. Press.

Barzun, Jacques. 1959. *The House of Intellect*. New York: Harper.

———. 1963. "What Is a Dictionary?" *American Scholar* 32: 176–81.

———. 1986. *A Word or Two before You Go . . . : Brief Essays on Language*. Middletown, Conn.: Wesleyan Univ. Press.

Baugh, John. 2000. *Beyond Ebonics: Linguistic Pride and Racial Prejudice*. New York: Oxford University Press.

Bernstein, Theodore M. 1962. *More Language That Needs Watching: Second Aid for Writers and Editors, Emanating from the News Room of the "New York Times."* Manhasset, N.Y.: Channel.

Blank, Paula. 1996. *Broken English: Dialects and the Politics of Language in Renaissance Writings*. London: Routledge.

Bloomfield, Leonard. 1944. "Secondary and Tertiary Responses to Language." *Language* 20: 45–55.

Bonfiglio, Thomas Paul. 2002. *Race and the Rise of Standard American*. Berlin: de Gruyter.

Calef, Robert. 1700. *More Wonders of the Invisible World*. London: Hillar and Collyer. Repr. in *Narratives of the Witchcraft Cases, 1648–1706*, ed. George Lincoln Burr, 291–393. New York: Scribner's, 1914. Available from http://etext.lib.virginia.edu/toc/modeng/public/Bur5Nar.html (accessed 6 May 2003).

Cameron, Angus, Roberta Frank, and John Leyerle, eds. 1970. *Computers and Old English Concordances.* Toronto: Univ. of Toronto Press.

Chamberlin, J. Edward. 1993. *Come Back to Me My Language: Poetry and the West Indies.* Urbana: Univ. of Illinois Press.

Clark, Thomas L. 1984. "Historical Perspective." In *Needed Research in American English (1983),* 1–3. Publication of the American Dialect Society 71. University: Univ. of Alabama Press.

Cmiel, Kenneth. 1990. *Democratic Eloquence: The Fight over Popular Speech in Nineteenth-Century America.* New York: Morrow.

Crawford, James, ed. 1992. *Language Loyalties: A Source Book on the Official English Controversy.* Chicago: Univ. of Chicago Press.

Crowley, Tony. 1989. *The Politics of Discourse: The Standard Language Question in British Cultural Debates.* Basingstoke: Macmillan Education.

Crumpton, Claudia E. 1917. "Speech Betterment in Alabama." *English Journal* 6: 96–102.

Cukor-Avila, Patricia. 2000. "Linguistic Diversity in the Workplace: How Regional Accent Affects Employment Decisions." Paper presented at the 29th Annual Conference on New Ways of Analyzing Variation (NWAV-29), East Lansing, Mich., 5–8 Oct.

Cukor-Avila, Patricia, and Dianne Markley. 2002. "If You Don't Sound Like Me, Then You Must Not Be as Good as I Am: Linguistic Security and the Decision to Hire." Paper presented at the annual meeting of the American Dialect Society, San Francisco, 3–5 Jan.

Dreiser, Theodore. 1900. *Sister Carrie.* New York: Doubleday, Page.

Dictionary of American Regional English. 1985–. Vol. 1 (A–C), ed. Frederic G. Cassidy. Vols. 2 (D–H) and 3 (I–O), ed. Frederic G. Cassidy and Joan Houston Hall. Vol. 4 (P–Sk), ed. Joan Houston Hall. 4 vols. to date. Cambridge, Mass.: Belknap Press of Harvard Univ. Press.

Edwards, Walter F. 1992. "Sociolinguistic Behavior in a Detroit Inner-City Black Neighborhood." *Language in Society* 21: 93–115.

Follett, Wilson. 1966. *Modern American Usage: A Guide.* Ed. and completed by Jacques Barzun. New York: Hill and Wang.

Giles, Howard, Justine Coupland, and Nikolas Coupland, eds. 1991. *Contexts of Accommodation: Developments in Applied Sociolinguistics.* Cambridge: Cambridge Univ. Press.

Gilman, E. Ward. 1989. *Webster's Dictionary of English Usage.* Springfield, Mass.: Merriam-Webster.

Gregory, Stanford W., Jr., and Stephen Webster. 1996. "A Nonverbal Signal in Voices of Interview Partners Effectively Predicts Communication Accommodation and Social Status Perceptions." *Journal of Personality and Social Psychology* 70: 1231–40.

Gregory, Stanford W., Jr., and Timothy J. Gallagher. 2002. "Spectral Analysis of Candidates' Nonverbal Vocal Communication: Predicting U.S. Presidential Election Outcomes." *Social Psychology Quarterly* 65: 298–308.

Jones, Gavin. 1999. *Strange Talk: The Politics of Dialect Literature in Gilded Age America*. Berkeley: Univ. of California Press.

Kamensky, Jane. 1997. *Governing the Tongue: The Politics of Speech in Early New England*. New York: Oxford Univ. Press.

Kramer, Michael P. 1992. *Imagining Language in America: From the Revolution to the Civil War*. Princeton, N.J.: Princeton Univ. Press.

Kretzschmar, William A., Jr. 1998. *Linguistic Atlas Projects* (Web site). Accessed 4 May 2003. Available from http://hyde.park.uga.edu/index.html.

Labov, William, Sharon Ash, and Charles Boberg. 2003. *TELSUR Project* (Web site). Accessed 17 May. Available from http://www.ling.upenn.edu/phono_atlas/home.html.

———, eds. Forthcoming. *Atlas of North American English: Phonetics, Phonology, and Sound Change*. Berlin: de Gruyter.

Lance, Donald M. 1999. "Regional Variation in Subjective Dialect Divisions in the United States." In Preston, 293–314.

Lesher, Stephan. 1972. "Who Knows What Frustrations Lurk in the Hearts of X Million Americans? George Wallace Knows—and He's Off and Running." *New York Times Magazine*, 2 Jan., 35. Quoted by editors in *Varieties of Present-Day English*, ed. Richard W. Bailey and Jay L. Robinson, 271. New York: Macmillan.

Lippi-Green, Rosina. 1997. *English with an Accent: Language, Ideology, and Discrimination in the United States*. London: Routledge.

Marckwardt, Albert H. 1964. "Report to the Commission on the Humanities." In "Needed Research in American English (1963)," 23–27. *Publication of the American Dialect Society* 41: 22–41.

Markley, Dianne. 2000. "Regional Accent Discrimination in the Hiring Process: A Language Attitude Study." M.A. thesis, Univ. of North Texas.

McDavid, Raven I., Jr. 1984. "Linguistic Geography." In *Needed Research in American English (1983)*, 4–28. Publication of the American Dialect Society 71. University: Univ. of Alabama Press.

Metcalf, Allan. 2002. *Predicting New Words: The Secrets of Their Success*. Boston: Houghton Mifflin.

Middle English Dictionary. 1952–2001. Vols. A–F, ed. Hans Kurath. Vols. G–P, ed. Sherman Kuhn. Vols. Q–Z, ed. Robert E. Lewis. Ann Arbor: Univ. of Michigan Press.

Milroy, James, and Lesley Milroy. 1999. *Authority in Language: Investigating Standard English.* 3d ed. London: Routledge.

Milroy, Lesley. 1999. "Standard English and Language Ideology in Britain and the United States." In *Standard English: The Widening Debate*, ed. Tony Bex and Richard J. Watts, 173–206. London: Routledge.

Niedzielski, Nancy. 1999. "The Effect of Social Information on the Perception of Sociolinguistic Variables." *Journal of Language and Social Psychology* 18: 62–85.

Parakrama, Arjuna. 1995. *De-hegemonizing Language Standards: Learning from (Post-)Colonial Englishes about "English."* New York: St. Martin's.

Pederson, Lee, ed. 1986–92. *Linguistic Atlas of the Gulf States.* 7 vols. Athens: Univ. of Georgia Press.

Phillipson, Robert. 1992. *Linguistic Imperialism.* Oxford: Oxford Univ. Press.

———. 2003. *English-Only Europe? Challenging Language Policy.* London: Routledge.

Pratt, Mary Louise. 1984. "Linguistic Utopias." In *The Linguistics of Writing: Arguments between Language and Literature*, ed. Nigel Babb, Derek Attridge, Alain Durant, and Colin MacCabe, 48–66. Manchester: Manchester Univ. Press.

Preston, Dennis R. 1989. *Perceptual Dialectology: Nonlinguists' Views of Areal Linguistics.* Dordrecht: Foris.

———. 1993. "Folk Dialectology." In *American Dialect Research*, ed. Dennis R. Preston, 333–77. Amsterdam: Benjamins.

———. 1998. "'They Speak Really Bad English Down South and in New York City.'" In *Language Myths*, ed. Laurie Bauer and Peter Trudgill, 139–58. London: Penguin.

———. 2002. "The Story of Good and Bad English in the United States." In *Alternative Histories of English*, ed. Richard Watts and Peter Trudgill, 134–51. London: Routledge.

———, ed. 1999. *Handbook of Perceptual Dialectology.* Vol. 1. Amsterdam: Benjamins.

Queen, Robin M. 1997. "'I Don't Speak Spritch': Locating Lesbian Language." In *Queerly Phrased: Language, Gender, and Sexuality*, ed. Anna Livia and Kira Hall, 233–56. New York: Oxford Univ. Press.

Reynolds, David S. 1988. *Beneath the American Renaissance: The Subversive Imagination in the Age of Emerson and Melville.* New York: Knopf.

Rickford, John R. 1999. *African American Vernacular English: Features, Evolution, Educational Implications.* Malden, Mass.: Blackwell.

Rickford, John Russell, and Russell John Rickford. 2000. *Spoken Soul: The Story of Black English.* New York: Wiley.

Schine, Cathleen. 1993. "'Hopefully' Springs Eternal." *New York Times Magazine,* 20 June, 12.

Shurtleff, Nathaniel B., ed. 1857. *Records of the Colony of New Plymouth in New England.* Vol. 7, *Judicial Acts, 1636–1692.* Boston: White. Repr. New York: AMS, 1968.

Skutnabb-Kangas, Tove. 2000. *Linguistic Genocide in Education, or World-Wide Diversity and Human Rights?* Mahwah, N.J.: Erlbaum.

Smith, Olivia. 1984. *The Politics of Language, 1791–1819.* Oxford: Clarendon.

Swift, Jonathan. 1712. *A Proposal for Correcting, Improving, and Ascertaining the English Tongue.* London: Tooke. Repr. English Linguistics, 1500–1800. Menston: Scolar, 1969.

Talib, Ismail S. 2002. *The Language of Postcolonial Literatures: An Introduction.* London: Routledge.

Tucker, G. Richard, and Wallace Lambert. 1969. "White and Negro Listeners' Reactions to Various American-English Dialects." *Social Forces* 47: 463–68. Repr. in *Varieties of Present-Day English,* ed. Richard W. Bailey and Jay L. Robinson, 293–301. New York: Macmillan, 1973.

Webster's Third New International Dictionary of the English Language, Unabridged. 1961. Editor in chief, Philip Babcock Gove. Springfield, Mass.: Merriam.

Worrell, A. S. 1861. *The Principles of English Grammar.* Nashville, Tenn.: Graves, Marks.

8. SLANG, METAPHOR, AND FOLK SPEECH

CONNIE C. EBLE

University of North Carolina at Chapel Hill

Over a period of about four months, I routinely consulted the indices of linguistics books that I had occasion to pick up for the occurrence of the three key terms of this essay. Finding in my haphazard search only three or four occurrences each of SLANG and METAPHOR and none of FOLK SPEECH, I continued the exercise in a more systematic way by consulting dictionaries and encyclopedias of linguistics and sociolinguistics, as well as textbooks and handbooks.[1]

Slang is an entry in two of the three dictionaries consulted and in one of the two encyclopedias. Asher and Simpson (1994) contains a good article on slang by sociologist Irving Lewis Allen, but Frawley (2003) has no entry at all on the topic. Of 11 recent sociolinguistics textbooks, *slang* appears in the indices of five. Holmes (2001) incorporates slang into the discussion of the greatest number of different topics, though that is only six. The term *metaphor* fares better. It is listed in all three dictionaries and both encyclopedias, where the emphasis is on cognitive metaphor, although Frawley (2003) contains two entries, one on metaphor and semantics by George Lakoff and one on metaphor in literature by Samuel R. Levin. Of the 11 textbooks, three have entries for *metaphorical code switching* and two for *metaphor*. Stockwell (2002) has the fullest treatment of metaphor, a chapter of about 20 pages. No work consulted has an entry or index item for *folk speech*. Even *American Dialect Research* (Preston 1993) of a decade ago has no index entry for any of the three terms addressed in this essay.

From the perspective of mainstream linguistics and sociolinguistics, then, slang, metaphor, and folk speech are not overworked topics.

These three types of lexis are similar insofar as all three are generally described, by linguists and nonlinguists alike, as a special, peculiar, or restricted kind of vocabulary as opposed to some neutral norm or standard. Research on them to this point reflects that deviant status. In current professional research about language, slang, metaphor, and folk speech are marginal topics and seldom enter the discussion of important issues like the intersection of language variation and change with speaker characteristics (age, ethnicity, socioeconomic class, and so forth) or with sociosituational factors (topic, audience, purpose, and so forth).

SLANG. Twenty years ago in *Needed Research in American English (1983)*, a half page in I. Willis Russell's (1984) section "New Words" was devoted to slang. There he called for the collection of slang in the same environment over a period of years and its analysis according to word-making processes (55). Such a study has been done (Eble 1996). Russell also encouraged exploration of "the less formal criteria" for defining slang that had been proposed by Bethany Dumas and Jonathan Lighter (1978). This too has been done. Dumas and Lighter's extended definition, characterizing slang by its effects on the hearer and on the speaker-hearer interaction, has proven to be the first step in moving the study of slang beyond lexicography (Nunnally 2001, 159–68). Discussions of the definition of slang and the relationship of slang to other socially salient and ephemeral types of vocabulary like vogue words are ongoing. Eastern Europeans are particularly interested in slang, to the extent that in 1999 a volume containing 11 essays on defining slang was published, with contributions from scholars from eight countries, all translated into Hungarian (Fenyvesi, Kis, and Varnai 1999).

Slang and kinds of lexis that share some characteristics with slang (e.g., colloquialisms, jargon, and vogue words) have largely been the purview of lexicography. Several substantial dictionaries by knowledgeable authors do a remarkably good job of documenting American slang for the twentieth century. Wentworth and Flexner (1960, 1967, 1975) contains an excellent preface by Flexner on the sociocultural context of American slang that has been reprinted many times. In it, he maintains that slang is associated primarily with males. To my knowledge, no study has ever been done to test the accuracy of this characterization from more than a quarter of a century ago or to assess the effects of expanding opportunities for women on the creation and use of slang in the United States. Chapman's (1986) updated and revised edition of Wentworth and Flexner likewise contains a valuable preface in which Chapman distinguishes between the primary slang of subculture members and the secondary slang that temporarily allies its users with a subculture or a trend in society. Chapman predicts that "in the future secondary or acquired slang will be our major variety" (xii). He also suggests that "the black influence on American slang has been more pervasive in recent times than that of any other ethnic group in history" (xi). Both of Chapman's conjectures appear to be important and true, but close analysis of them remains to be done.

Nunnally (2001) reviews six lexical works on American slang and Americanisms that were published from 1997 to 1999. Of them, Jonathan Lighter's incomparable historical dictionary of American slang stands apart. Two volumes of four have been published as the *Random House Historical Dictionary of American Slang* (1994–). The greatest need in slang research in the United States today is the publication of Lighter's dictionary in its entirety. That event now seems likely. In 2003 the National Endowment for the Humanities announced a grant that will allow Oxford University Press to bring the project to completion by 2010. The project director will be Jesse Sheidlower. Another valuable dictionary-in-the-making is *The New Partridge Dictionary of Slang and Unconventional English* (Dalzell and Victor forthcoming). However, lexicographical work in slang—no matter how good it is—will not move the study of slang from the margins of the scientific study of language to a more central position. Slang must be seen as a component of a number of issues of interest to linguists—aging, identity, register shifts, innovation and diffusion, and pragmatics, to name a few. Furthermore, it is possible that the controlled experiment model standard in psychology could be advantageously applied to the study of subjects producing, processing, and reacting to slang. Among the very few studies of this sort is one by Friendly and Glucksberg (1970), which gives a quantitative description of the acquisition of campus slang by Princeton undergraduates.[2]

Slang must also be viewed as part of the continuum of kinds of vocabulary that people use every day to greet others, make small talk, communicate in the workplace, buy groceries, make medical appointments, and perform the many other unplanned language acts occasioned by living. Among these are widely known VOGUE WORDS, such as *senior moment* 'temporary mental lapse' and the euphemistic *regime change* 'overthrow of Saddam Hussein by U.S. military aggression', and FLIPPANT SAYINGS such as *Been there. Done that. Got the tee-shirt.* and the tough guy allusion *I'll make you an offer you can't refuse.* Also not to be excluded are many other words and expressions used within groups or limited networks that require insider knowledge, such as nicknames and allusions.

Slang as ordinary English usage is often minimized or omitted in descriptions of the language. However, one of the fourteen chapters that together characterize English in North America in volume 6 of *The Cambridge History of the English Language* (Algeo 2001) is an original essay on slang by Jonathan Lighter (2001). In the final section, Lighter interprets the preponderance of slang and other kinds of informal vocabulary in ordinary speech as a way of coping with an increasingly "urban, mobile, stratified, industrialized, . . . competitive, and impersonal" society (249). In broad perspective, the creation and use of slang and its kin are adaptations to the strong currents of material, technological, social, and cultural change that have swept over the United States since the beginning of the twentieth century. The details of Lighter's sketch need to be worked out and filled in. To use a vogue expression of 2002, research needs to "connect the dots." This will require rigorous analysis of the social psychology of slang as well as mapping specific relationships among mass media, popular culture, and linguistic fashion. Perhaps most important, and most difficult, is that successful research concerning slang must tap into the perspectives and empirical work of other disciplines. For example, the role of fashion in language should be seen as a particular manifestation of the importance of fashion in other kinds of human expression (Eble 2000). In the disciplines of sociology, anthropology, and psychology, the large body of professional literature devoted to analysis of fashion undoubtedly holds insights for understanding slang and vogue words. Diffusion of innovation is another topic treated by both natural and social scientists that is relevant to slang.

The earliest records and observations about English slang characterize it as primarily oral and linked to subcultures within society. However, slang now faces the prospect of being transmitted in writing, instantaneously, and across continental and cultural borders. As the twenty-first century begins, the Internet has propelled American slang to the global stage, giving it unprecedented opportunities for diffusion across boundaries of geography, age, gender, education, occupation, and so forth. A search for the word *slang* on google.com on a single day (24 July 2002) yielded 873 hits. In a 10% sampling of these, the overwhelming majority were sites written in English. They ranged from personal collections of the slang of Australia, the Civil War, and the Royal Navy to commercial sites that used slang to sell goods or services, including tattoos, pornography, coins, and English lessons. A site in Spanish provided teenagers with a list of U.S. slang defined in Spanish to help them appear "cool"; and on a site in Russian, amid Cyrillic characters, could be seen *kewl* 'cool', *rules, prob,* and *snailmail.* Analysis of slang on the Internet can reveal much about lay folks' awareness and understanding of socially salient vocabulary (Eble 2002).

As people around the world choose to learn American English as their second or third language, American slang is attaining an international cachet. More and more, American slang is being learned not by transmission from speaker to speaker but from song lyrics, films, and Web sites—and in the ESL classroom. *An Introduction to American English* (Tottie 2002), for non-native speakers, includes a well-informed description of the nature and function of slang vocabulary along with a list of about 30 items of current American slang. The desire of international students to be in the know about American slang, its nuances, and the appropriate situations for its use is a growing challenge in ESL pedagogy.

METAPHOR. Unlike slang or folk speech—vocabulary types traditionally associated with marginal subcultures or with unsophisticated rural speakers—metaphor has always been regarded in western Europe as an elevated type of diction. One of the classical tropes, metaphor provides a way for literary artists to express their thoughts in new images. Metaphors have been considered such a special instance of language use that they have been routinely excluded from grammatical descriptions. Evaluation of the originality, aptness, and sonority of metaphors has long been the business of literary criticism, where a distinction is made between dead metaphors, which have become drab and conventional, and valued literary ones. The verb *run*, for instance, is often cited as a dead metaphor in collocations like *the river runs* or *the machine runs*. Another common example is the noun *foot* in expressions like *the foot of the bed*. Since the 1970s, however, the view among linguists has been that metaphor, rather than being a special effect of language cultivated by the intellectual and well-read, is pervasive in the conversation of all classes of speakers. By that measure, metaphor is said to be characteristic of ordinary language.

In the past 25 years metaphor (but not literary metaphor) has received much attention from linguists. The new approach, made famous by Lakoff and Johnson's *Metaphors We Live By* (1980), locates metaphor in the conceptual system and makes metaphor the basis for thought and action. "Each metaphor is a structural mapping from one conceptual domain to another. When a metaphor is conventional, it forms a part of our everyday understanding of experience: it is processed automatically, effortlessly, and without notice" (Lakoff 2003, 53). Because of the popularity and accessibility of Lakoff and Johnson (1980), several of the metaphors identified there are widely known and accepted as explanatory, such as *The mind is a container, Death is departure, Argument is war*. Conventional metaphors that cause little admiration among literary critics have become the important sort of metaphors for linguists seeking to understand language and cognition.

Despite its widespread appeal among linguists, the notion of cognitive metaphors underlying thought and speech has not gone unchallenged. Sam Glucksberg and his associates offer experiments based on reading-time measurement that suggest that "people need not rely on conceptual mappings for conventional expressions, although such mappings may be used to understand *nonconventional* expressions" (Keysar et al. 2000, 576). McGlone (2001), in a chapter devoted to concepts as metaphors, concludes that "the conceptual metaphor view has not fared well theoretically or empirically" (105). Until the process of constructing conceptual mappings is verified and the dichotomy of literal versus figurative language better understood, the direction and potential of the study of metaphor for understanding language variation and change are difficult to predict.

FOLK SPEECH. The term *folk speech* is associated with dialect geography as it was formulated for the linguistic atlas projects of Europe and the United States early in the last century, and today it sounds somewhat old-fashioned. In the atlas projects of the United States, Type I informants were the "folk speakers," whose usage was least affected by education or by influence from outside the local community. Their lives were bounded locally, and they tended to be old. In traditional dialect geography, folk speech had an aura of primacy and authenticity about it, and field-workers went to great trouble to record it. Recognizing that the rural and agrarian society that favors folk speech was fast disappearing, Frederic Cassidy (1985) decided that the *Dictionary of American Regional English* (*DARE*) would include "any word or phrase whose form or meaning is distinctively a folk usage . . . that which is learned in the home and in the community, from relatives and friends, not from schooling, books, or other outside forms of communication" (xvi). Because of the pervasiveness of mass media like radio and television, most Americans are no longer isolated from influence beyond the circle of family, friends, and acquaintances in their local community, and the number of speakers who readily fit the characteristics of a Type I informant is certainly smaller than ever.

It is probable that folk speakers as traditionally conceived and their speech no longer constitute a significant part of American regional dialects. However, the loss of the folk category of speakers does not entail the loss of a vocabulary of local identity. The conservation of local identity via speech may now have shifted to a different group. Those who consider themselves the folk of an area may now be native-born or transplanted and of various ages and with various levels of education and experience of the larger world. Some, for example, are retirees moving "home" after decades of a life of work spent far away. The observations of Johnstone, Bhasin, and Wittkofski (2002) for Pittsburgh, Tillery (1997) for Texas, Wolfram and Schilling-Estes (1997) for the Outer Banks of North Carolina, and Eble (2001) for New Orleans suggest that communities are creating a new kind of folk speech for people who live in a highly connected world by selecting a small set of pronunciations and vocabulary items as markers of local identity. Some of the features selected are old regional hallmarks; others are associated with a particular local class or ethnicity; others are innovations. Some are easy for transplants to acquire—like *y'all* in the South or the local pronunciation of place names; others are harder, like the monophthongization of the /aj/ diphthong in Texas. The development of such local linguistic responses to the threat of the homogenization of American culture is an excellent example of how humans subtly code their reactions to a changing world into language. These new linguistic expressions of localness are influenced by a range of external factors, many of which are economic, and need to be studied from a broad perspective.

Slang, metaphor, and folk speech have by and large been well-served by lexicography, and the process of collecting and fully and accurately documenting these kinds of vocabulary will always be an important need in language research in America. Now, however, these types of lexis must be situated within the social and psychological dimensions of language use, and the accumulated knowledge of allied disciplines must be brought to bear in the process. Furthermore, to fit with prevailing standards of description and explanation in linguistics, the occurrence and effects of slang, metaphor, and folk speech must be extracted, quantified, and correlated much like other internal linguistic variables.

NOTES

1. In addition to those cited in the text that follows, the following works were consulted—dictionaries: Bussmann (1996), Crystal (1997, 2001); sociolinguistics textbooks: Bell (1976), Macaulay (1994), Romaine (1994), Montgomery (1995), Hudson (1996), Downes (1998), Wolfram and Schilling-Estes (1998), Trudgill (2000), and Wardhaugh (2002).

2. I am grateful to Ruth Day, professor of psychology at Duke University, for directing me to the work of Sam Glucksberg, who has been studying ordinary kinds of language for several decades using the experimental methods of psychology.

REFERENCES

Algeo, John, ed. 2001. *English in North America*. Vol. 6. of *The Cambridge History of the English Language*. Cambridge: Cambridge Univ. Press.

Allen, Irving Lewis. 1994. "Slang: Sociology." In Asher and Simpson, 7: 3960–64.

Asher, R. E., and J. M. Y. Simpson, eds. 1994. *The Encyclopedia of Language and Linguistics*. 10 vols. Oxford: Pergamon.

Bell, Roger T. 1976. *Sociolinguistics: Goals, Approaches, and Problems*. London: Batsford.

Bussmann, Hadumod. 1996. *Routledge Dictionary of Language and Linguistics*. Trans. and ed. Gregory Trauth and Kerstin Kazzazi. London: Routledge.

Cassidy, Frederic G., ed. 1985. *Dictionary of American Regional English*. Vol. 1 (A–C). Cambridge, Mass.: Belknap Press of Harvard Univ. Press.

Chapman, Robert L. 1986. *New Dictionary of American Slang*. New York: Harper and Row.

Crystal, David. 1997. *A Dictionary of Linguistics and Phonetics*. 4th ed. Oxford: Blackwell.

———. 2001. *A Dictionary of Language*. 2d ed. Chicago: Univ. of Chicago Press.

Dalzell, Tom, and Terry Victor, eds. Forthcoming. *The New Partridge Dictionary of Slang and Unconventional English*. London: Routledge.

Downes, William. 1998. *Language and Society*. 2d ed. Cambridge: Cambridge Univ. Press.

Dumas, Bethany K., and Jonathan Lighter. 1978. "Is *Slang* a Word for Linguists?" *American Speech* 53: 5–17.

Eble, Connie C. 1996. *Slang and Sociability.* Chapel Hill: Univ. of North Carolina Press.

———. 2000. "Fashion as a Linguistic Variable." Paper presented at the meeting of the Southeastern Conference on Linguistics, Oxford, Miss., Apr.

———. 2001. "Local Language and Local Identity in New Orleans." Paper presented at the meeting of the Modern Language Association, New Orleans, La., Dec.

———. 2002. "The Expanding World of English Slang." Paper presented at the meeting of the Linguistic Association of Canada and the United States, Toledo, Ohio, 31 July.

Fenyvesi, Anna, Tamas Kis, and Judit Szilvia Varnai, eds. 1999. *Mi a szleng?* Debrecen: Kossuth Egyetemi Kiado.

Frawley, William J., ed. 2003. *International Encyclopedia of Linguistics.* 2d ed. 4 vols. Oxford: Oxford Univ. Press.

Friendly, Michael L., and Sam Glucksberg. 1970. "On the Description of Subcultural Lexicons: A Multidimensional Approach." *Journal of Personality and Social Psychology* 14: 55–65.

Holmes, Janet. 2001. *An Introduction to Sociolinguistics.* 2d ed. London: Longman.

Hudson, R. A. 1996. *Sociolinguistics.* 2d ed. Cambridge: Cambridge Univ. Press.

Johnstone, Barbara, Neeta Bhasin, and Denise Wittkofski. 2002. "'Dahntahn' Pittsburgh: Monophthongal /aw/ and Representations of Localness in Southwestern Pennsylvania." *American Speech* 77: 148–66.

Keysar, Boaz, Yeshayahu Shen, Sam Glucksberg, and William Horton. 2000. "Conventional Language: How Metaphorical Is It?" *Journal of Memory and Language* 43: 576–93.

Lakoff, George. 2003. "Metaphor and Semantics." In Frawley, 3: 53–54.

Lakoff, George, and Mark Johnson. 1980. *Metaphors We Live By.* Chicago: Univ. of Chicago Press.

Levin, Samuel R. 2003. "Metaphor." In Frawley, 2: 480–83.

Lighter, Jonathan E. 1994–. *Random House Historical Dictionary of American Slang.* 2 vols. to date. New York: Random House.

———. 2001. "Slang." In Algeo, 219–52.

Macaulay, Ronald. 1994. *The Social Art: Language and Its Uses.* New York: Oxford Univ. Press.

McGlone, Matthew S. 2001. "Concepts as Metaphors." In *Understanding Figurative Language: From Metaphor to Idioms*, ed. Sam Glucksberg, 90–107. Oxford: Oxford Univ. Press.

Montgomery, Martin. 1995. *An Introduction to Language and Society*. 2d ed. London: Routledge.

Nunnally, Thomas E. 2001. "Glossing the Folk: A Review of Selected Lexical Research into American Slang and Americanisms." *American Speech* 76: 158–76.

Preston, Dennis, ed. 1993. *American Dialect Research*. Amsterdam: Benjamins.

Romaine, Suzanne. 1994. *Language in Society: An Introduction to Sociolinguistics*. Oxford: Oxford Univ. Press.

Russell, I. Willis. 1984. "New Words." In *Needed Research in American English (1983)*, 54–59. Publication of the American Dialect Society 71. University: Univ. of Alabama Press.

Stockwell, Peter. 2002. *Sociolinguistics: A Resource Books for Students*. London: Routledge.

Tillery, Jan. 1997. "The Role of Social Processes in Language Variation and Change." In *Language Variety in the South Revisted*, ed. Cynthia Bernstein, Thomas Nunnally, and Robin Sabino, 431–46. Tuscaloosa: Univ. of Alabama Press.

Tottie, Gunnel. 2002. *An Introduction to American English*. Oxford: Blackwell.

Trudgill, Peter. 2000. *Sociolinguistics: An Introduction*. 4th ed. New York: Penguin.

Wardhaugh, Ronald. 2002. *An Introduction to Sociolinguistics*. 4th ed. Oxford: Blackwell.

Wentworth, Harold, and Stuart Berg Flexner, eds. 1960. *Dictionary of American Slang*. New York: Crowell. Supplemented ed., 1967. 2d supplemented ed., 1975.

Wolfram, Walt, and Natalie Schilling-Estes. 1997. *Hoi Toide on the Outer Banks: The Story of the Ocracoke Brogue*. Chapel Hill: Univ. of North Carolina Press.

———. 1998. *American English*. Oxford: Blackwell.

9. LANGUAGES OTHER THAN ENGLISH IN CANADA AND THE UNITED STATES

ROBERT BAYLEY

University of Texas at San Antonio

RUTH KING

York University

THE PAST TWO DECADES have witnessed substantial growth in research on languages other than English in North America. As a consequence of the growth in scholarly activity prompted by the increasing linguistic diversity of Canada and the United States, it is impossible for us to address all that has been accomplished and all that remains to be done. Such a task would require several volumes rather than a single chapter. In this chapter, therefore, we concentrate on U.S. Spanish, Canadian and U.S. French, and American Sign Language. Whenever possible, we also take account of other languages. We exclude discussion of indigenous languages of North America because the research on these languages has recently been summarized by Cook (1998), Drapeau (1998), and Mithun (1999). Although our treatment of a very wide-ranging topic is necessarily incomplete, we hope that it will provide an indication of the kind of work that has been done as well as work that might be done on the many languages and language varieties currently spoken in North America.

LINGUISTIC DIVERSITY IN NORTH AMERICA

LINGUISTIC DIVERSITY IN THE UNITED STATES. In the United States, the number of speakers of languages other than English increased dramatically in the last two decades of the twentieth century, reaching levels not seen since the great migrations of the pre–World War I period. As it had been in the early period and has been in the first decade of the twenty-first century, immigration was the primary factor in the increase in languages other than English during the 1980s and 1990s. However, in a change from the earlier period, immigrants came not from Europe, but primarily from Latin America, especially Mexico, and from Asia. Thus, Spanish speakers over the age of four increased from approximately 11.5 million in 1980 to more than 17 million in 1990 to more than 28 million in 2000 (U.S. Bureau of the Census, 1984, 1993, 2003). And, although the increases of speakers of other languages are not nearly as great when viewed in terms of absolute numbers, they are impressive. For example, in the 1980 U.S. census, approximately 630,000 people aged five and older reported speaking Chinese at home (the data do not distinguish between different Chinese varieties). The number had increased to 1.25 million by 1990 and to slightly more than 2 million by 2000. Other Asian languages also showed robust increases. The number of speakers of Tagalog, for example, increased from 452,000 in 1980 to more than 1.2 million in 2000, and speakers of Vietnamese increased from a little more than 200,000 in 1980 to more than a million in 2000. Table 1 provides details about the most commonly spoken languages other than English from the 1990 and 2000 censuses.

While Spanish and Asian languages gained speakers in the United States since 1980, the number of speakers of most European languages either remained static or declined, indications of aging populations in communities undergoing language shift. Among languages spoken primarily in Europe, only Russian showed a robust increase. As shown in table 1, in the 1990s, the number of Russian speakers in the United States nearly tripled.

LINGUISTIC DIVERSITY IN CANADA. Canada has two official languages, English and French. In 2001, 17.4 million people, 60.4% of the population, reported English as their sole mother tongue, defined as the language they learned first and still understood at the time of the census; 6.7 million respondents, 22.9% of the population, reported French. As table 2 shows, English is the majority language in every province but Quebec, where the population is 82% francophone, a proportion virtually unchanged over the last 50 years.

TABLE 1

Most Commonly Spoken Languages in the United States
Other than English, 1990 and 2000
(U.S. Bureau of the Census 1993, 2003)

2000 Rank	Language	1990	2000	Change, 1990–2000
1	Spanish	17,862,477	28,101,052	+10,238,575
2	Chinese[a]	1,249,213	2,022,143	+772,930
3	French, incl. Patois, Cajun	1,702,176	1,643,838	−58,338
4	German	1,547,099	1,383,442	−163,657
5	Tagalog	843,251	1,224,241	+380,990
6	Vietnamese	507,069	1,009,627	+502,558
7	Italian	1,308,648	1,008,370	−300,278
8	Korean	626,478	894,063	+267,585
9	Russian	241,798	706,242	+464,444
10	Polish	723,483	667,414	−56,069
11	Arabic	355,150	614,582	+259,432
12	Hindi and Urdu	331,484	579,957	+248,473
13	Portuguese or Portuguese Creole	429,860	564,630	+134,770
14	Japanese	427,657	477,997	+50,340
15	French Creole	187,658	435,368	+247,710
16	Greek	388,260	365,436	−22,824

a. Includes all dialects of Chinese.

While nationally the numbers of anglophones and franco-phones increased slightly from the 1996 to the 2001 census, their proportions in the population as a whole declined somewhat, the result of an aging population. The main source of population growth is allophones, those whose first childhood language is neither English nor French. Allophones are concentrated in multi-lingual, multicultural urban centers in just four provinces: Ontario, Quebec, British Columbia, and Alberta. For example, while Chinese speakers made up 2.9% of the total population of Canada in 2001, three-quarters of them lived in Vancouver or Toronto. In Vancouver they made up 15.2% of the population, and in Toronto, 7.6%. Further, 79% of the 97,670 Tamils living in Canada live in Toronto. Thirty-six percent of the 220,535 Arabic speakers live in

TABLE 2
Population of Mother Tongue Language Groups
by Province and Territory, 2001
(Statistics Canada 2002)

	Anglophone	Francophone	Other
Newfoundland & Labrador	500,400	2,520	5,815
Prince Edward Island	125,650	6,190	2,150
Nova Scotia	836,910	36,740	28,330
New Brunswick	471,010	242,060	12,625
Quebec	627,500	5,844,070	756,710
Ontario	8,119,835	533,965	2,797,560
Manitoba	839,765	47,560	232,775
Saskatchewan	827,355	19,520	126,045
Alberta	2,412,190	65,990	497,205
British Columbia	2,872,830	63,630	981,920
Yukon Territory	24,925	975	2,955
Northwest Territories	29,080	1,060	7,425
Nunavut	7,400	435	19,325
TOTAL	17,694,835	6,752,040	5,470,820

NOTE: This table includes single and multiple responses, e.g., speakers claiming both English and French as mother tongues were counted twice.

Montreal, and 32% of the 284,750 Punjabi speakers live in Vancouver (Statistics Canada 2002). As in the United States, the growth in the allophone population is driven by immigration. Asia is the primary source of immigration to Canada. The number of residents speaking Chinese, Punjabi, Arabic, Urdu, and Tagalog rose by more than 18% from 1996 to 2001. Table 3 shows the most commonly spoken languages in Canada by mother tongue.

In addition to English, French, and immigrant languages, 187,675 people identified themselves as speaking an aboriginal language as their mother tongue in 2001, 2,000 less than in the 1991 census. The figures for some of the more than 30 languages spoken are quite low, for example, Haida had only 165 speakers in 1991 and that number was reduced to 145 in 2001. Cree has the greatest number of mother tongue speakers (almost 73,000 speakers), followed by Inuktitut (29,005) and Ojibway (21,000).

TABLE 3

Most Commonly Spoken Languages in Canada by Mother Tongue

(Statistics Canada 2002)

Mother Tongue	Total	1996 Census % of pop.	2001 Census % of pop.	% Change
English	17,694,835	60.49	59.70	–0.79
French	6,864,615	23.80	23.16	–0.64
Chinese[a]	853,745	2.51	2.88	0.37
Cantonese	322,310			
Mandarin	101,790			
Hakka	4,560			
Chinese, n.o.s.	425,085			
Italian	469,485	1.70	1.58	–0.12
German	438,080	1.58	1.48	–0.10
Punjabi	271,220	0.71	0.92	0.21
Spanish	245,495	0.75	0.83	0.08
Portuguese	213,810	0.74	0.72	0.02
Polish	208,375	0.75	0.70	–0.05
Arabic	199,940	0.52	0.67	0.15
Others	2,179,435	6.46	7.35	0.89

a. Since many respondents chose the designation "Chinese" rather than identifying a specific Chinese variety, we have given overall numbers for Chinese as well as individual numbers for those Chinese dialects named.

In the following sections, we review some of the more important findings on research on individual languages, with a focus on Spanish in the United States, French in Canada and Louisiana, and American Sign Language.

SPANISH IN THE UNITED STATES

Spanish is by far the most commonly spoken language other than English in the United States. Primarily as a result of large-scale immigration in recent decades, the Latino population now numbers more than 35 million, 80% of whom claim to speak at least some Spanish at home, and the United States is now the world's fifth most populous Spanish-speaking country, trailing only Mexico, Spain, Colombia, and Argentina. Given the number of speakers involved and the deeply rooted nature of many Spanish-speaking communities, some of which long antedate U.S. independence, it is not surprising to find that Spanish varieties have received more scholarly attention than other minority languages. Although much remains to be done, research on U.S. Spanish varieties has progressed steadily in the last 20 years. An annual conference, El español en los EE.UU., Spanish in the United States, has provided a convenient venue for researchers to present their work and to interact with other scholars. In addition, descriptions of different varieties of U.S. Spanish (e.g., Silva-Corvalán 1994, forthcoming) and a substantial number of edited volumes have appeared (e.g., Elías-Olivares 1983; Bergen 1990; Roca and Lipski 1993; Silva-Corvalán 1995; Roca 2000). Studies have dealt with language maintenance and shift at the community level and beyond from a variety of perspectives (e.g., Veltman 1988; Hakuta and D'Andrea 1992; Vasquez, Pease-Alvarez, and Shannon 1994; Bills, Hernández Chávez, and Hudson 1995; Bills 1997; Schecter and Bayley 2002). Other studies have focused on linguistic systems at all linguistic levels, from relatively small-scale studies of individual forms (e.g., García 1995, 1999) to large-scale community-based accounts of language variation (e.g., Silva-Corvalán 1994) to longitudinal studies of individuals' developing linguistic competencies in several varieties of Spanish and English (e.g., Zentella 1997). In addition, scholars have begun to focus on the linguistic consequences of contact among Spanish dialects in U.S. cities (e.g., Amastae and Satcher 1993 on Hondurans in El Paso, Texas; Parodi and Santa Ana 2002 on Salvadorans in Los Angeles; Otheguy and Zentella 2002 on New York City Spanish). Code-switching has also figured prominently in sociolinguistic studies of U.S. Latino communities, with numerous studies of both Mexican American and Puerto Rican communities (e.g., Poplack 1980, 1981, 1985; Zentella 1981, 1997; Jacobson 1982; Pfaff 1982; Reyes 1982; Valdés 1982; Bayley and Zapata 1993; Toribio 2002, to name just a few). Finally, scholars have paid considerable attention to Spanish varieties that developed in the Southwest under Spanish and Mexican rule, particularly the varieties spoken in northern New Mexico and southern Colorado (Bills 1997; Bills and Vigil 1999), and to moribund dialects, among them the Isleño and Brule dialects spoken by very small numbers of descendants of Spanish settlers in Louisiana (Lipski 1987, 1990; Coles 1993; Holloway 1997).

It is beyond the scope of this chapter to examine in detail all the work that has been accomplished. Rather, we will outline some of the more important findings that research has revealed and suggest areas where further work would seem most fruitful. In particular, we will focus on language maintenance and shift, contact between Spanish and English, and Spanish/English code-switching.

SPANISH LANGUAGE MAINTENANCE AND SHIFT. Fifteen years ago, demographer Calvin Veltman (1988) suggested that continuing immigration from Spanish-speaking countries was the primary reason for the apparent vitality of Spanish in the United States. His conclusion was based on large-scale surveys that showed that U.S. Latinos tended to follow the pattern that has characterized many immigrant communities. Typically, for immigrants to the U.S., the immigrant generation is monolingual, or at least dominant, in the language of the country of origin. The first U.S.-born generation is bilingual in the immigrant language and English, although usually their literacy skills are stronger in English as a result of attending English-medium schools. The second U.S.-born generation is often monolingual in English, or at least strongly English-dominant, with only receptive knowledge of the immigrant language.

Despite the extremely rapid growth of the U.S. Latino population over the last 20 years, substantial evidence suggests that language shift to English is continuing, although perhaps at a somewhat slower pace than with earlier immigrant communities. Bills (1997), for example, used data from the 1990 census to examine the numbers of people who claimed to use Spanish at home in five states with traditionally large Mexican-origin populations: Arizona, California, Colorado, New Mexico, and Texas. Table 4 shows the results by state and age group. These 1990 census data are consistent with the trends discussed by Veltman (1988). In all five states that Bills studied, far more adults (18 years and older) claimed to use at least some Spanish at home than did the 5- to 17-year-olds. That is, despite the impressive percentages of Spanish-language claimants in some states, the 1990 census provides an illustration of the gradual replacement of Spanish by English. Moreover, as Bills points out, the home is usually the last domain of an ethnic language to undergo shift. The 1990 census data do not provide information about language use in domains outside the home, but it seems reasonable to infer that many of those who report using Spanish at home use English in most of their interactions outside the home.

Bills's results have been confirmed by more recent work. Brodie et al. (2002), for example, reports the results of a general survey of education, income, and language use of a broad, well-stratified sample of U.S. Latinos. According to Brodie et al., 61% of U.S.-born respondents regarded themselves as English-dominant and 35% considered themselves bilingual (13). Fully 78% of third-generation and higher respondents considered themselves English-dominant, and only 22% considered themselves bilingual (16).

Large-scale studies such as those by Veltman (1988), Bills (1997), and Brodie et al. (2002) are highly useful in providing an overall view of language use by U.S. Latinos. Nevertheless, such studies, whether based on census data or on well-stratified samples

TABLE 4

Spanish Home Language Claimants as a Percentage
of the Hispanic Population in Five Southwestern States
(U.S. Bureau of the Census 1993, as adapted by Bills 1997, 157)

	Total	Age 18+	Age 5–17
Arizona	79.6	87.1	62.4
California	81.7	84.9	73.3
Colorado	54.5	63.2	32.3
New Mexico	74.7	84.6	49.4
Texas	89.9	95.0	77.9
TOTAL	83.1	87.4	72.0

of the entire U.S. Latino population, tell us little about the quality of Spanish used by Spanish-language claimants. Recent work on language practices in Latino families, however, reveals, considerable variation in both the quantity and quality of Spanish used (Vasquez, Pease-Alvarez, and Shannon 1994; Bayley, Schecter, and Torres-Ayala 1996; Lambert and Taylor 1996; Zentella 1997; Schecter and Bayley 2002). In some families, interactions in Spanish between parents and children, which are critical for maintaining the minority language (Hakuta and D'Andrea 1992; Hakuta and Pease-Alvarez 1994), are restricted to occasional endearments or to specific times set aside precisely to revive the minority language (Schecter and Bayley 1997). In other families and communities, children acquire a broad range of Spanish and English dialects. For example, Zentella (1997, 41–48), in an ethnographic study that spanned 14 years, documents how young people growing up in a New York City *barrio* use standard Puerto Rican Spanish, popular Puerto Rican Spanish, African American Vernacular English, standard New York City English, and Hispanicized English for a range of expressive purposes. Youngsters such as those studied by Zentella are socialized to become competent in many of the varieties spoken in the community, and they learn to switch from one variety to another according to the image they wish to present.

Ethnographic research on Spanish language maintenance and shift such as that reported in Schecter and Bayley (2002) and Zentella (1997) has shown that U.S. Latinos place a high value on minority language maintenance. For Latino families, pressures to shift to English monolingualism also remain strong, particularly in light of political developments such as the passage of English-only laws in many states (Crawford 2000) and successful ballot initiatives to ban bilingual education in Arizona, California, and Massachusetts. The Torres family of San Antonio, Texas, provides an example of the obstacles faced by parents who wish to transmit a minority language to their children (for a detailed account see Bayley, Schecter, and Torres-Ayala 1996). José and Elena Torres and their three daughters, ages 10, 11, and 12, lived in an overwhelmingly Latino neighborhood on the south side of San Antonio. Sr. and Sra. Torres acquired Spanish at home from their own parents, who had immigrated from northern Mexico as young adults, and both of them continued to use Spanish with their mothers. Like many Mexican Americans of their generation, the Torreses acquired English at school when use of Spanish on school grounds was a punishable offense (Hurtado and Rodríguez 1989). As a consequence, they never learned to read or write in Spanish. At home, José and Elena spoke both Spanish and English with one another. Outside of the home, they accommodated to the language preferences of their interlocutors or to the demands of the situation.

In their daughters' formative years, José and Elena spoke only English with the girls because they wanted to ease their transition to formal schooling and to spare them the difficulties they themselves had experienced as Spanish-speakers entering English-medium schools. As the girls grew older, however, the Torreses became increasingly concerned about their lack of Spanish proficiency, which they associated with loss of cultural continuity and intergenerational communication. To address their concerns, José and Elena set aside one day a week where Spanish was to be used at home, and they arranged for their daughters to spend more time with one of their Spanish-speaking grandmothers. In addition, they regularly attended church services conducted in Spanish. Although they sought assistance from the schools their children attended, none was available. After more that a year of attempts to revive Spanish at home, the Torreses' daughters' ability to speak Spanish remained at a rudimentary level, although they had acquired some ability to understand their parents' first language.

To summarize, the preponderance of the evidence from large-scale surveys and detailed studies of language minority communities and families suggests that the traditional pattern of intergenerational shift to English continues among U.S. Latinos. However, large-scale demographic changes as well as the increasing economic influence of Spanish speakers may well act to encourage Spanish language maintenance. In fact, the increasing presence of Latinos in areas of the United States outside of the Southwest and the East Coast presents a number of areas for research, not only on language maintenance and shift, but on other areas of language contact as well. Finally, most studies of language maintenance and shift among U.S. Latinos have focused on people of Mexican or Puerto Rican descent, as have studies of U.S. Spanish. Given the distribution of the U.S. Latino population, such a focus is understandable. However, recent decades have seen the development of numerous other Latino communities. Beginning in the 1960s, numerous Cubans settled in southern Florida following the Cuban revolution. In the 1980s and following decades, large numbers of speakers from other Latin American countries settled in various areas of the United States. For example, Moriello and Wolfram (forthcoming) report that the Latino population of Siler City, North Carolina, a small town in the center of the state, increased from 3% to 40% in the 1990s, with new arrivals coming from El Salvador and other Latin American countries as well as from Mexico. To take another example, Los Angeles, which has more people of Mexican background than any other U.S. city, is also home to numerous Salvadorans. Finally, in addition to a very substantial Puerto Rican community, New York City is home to large numbers of Colombians, Cubans, Dominicans, Ecuadoreans, and Mexicans, many of the latter from the state of Puebla in central Mexico. These diverse Latino communities provide numerous opportunities for research, not only on maintenance and shift and English-Spanish contact, but also on contact between different dialects of Spanish.

THE SPANISH/ENGLISH BILINGUAL CONTINUUM. It is well established that a bilingual continuum may develop among speakers in immigrant communities (Elías-Olivares 1979; Dorian 1981; Silva-Corvalán 1994). Silva-Corvalán observes that "one can identify a series of lects which range from standard or unrestricted Spanish to an *emblematic* use of Spanish. . . . Speakers can be located at various points along this continuum depending on their level of dominance in one or other of the languages or both" (1994, 11; emphasis in original). The existence of such a continuum has provided a rich source for research on language change, primarily focused on questions of simplification and adaptation in conditions of language contact. Silva-Corvalán's study of the Spanish spoken by Mexican immigrants and Mexican Americans in Los Angeles is perhaps the most extensive study of a U.S. immigrant Spanish variety yet completed and illustrates the way that these questions have been addressed.

Among other questions, Silva-Corvalán investigated the loss of tense-aspect distinctions among speakers of varying levels of Spanish proficiency. She distinguished five stages of simplification and loss, which fell into an implicational pattern, summarized in table 5. The pattern illustrated in table 5 provides evidence in support of the notion of a bilingual continuum on which immigrants are more fluent in the standard variety of the immigrant language, while succeeding generations are less fluent. As Silva-Corvalán notes, however, the process illustrated in table 5 is not unique to U.S. Spanish. Rather, similar processes can be observed among varieties of rural Mexican Spanish (see, e.g., Santa Ana and Parodi 1998).

Other studies have also examined changes in the Spanish verbal system across the bilingual continuum. Bayley (1999), for example, tested the predictions of the primacy of aspect hypothesis (Andersen and Shirai 1996) using narratives elicited from three groups of Mexican-background children and early adolescents in communities undergoing language shift. Results showed a clear implicational pattern for use of aspectual categories in both the preterit and imperfect tenses. Crucially, all participants who preserved the full Spanish tense/aspect system in both the preterit and the imperfect used Spanish in the majority of home interactions.

In addition to examining the Mexican-American Spanish verbal system, scholars of U.S. Spanish have studied other variables across the bilingual continuum, including the use of overt and null pronouns (*yo/Ø quiero ir a la playa* 'I want to go to the beach') (e.g., Silva-Corvalán 1982, 1994; Hochberg 1986; Bayley and Pease-Alvarez 1996, 1997; Flores 2002; Otheguy and Zentella 2002; Parodi and Santa Ana 2002). The patterns of variation observed for this often-studied sociolinguistic variable are of particular interest for several reasons. First, from the point of view of linguistic theory, variable subject pronoun use provides a convenient testing

TABLE 5
Tense Systems across the Spanish Continuum
(Silva-Corvalán 1994, 31)

Absolute-Relative Tenses	Mexico-Born Bilinguals		U.S.-Born Bilinguals		
	I	II	III	IV	V
Relative tenses					
Infinitive	+	+	+	+	+ .
Present participle	+	+	+	+	+
Past participle	+	+	+	+	−
Absolute tenses					
Present indicative	+	+	+	+	+
Preterit indicative	+	+	+	+	+
Imperfect indicative	+	+	+	+	+
Future periphrastic	+	+	+	+	+
Present perfect indicative	+	+	+	+	−
Future	+	+	−	−	−
Absolute-relative tenses					
Periphrastic conditional	+	+	+	+	+
Present subjunctive	+	+	+	+	−
Imperfect subjunctive	+	+	+	−	−
Pluperfect subjunctive	+	+	+	−	−
Pluperfect indicative	+	+	+	−	−
Present perfect subjunctive	+	−	−	−	−
Conditional pluperfect	+	−	−	−	−
Conditional	−	−	−	−	−
Future perfect	−	−	−	−	−

ground for functionalist explanations of linguistic variation. No information is lost, for example, if the pronoun is absent in a first person singular form such as *quiero* 'I want', because the person and number are recoverable from the unique verb inflection. However, in the case of a form such as *quería* 'I' or 's/he wanted' (imperfect), the subject is not recoverable from the verb. Therefore, a functionalist view of variation would lead us to predict greater subject pronoun absence with first person singular present tense forms than with first/third person imperfect verbs. Second, and of more relevance to the possible influence of contact between Spanish and English, the fact that subject pronoun expression is obligatory in English but optional in Spanish suggests that English-dominant speakers might use more subject pronouns in Spanish than do Spanish-dominant speakers. Third, subject pronouns provide a convenient way to examine the possible influence of Spanish dialects on one another. To generalize, in New World Spanish, highland dialects such as those spoken in most of Mexico and the Andean countries are characterized by a relatively low incidence of subject pronoun use. Lowland dialects, including those of Cuba, the Dominican Republic, Puerto Rico, and certain coastal areas of Colombia and Mexico, are characterized by a relatively high incidence of subject pronoun use. Lowland dialects are also characterized by variable /s/ aspiration and deletion (e.g., *más* 'more' → *máh* → *máØ*), which may neutralize the distinction between second and third person verb forms. In areas such as New York City, then, where speakers of lowland varieties have predominated historically, we might expect to see increased use of subject pronouns by more recent arrivals from central Mexico if the new arrivals are converging with the norms of the traditional Spanish-speaking population of the area. In contrast, in areas such as San Antonio or Los Angeles, where speakers of highland varieties from Mexico have historically predominated, we might expect to see decreased use of subject pronouns by lowland speakers such as Puerto Ricans or Salvadorans, again, assuming that speakers of nonpredominant Spanish varieties are converging with the regional norm.

　　Recent research on U.S. and Puerto Rican Spanish has provided evidence regarding the first two of these issues, and ongoing research promises results on the third. First, with respect to functionalist explanations, Bayley and Pease-Alvarez (1997) and especially Cameron (1996) have shown that functionalism cannot explain differences in variable pronoun use. Bayley and Pease-Alvarez (1997) appeal to discourse constraints, while Cameron (1996) attributes the difference in pronoun use between Puerto Rican Spanish and Madrid Spanish (a highland variety) to differences in the treatment of specific and nonspecific *tú* 'you'. The second issue, the possible influence of English in promoting overt pronoun use in the Spanish of English-dominant speakers, has been addressed by Bayley and Pease-Alvarez (1996, 1997) and Silva-

Corvalán (1994) in studies of Chicanos and Mexican immigrants in California and by Flores (2002) in a study of Puerto Ricans in New York City. Bayley and Pease-Alvarez and Silva-Corvalán found no overall increase in the use of subject pronouns across the bilingual continuum, although Silva-Corvalán did note a weakening of several constraints. The results of Flores's (2002) study, on the other hand, are somewhat ambiguous. She found that Puerto Ricans born in New York City consistently used more overt pronominals than those born on the island. However, she also found that age of arrival, language use at home, and total years in New York City, all of which are presumably correlated with exposure to English, had no significant effect. Thus, although studies of Mexican-background speakers in California suggest that patterns of overt and null pronoun use are resistant to the influence of English, the question remains open, particularly with regard to speakers of other Spanish varieties.

The third issue raised by the study of subject pronouns concerns the possible influence of different Spanish varieties on one another. That is, in areas in which speakers of a number of Spanish dialects live in close proximity, are we witnessing the development of Spanish koinés or are speakers maintaining their linguistic distinctiveness? That question is currently being addressed by Ricardo Otheguy and Ana Celia Zentella in a large-scale study of New York City Spanish. Otheguy and Zentella (2002) are investigating pronoun use by speakers of three highland dialects (Colombian, Ecuadorean, and Mexican) and three lowland dialects (Cuban, Dominican, and Puerto Rican). In another study, Parodi and Santa Ana (2002) are investigating the use of subject pronouns by Salvadorans in Los Angeles. Studies such as those by Otheguy and Zentella and by Parodi and Santa Ana are particularly well-suited to answer the question of whether a pan-Latino identity is developing in the United States. In addition, such studies have considerable potential to expand our views of language contact, which have too often been restricted to examinations of the influence of a socially dominant language on a socially nondominant language. Clearly, there is much more to be learned about how immigrant dialects interact in contact with one another, and Spanish subject pronouns represent only one variable for such study. In fact, as Amastae and Satcher (1993) show in their study of the assimilation of two phonological variables by Hondurans in the predominantly Mexican environment of El Paso, Texas, the study of possible convergence of patterns of phonological variation is a particularly promising area of research on Spanish dialect contact.

SPANISH/ENGLISH CODE-SWITCHING. Research on code-switching, the alternate use of two (or more) languages within the same discourse, has progressed greatly during the past two decades, and a considerable body of basic research has focused on Spanish/ English code-switching in U.S. Latino communities. Much of the work published during the 1980s sought to counter the prevalent deficit notion that code-switching was a consequence of a bilingual's failure to master fully either language. Jacobson (1982), for example, explored the social implications of code-switching among bilingual Mexican Americans in south Texas and concluded that the utterances in interactions in which code-switching is frequent "reveal a grammar of their own and do not reflect the speaker's ignorance of either/both languages as has often been suggested" (206). Valdés (1982) made a similar point in her case study of a young Mexican American woman who used Spanish exclusively with some interlocutors, English with others, and a combination of English and Spanish with still others. Valdés's subject's choice of code depended on the linguistic preferences and proficiencies of her interlocutor rather than on a linguistic deficit on her part. Zentella (1981, 1982) extended the study of Spanish/English code-switching, which previously had focused mainly on adolescents and adults, to Puerto Rican children in New York City and examined the way a group of third-graders used code-switching according to perceived rules of interaction.

Poplack's (1980, 1981) seminal study of code-switching among New York Puerto Ricans appeared during the same period. In an attempt to create a general model of code-switching, Poplack proposed two constraints: the free morpheme constraint, which holds that "codes may be switched after any constituent in a discourse provided that constituent is not a bound morpheme," and the equivalence constraint, which predicts that "code-switches will tend to occur at points in discourse where juxtaposition of L1 and L2 elements does not violate a syntactic rule of either language" (1980, 234). Other scholars have found that Poplack's proposed constraints do not hold for all pairs of languages, and violations may be found even in Spanish/English code-switching. Nevertheless, her study remains important because it represents one of the first attempts to develop a grammar of code-switching and to test that grammar quantitatively with a substantial naturalistic corpus.

In recent years, research has explored Spanish/English code-switching from formal perspectives as well as those which have added to our understanding of the social functions of language mixing. D'Introno (1996), for example, attempts to show how Chomsky's (1981, 1986) government and binding theory can explain the ungrammaticality of impossible cases of code-switching. D'Introno argues that bilingual grammars constitute a very good testing ground for theories of grammar because "they allow testing of grammatical aspects and conditions which are not obvious or do not have clear empirical consequences in monolingual grammars" (199). Belazi, Rubin, and Toribio (1994) and Toribio and Rubin (1996) develop their analysis within the framework of Chomsky's (1995) minimalist program. They focus on the Functional Head Constraint (FHC), which predicts that "the complements of a verb and the verb itself will be in the same language, i.e., that complement clauses, direct and indirect objects, and complement prepositional phrases must be in the same language as the verb" (Toribio and Rubin 1996, 204). The FHC further predicts that "adjectives must be in the same language as the noun modified and that complements of a preposition must have the same language index as the preposition itself" (204). Toribio and Rubin argue that the FHC subsumes Di Sciullo, Muysken, and Singh's (1986) Government Constraint, Poplack's (1980, 1981) Free Morpheme and Equivalence Constraints, and Joshi's (1985) Constraint on Closed-Class Items and offers a new paradigm for research.

Other recent work on code-switching has focused on the social aspects of language mixing. Zentella (1997), for example, in her analysis of the grammar of code-switching used by the New York

City Puerto Rican children she studied, found that individual patterns "exposed each girl's vantage point in the NY-PR cross-cultural intersection, and communicated unique aspects of the process of growing up bilingual" (136). To take another example, Bayley and Zapata (1993) examined the pervasive code-switching on a popular south Texas radio station shortly after the station had changed to a bilingual format. They found that prerecorded commercial announcements were likely to be either in English or in Spanish exclusively or to employ intersentential switching. Disc jockeys, in contrast, who were San Antonio natives, used far more intrasentential switches. Recently Kobel (2003) investigated code-switching on the same station that Bayley and Zapata had studied ten years earlier and compared code-switching patterns on the San Antonio station with the patterns used by announcers on a popular Tejano station in a border community. Kobel found that code-switching had become much less frequent than it had been a decade before. On both stations, the type of complicated intrasentential switching that Bayley and Zapata found had been replaced by emblematic switches or set phrases that could easily be understood by listeners with even the most minimal command of Spanish. Interestingly, though, both the San Antonio and the border station continued to feature music sung in Spanish.

As even this brief and highly selective review indicates, code-switching continues to be a lively area of research, with implications both for linguistic theory and social identity. The prevalence of code-mixing in U.S. Latino communities provides an important source of data for testing hypotheses about proposed models of code-switching, including, of course, Myers-Scotton's (1993) influential Matrix-Language Frame Model and recent proposals such as that of Toribio and Rubin (1996), who seek to use English/Spanish code-switching data to clarify issues in formal linguistics. From a social perspective, English/Spanish code-switching offers a window into how speakers deploy their linguistic resources, including limited resources in the case of emblematic switchers, to express identities in fluid social contexts.

DIRECTIONS FOR FUTURE RESEARCH ON U.S. SPANISH. Research on Spanish in the United States has made great progress during the past two decades. However, many questions remain to be addressed. For example, how does the increasing concentration of Latinos in major cities such as Los Angeles, New York, and San Antonio change the outlook for Spanish language maintenance? Carreira (2002) has documented the increase in Spanish-language media outlets over the past ten years, a response not only to the growing numbers of Spanish speakers but to their increasing economic power. What is the effect of widespread availability of Spanish-language radio and television on language maintenance? According to Carreira, the number of companies publishing in Spanish in the United States has increased from 60 to 600 over the past decade, and in 2000, 342 Latino magazines were published in Spanish or in a bilingual format (42). How does the increase in the availability of Spanish printed material affect maintenance of Spanish literacy, if indeed it has such an effect? Other issues where research is needed concern how Spanish dialects are impacted by contact with English on the one hand and with other Spanish dialects on the other. A related question concerns the relationship between varieties of Spanish and identity. Are there emerging Spanish koinés in different areas of the United States, or are speakers of different national, regional, and social varieties maintaining their linguistic distinctiveness? Finally, as we have noted, most research on U.S. Spanish has focused on speakers of Mexican or Puerto Rican origin. However, given the great diversity of Latino groups in the United States, research on other Latino varieties is clearly needed if we are to have a full understanding of the many dialects of Spanish spoken in the United States today.

FRENCH IN CANADA AND LOUISIANA

FRENCH IN CANADA. Since the bulk of linguistic research on languages other than English spoken in Canada has been concentrated on French, we will provide a summary of recent research on that language before turning to research on other languages.

Varieties of Canadian French are traditionally divided into two major dialects, Quebec and Acadian French. Quebec French includes not only the French spoken in the province of Quebec but also Ontario French, the French of western Canada, and some small francophone enclaves in the northeastern United States, all the result of immigration from Quebec. Acadian French includes the French spoken in the three Maritime Provinces (Prince Edward Island, New Brunswick, and Nova Scotia) and in Newfoundland as well as in a few areas of Quebec. The structural differences which distinguish these two dialects are due to the different European origins of the colonists and to the relative degree of isolation of their speakers over the course of more than three centuries (see Mougeon and Beniak 1994 for information on the origins of varieties of Canadian French).

Sociolinguistic Research. There is a long history of dialectological and lexicographical work on French spoken in the province of Quebec, dating from the turn of the last century (see Sabourin and Lamarche 1985). Outside of French linguistics, Canadian French is perhaps best known through the foundational research in sociolinguistics that focused on this variety, in particular studies of Montreal French that began in the early 1970s conducted under the direction of Henrietta Cedergren, David Sankoff, Gillian Sankoff, and their associates (e.g., Sankoff and Cedergren 1973; Sankoff et al. 1976; Laberge 1977; Sankoff and Thibault 1980; Lemieux and Cedergren 1985; Sankoff et al. 1989). Much less research has been devoted to Acadian French, although there were a number of important works in lexicography and dialectology dating from the 1960s (see Gesner 1986 for an annotated bibliography); however, as we shall see, interest in Acadian French has greatly increased over the last two decades. Since sociolinguistic research on Canadian French has been so prominent, we will begin with an overview of research in that tradition.[1]

In the 1970s, a number of sociolinguistic corpora were constructed, the best known of which is the Montreal French corpus of sociolinguistic interviews with a random sample of 120 speakers, stratified according to social class, sex, and age. The methodology now standard to the quantification of sociolinguistic data involving use of the VARBRUL program (Cedergren and Sankoff 1974; Rousseau and Sankoff 1978) was developed during the course of work on this corpus. Other sociolinguistic corpora dating from this period are representative of the French of the eastern townships of Quebec (Beauchemin 1983), Quebec City (Deshaies 1986), and a number of Ontario communities in which the sociolinguistic circumstances of French vary considerably, for example, Pembroke, North Bay, Cornwall, and Hawkesbury (Mougeon et al. 1982). In the 1980s, a corpus for the nation's capital, Ottawa, located in Ontario, and nearby Hull, in the province of Quebec (Poplack 1989), and corpora for some smaller Ontario communities, Welland (Beniak, Mougeon, and Valois 1985), Sudbury, and Rayside (Thomas 1986), were also constructed. Like the Montreal French corpus in the 1970s, the Ottawa-Hull corpus has served as a model for subsequent research involving the collection and manipulation of large amounts of sociolinguistic data. The 1980s also saw the construction of sociolinguistic corpora for communities in all four Atlantic provinces in which Acadian French is spoken, New Brunswick (Flikeid 1984), Nova Scotia (Flikeid 1989), Prince Edward Island (King and Ryan 1989), and Newfoundland (King 1985). These corpora provide important data for comparative research on Canadian French and also provide a testing ground for theories of language variation and change more generally. For instance, the communities studied range from ones in which there is very little contact with English (e.g., Quebec City) to those in which almost all speakers are bilingual but French remains the majority language (e.g., Hawkesbury, Ont.) to those in which French is spoken by a minority of the population (e.g., Pembroke, Ont.). Data from varieties with little contact with English, such as the Quebec City variety, provide an important baseline for measuring the effects of contact with English and degree of French language use restriction (see, e.g., Mougeon and Beniak 1991).

The specific features of Canadian French varieties investigated using variationist sociolinguistic methodology are many, and include such diverse topics as metrical structure and vowel deletion (Cedergren 1986), stress assignment (Paradis and Deshaies 1990), use of future tense marking (Poplack and Turpin 1999; King and Nadasdi forthcoming), subject-verb agreement (King 1994), and subject doubling (Nadasdi 2000). In addition to investigating phonological and grammatical variation, scholars have also examined various discourse features including the use of exemplification particles (Vincent 1992), phrase-terminal extension particles such as *tout ça* 'all that' and *des affaires de même* 'things like that' (Dubois 1992), punctors such as *là* 'there', *tu sais* 'you know', *n'est-ce pas* 'isn't it', and *hein* 'eh' (Vincent and Sankoff 1992), and the relationship between age and the use of *comme* 'like' (Chevalier 2002). Many variables initially investigated for French in Montreal have also been studied in other communities, such as choice of auxiliary (Sankoff and Thibault 1980). Auxiliary choice has also been the subject of research in Ottawa-Hull French (Willis 2000), other Ontario French varieties (Canale, Mougeon, and Bélanger 1978), Acadian French (King and Nadasdi 1998), and Vermont French (Russo and Roberts 1999). An exhaustive presentation is beyond the scope of this chapter. We have therefore focused on a number of representative studies that illustrate the directions research has taken.

The construction of new corpora in the last 20 years has also involved Montreal French. In 1984, 60 of the original 120 speakers of the 1971 corpus were reinterviewed and an additional 14 younger speakers, born between 1959 and 1969, were added (Thibault and Vincent 1990). In 1995, 12 of the original speakers were interviewed again, in a variety of conversational situations, along with two of the new speakers from 1984 (Vincent, Laforest, and Martel 1995). Such follow-up studies allow the examination of change in real time and verification (or refutation) of earlier apparent-time results. In research on a number of discourse markers, Thibault and Daveluy (1989) compared usage in the 1971 and 1984 corpora and found that *alors* 'then' was age-graded, being associated with speakers of bourgeois origin, who increased their usage of this form as they got older. On the other hand, they found a clear rise in the usage of *tu sais* 'you know', a change that went far beyond what the shift to use of the familiar form *tu* in a variety of contexts would predict. Another instance of real-time change involves the pronominal system, whereby Blondeau's (2001) comparison of data for all three corpora, 1971, 1984 and 1995, shows the decline of compound forms such as *vous-autres* 'you' and rise of their simple variants, such as *vous*.

A particularly interesting result of such longitudinal studies involves the possibility of linguistic change across the lifespan. For instance, in a 1979 study, Clermont and Cedergren had compared (r) usage in the 1963 Bibeau-Dugas Montreal corpus on the part of speakers born before 1925 with that of speakers born between 1937 and 1956 who formed part of the 1971 Montreal French corpus. They found that the older group were almost categorical users of alveolar [r], the traditional variant, while over half of the younger group were almost categorical users of velar or uvular [ʀ] with the remainder displaying variable usage. It is evident that the articulation of (r) has changed in the course of the last century in Quebec French. Interestingly, a recent study by Sankoff, Blondeau, and Charity (2001) shows that some of those speakers who had variable usage in 1971 had significantly increased their use of [ʀ] by 1984, moving away from the variant they had acquired in childhood. Such results challenge the notion of the stable linguistic system acquired in childhood remaining unchanged throughout adulthood.

As noted earlier, a wide array of French-English contact situations obtain in Canada. They have received considerable attention from sociolinguists, resulting in a body of work that deals with both grammatical (Poplack 1985; Poplack, Sankoff, and Miller 1988) and pragmatic aspects of code-switching (Poplack 1988; Heller 1992; Heller and Lévy 1994; King and Nadasdi 1999b), the politics of language choice (Heller 1992, 1994, 1995), and the structural effects of language contact on the minority language (Flikeid 1989; Mougeon and Beniak 1991; Poplack 1996; King 2000). We will review some of the themes of this research.

Shana Poplack's work on the French of Ottawa-Hull investigates the effects of language contact in the region of the national capital. Her 1988 quantitative study of code-switching and borrowing in five neighborhoods, in collaboration with David Sankoff and Christopher Miller, involves the analysis of some 20,000 loan tokens for 120 speakers. Solid empirical support for hierarchies of borrowability (involving the notion that more grammatical morphemes are less easily borrowed than content words; cf. Weinreich 1968, 35) was found, as well as correlation between overall borrowing rates and a number of social factors, such as the status of French in the neighborhood (minority or majority), occupation, class, and degree of bilingual proficiency. This work also operationalized and provided empirical support for the classification "nonce borrowings," that is, lexical items borrowed on the spur of the moment which do not have an established status in the borrowing language, first discussed by Haugen (1950). In another thread of this research program, Poplack has investigated claims of structural borrowing from English. For instance, in her study of the subjunctive in Ottawa-Hull French, reportedly disappearing from Canadian French under the influence of English, Poplack (1996) found that there is no empirical support for such a change; rather the variability that exists in the present day is simply a reflection of changes that have been ongoing for centuries. King (2000) also addresses the issue of direct structural borrowing. She analyzes innovations in the Acadian French of Prince Edward Island which at first glance appear to be bona fide cases of structural borrowing but finds compelling evidence that what is at issue is lexical borrowing, which in turn triggers grammatical reanalysis in the borrowing language, as in the case of the emergence of preposition stranding in this variety. In this work she argues for a theory whereby borrowing is mediated by the lexicon.

In a series of studies over 25 years on variation in Ontario French, Raymond Mougeon and his collaborators have investigated the effects of bilingualism and concomitant language restriction. Their findings include the fact that vernacular features are best maintained when language use restriction is minimal, equal use of the two languages promotes linguistic innovation, and significant language use restriction leads to stylistic reduction and structural simplification. Some of the variables investigated by these researchers include use of the vernacular possessive with *à*, the innovative third person plural imperfect form of the verb *être* 'to be', *sontaient*, and auxiliary choice. Extensive sociolinguistic research in bilingual communities led Mougeon and Nadasdi (1998) to a reexamination of a central tenant of variationist research, the idea that members of the same speech community display uniform linguistic and social constraints on variation. Citing numerous counterexamples, they argue for a reformulation of the notion of speech community to allow for discontinuous patterns of variation.

As noted earlier, over the past 20 years there has been a great upsurge of research on Acadian French, which is particularly interesting for language contact research because in some communities borrowing is much more advanced than in the Quebec varieties investigated. For instance, while all Canadian varieties borrow verbs, only (certain) Acadian varieties borrow prepositions (King 2000). On the other hand, Acadian French tends to better preserve vernacular features of the language than does Quebec French. For instance, in Acadian French communities in which there is low normative pressure, the first person plural form *je . . . ons* (e.g., *je parlons* 'I speak'), an example of older usage which has disappeared from Quebec French, is the variant of choice (Flikeid and Péronnet 1989; King and Nadasdi 1999a). Research on Acadian French has been concerned with both documenting vernacular usage and analyzing variation and change. Research over the past two decades has shown not only that Acadian differs dramatically from its more studied neighbor but also that there exists a great deal of variation across Acadian varieties, not only in terms of the effects of contact with English (e.g., Flikeid 1989; King 2000), but in other ways as well. For instance, King and Nadasdi (1997) present evidence that subject pronouns in Newfoundland Acadian are syntactic subjects rather than verbal affixes (as they have been analyzed in Quebec French, cf. Auger 1998; for Ontario French, cf. Nadasdi 1995). However, Beaulieu and Balcom (1998) show that their status in the grammar of the French of northeastern New Brunswick is closer to the Quebec/Ontario case, that is, they behave as verbal affixes. In the face of such variation, current Acadian research tends to proceed one variety at a time and to generalize across varieties only when there is compelling evidence to do so.

In addition to examining various aspects of French as spoken by francophones, scholars have also investigated sociolinguistic variation in the French varieties spoken by anglophones. Sankoff et al. (1997), for example, studied the use of discourse markers such as *tu sais* 'you know', *là* 'there', *bon* 'good', and *alors* 'so' in the French of 17 anglophone residents of Montreal. They found a correlation between the use of discourse markers, which are not taught in school, and fluency in French. Sankoff et al. concluded that appropriate use of discourse markers provided an indication of the speaker's integration into the local French-speaking community. Other recent studies of the French of anglophone Montreal residents include Nagy and Blondeau's (1999) and Nagy, Blondeau, and Auger's (forthcoming) work on subject doubling, a feature that, like discourse markers, is not taught in school. As in the case of use of discourse markers, Nagy, Blondeau, and Auger found that speakers who were more native-like with respect to the rate of subject doubling had more contacts with the local francophone community than those who were less native-like.

Raymond Mougeon and his colleagues have undertaken the most extensive work on L2 French in Canada. Mougeon and his colleagues studied the acquisition of sociolinguistic variation by students in Ontario's widely admired French immersion programs. As with the work of Nagy, Blondeau, and Auger (forthcoming) and Sankoff et al. (1997), Mougeon and his colleagues sought to determine to what extent L2 speakers of French, including students who used Italian or Spanish at home as well as native-born anglophones, approximated native-speaker sociolinguistic norms. Among the variables investigated are *ne* deletion (Rehner and Mougeon 1999), subject-verb agreement (Nadasdi 2001), variation in the use of *nous* 'we' versus *on* 'one' (Rehner, Mougeon, and Nadasdi 2003), *seulement* versus *juste* versus *rien que* (Mougeon and Rehner 2001), schwa deletion (Mougeon et al. 2002), discourse markers (Rehner 2002), and use of the future tense (Nadasdi, Mougeon, and Rehner forthcoming). The overall results reveal a complex patterning of variation. For a number of variables, for example, use of the restrictive adverb *seulement* versus *juste* and schwa deletion, the constraints follow those of native speakers.

And, as we might expect, for several variables, such as *ne* deletion and restrictive adverb *juste* for *seulement,* interaction with francophones has a favorable effect on students' use of vernacular variants. Other factors also play a role, however. For example, L2 speakers tend to overuse a number of formal variants and to use mildly marked variants such as *ne* deletion or schwa deletion at levels below native-speaker norms. The first language also plays a role. Thus, Spanish native speakers tend to overuse the formal variant *seulement,* perhaps influenced by the Spanish *solamente* 'only'.

To summarize, by focusing on acquisition of sociolinguistic norms that are not normally taught either in traditional language classrooms or in immersion programs, scholars investigating nonnative varieties have opened up a new area of research in second-language acquisition, which traditionally has been concerned with the acquisition of categorical structures. From the point of view of dialectology, which at least in North America has traditionally focused on monolingual speakers, work such as that by Mougeon and his colleagues, Sankoff et al. (1997), and Nagy, Blondeau, and Auger (forthcoming) provides a window into dialect formation in conditions of continuing language contact.

Traditional Dialectology. The last two decades have also seen more traditional work in dialectology, such as Louise Péronnet's (1991, 1992) studies of the speech of older residents of southeastern New Brunswick and Sandrine Hallion's (2000) description of the French of the Saint-Boniface neighborhood of Winnipeg, Manitoba. In 1990 Gérin published a critical edition of the nineteenth-century Acadian glossary compiled by Pascal Poirier, and in 1998, a dialect atlas of maritime vocabulary for Acadian varieties spoken in the provinces of New Brunswick, Nova Scotia, and Prince Edward Island appeared (Péronnet, Babitch, and Cichocki 1998). There is also a rich tradition of diachronic work in Quebec French lexicography, culminating in the appearance in 1998 of the *Dictionnaire historique du français québécois,* edited by Claude Poirier.

Directions for Future Research on Canadian French. In contrast to the wealth of studies on the French of central and eastern Canada, the French of western Canada has been almost totally neglected by linguists. In addition to the detailed description of a Manitoba variety (Hallion 2000, mentioned above), the literature includes two phonetic studies of Alberta French (Rochet 1993, 1994) and a number of short glossaries (e.g., Rodriguez 1984; Gaborieau 1985). We note the existence of a large French sociolinguistic corpus for three Alberta communities, including Edmonton, collected in 1976 under the direction of Bernard Rochet, Jo Ann Creore, and Robert Papen, but this database remains to be exploited (Beniak, Carey, and Mougeon 1984). Western Canadian French varieties, then, constitute an area of needed research.

Another area about which little is known is the new reality of the immigrant francophone presence in major Canadian cities such as Toronto, Ottawa, and Montreal. There does exist some important ethnographic research by Monica Heller in the area of language and education. For instance, Heller (1995) investigates the interplay of social class and ethnicity in a Toronto French-medium school, investigating the strategic use of linguistic resources, in particular language choice and code-switching, in the maintenance of and resistance to institutional power. Sociolinguistic research with foreign-born francophones might fruitfully investigate patterns of language variation and change in urban francophone communities.

In addition to these proposed new avenues of research, we point to a relatively new area of intensive research: the history of morphosyntactic variation in Quebec French. For instance, Martineau and Mougeon (2003) reconstruct the history of the negative particle *ne* in both European and Quebec French from the seventeenth century on. Such work requires representative corpora. Important in this regard is Martineau's computerized corpus of informal letters for Quebec French from the time of colonization and, for nineteenth-century French, the newly available *Récits du français québécois d'autrefois* (St.-Amand and Poplack 2002), both housed at the University of Ottawa, in the Laboratoire de français ancien (Pierre Kunstmann and France Martineau, directors) and the Sociolinguistic Laboratory (Shana Poplack, director), respectively.

FRENCH IN LOUISIANA. The French spoken in Louisiana is traditionally categorized into three distinct varieties: Colonial (the French of the descendants of the original European settlers), Cajun (evolved from the French spoken by the deported Acadians), and Creole (spoken by descendants of the slave population). However, it must be kept in mind that these distinctions do not take into account centuries of contact among the three francophone groups, contact which leads many modern researchers to propose varying degrees of dialect leveling. For instance, Brown (1993) maintains that present-day Louisiana francophones may display linguistic features commonly associated with all three varieties. Dubois (2003) argues that the early linguistic history was even more complex than previously thought, with many regional vernaculars spoken prior to the Civil War. Reflexes of features of these vernaculars may account for at least some of the diversity found in present-day Louisiana.

The actual number of speakers of these varieties is unclear. Census figures are not particularly helpful in establishing the size of the population since Louisianans may be reluctant to report speaking a stigmatized language (see Brown 1993 and Picone 1997a for discussion). While Neumann (1985) estimates that Colonial French has 3,000 to 4,000 speakers, Cajun 500,000 to 1,000,000, and Creole 60,000 to 80,000; and Ancelet (1988) between several hundred thousand to half a million Cajun French speakers, these numbers may be overly optimistic. Valdman and Klinger (1997, 110) suggest, on the basis of Klinger's fieldwork experiences in the 1990s (Klinger 1992), that Neumann's figures for Creole should be downgraded due to language loss. Landry, Allard, and Henry's (1996) self-report study of language use by high-school students of Cajun origin likewise points to language erosion, while Dubois's (1997) large-scale sociolinguistic survey (based on responses for almost 1,000 individuals) of the present-day situation in four parishes with substantial Cajun populations provides a wealth of data on both language attitudes and language use. She finds more positive attitudes than documented in the past, with fluent speakers of the variety (as opposed to passive bilinguals) emphasizing its relationship to Acadian French, rather than English influence. However, while the majority of respondents over 40 years old had Cajun French as their first language, and had most exposure to French, younger speakers tended to learn English first and had least exposure to Cajun.

A 1997 collection of articles, *French and Creole in Louisiana*, edited by Albert Valdman, provides an overview of the state of research in the 1990s.[2] While there are a fairly large number of studies of Louisiana French communities dating from the 1930s and 1940s, most tend to be, in Valdman's words, "narrowly descriptive" (1). They tend to concentrate on the speech of a particular parish and take as their focus divergences from standard French. A recent project which takes a much broader approach is Sylvie Dubois's study of language variation in a large sociolinguistic corpus of 120 Cajun French speakers, stratified by sex and age, for four parishes, Lafourche, St. Landry, Vermillion, and Avoyelles. One study arising from this project concerns the fate of linguistic features which would have been found in the speech of the Acadian settlers to this region. It is based on data from the speech of the oldest age group sampled, speakers over 60. Dubois (2000, forthcoming) finds loss, or near loss, of morphosyntactic forms associated with Acadian French (e.g., first person plural verbal morphology *je ... ons* is categorically absent, third person plural *ils ... ont* is infrequent) and, in the area of phonology, far better preservation of vocalic rather than consonantal features. Dubois's explanation of these findings lies in the fact that the vocalic features were more characteristic of colloquial French of the settlement period in general (unlike, for instance, a consonantal feature such as the pronunciation of /ʒ/ as [h], typically Acadian, with an origin in the center west of France). She suggests leveling of features not found in contact varieties of French, a claim supported by the fact that Acadian features are more frequent in parishes which historically had least contact with other French varieties (i.e., Lafourche and Avoyelles).

Given a situation of language shift, it is not surprising that considerable attention has been devoted to issues relating to language contact. For instance, Rottet (1998, 2001) is concerned with structural consequences of language contact for Cajun French, examining morphosyntactic decay in the speech of residents of the Terrebonne and Lafourche parishes. Variables investigated involve the pronominal and verbal paradigms, along with subordination structures. Rottet found significant results for generation, with younger speakers exhibiting stylistic reduction, such as loss of formal *vous*, and morphological leveling, such as loss of the second person plural ending *-ez*. An example of variation in subordination structures is Rottet's finding that younger speakers (under 30) used subjunctive forms far less frequently than did older (over 55) speakers. Similarly, Noetzel and Dubois (2003) document many generational patterns of linguistic attrition, including changes in the use of locative prepositions and definite articles. Other researchers have documented patterns of code-switching and borrowing (e.g., Brown 1986, 2003; Rottet and Golembeski 2000). One contact phenomenon which has attracted the attention of a number of researchers is the fact that in Cajun French verbs of English origin are frequently not morphologically integrated (Brown 1986; Picone 1994, 1997b; Dubois and Sankoff 1997; Klinger, Picone, and Valdman 1997). For example, whereas English *He retired (from his job)* would be rendered *il a retiré* in all Canadian French varieties of which we are aware, in Cajun one finds *il a retire* [riytayr] or *il a retired* [riytayrd]. A variety of characterizations have been offered, ranging from the idea of a code-intermediate phenomenon, belonging to the grammar of neither English nor French and requiring special morphological processing (Picone 1997b; Klinger, Picone, and Valdman 1997), to the postulation of a phonetically null suffix for borrowed verbs (Dubois and Sankoff 1997). Whatever the explanation, lack of morphological integration appears to go hand in hand with a language contact situation where there is reduction in Cajun French verbal morphology more generally.

Recent research on the French-based Creole spoken in Louisiana includes Neumann's (1985) description of the phonology and morphosyntactic structure of the Breaux Bridge variety and the *Dictionary of Louisiana Creole* (Valdman et al. 1998). As in the case of Cajun French, there is ongoing language shift, with Creole speakers largely confined to older generations. Despite the fact that many researchers view the two varieties not as discrete but as part of a continuum, Dubois and Melançon's (2000) study of language attitudes and use in two French Creole communities found clear divisions along ethnic lines in that the great majority of respondents who claim some level of proficiency in Creole French self-identify as African Americans. Further, respondents viewed having grandparents and parents who spoke the variety as the major criterion for Creole identity, with some proficiency in the language themselves rated as simply desirable. The relative lack of importance of native speaker fluency for such individuals raises important questions for language and identity. Dubois's research on issues of language and identity in French Louisiana has led her to an investigation of Cajun English and Louisiana African American Creole English, in particular of how the expression of ethnic identity is maintained in an adopted language. Results of this work (see, e.g., Dubois and Horvath 1999), including the documentation of complex sociolinguistic patterns such as the resurgence of "accented" English by young Louisiana residents of French ancestry as an index of Cajun identity, are important contributions to the study of language and identity in language contact situations.

AMERICAN SIGN LANGUAGE

Over the past two decades, research on the varieties of American Sign Language (ASL), the language commonly used in Deaf communities in both the United States and English-speaking Canada, has shown remarkable progress. In part this progress may be attributed to the increasing recognition of ASL, and by extension, other signed languages, as natural languages, independent in structure from English or from other languages with which they may coexist in the same community. And, just as the entrance of African American scholars into the field led to progress in our understanding of African American English, much of the progress on ASL and other signed languages has come about as a result of the entrance of Deaf people into the field. Work accomplished so far includes both small-scale studies of variation within the signing of a single individual (e.g., Hoopes 1998) as well as large-scale studies of phonological and lexical variation conducted in different sites across the United States (e.g., Lucas, Bayley, and Valli 2001). In this section we discuss work on various aspects of ASL.

Much of the early work on ASL concerns the lexicon. Shroyer and Shroyer (1984) is a typical and well-known example. They studied lexical variation and drew on signers from across the United States. Shroyer and Shroyer collected data on 130 words (the criterion for inclusion of a word being the existence of three signs for the same word) from 38 white signers in 25 states, for a total of 1,200 sign forms for the 130 words, including nouns, verbs, and some adverbs. Many of the forms that they present are actually related phonological variants of the same basic sign. Nevertheless, they present them as separate lexical items.

More recently, the focus of research on lexical variation has broadened considerably. Work undertaken in the 1990s includes small-scale studies of different social and occupational categories. Researchers have looked at gender differences (Mansfield 1993), differences in the use of signs for sexual behavior and drug use (Bridges 1993), and variation related to socioeconomic status (Shapiro 1993). Finally, Lucas, Bayley, Reed, and Wulf (2001) examined variation in 34 signs, using data elicited from more than 200 African American and white signers in seven sites ranging from Boston to Bellingham, Washington. Signs included both forms that were believed to be undergoing change, such as DEER, which has both one-handed and two-handed variants, as well as new signs for AFRICA and JAPAN, which are beginning to replace older signs that have been perceived as racist because they referred to physical characteristics.[3] Their results showed that for 28 of the 34 signs, African Americans used signs that white signers did not. Lucas et al. concluded that while African American and white signers share a lexicon to some extent, not all areas of the lexicon overlap.

Recently, Kleinfeld and Warner (1996) examined ASL signs used to denote gay, lesbian, and bisexual persons. Thirteen hearing interpreters and 12 deaf ASL users participated in the study. Kleinfeld and Warner focused on eleven lexical items and provided detailed analysis of phonological variation in two signs, LESBIAN and GAY. The analysis showed that the variation can be correlated to some extent with external constraints such as the signer's sexual identity (straight or gay/lesbian).

Variation in ASL phonology has also received considerable attention in recent years. Metzger (1993), for example, looked at variation in the handshape of second and third person pronouns, which can be produced either with the index finger or with an S handshape with the thumb extended. Metzger's data yielded one example of the thumb variant and one unexpected variant, the fingerspelled pronoun S-H-E. There is some indication that the sign that precedes the thumb variant, AGO, with its closed hand-shape, may play a role in the occurrence of the thumb variant.

Lucas (1995a) studied variation in location in the sign DEAF. In its citation form (the form of the sign that appears in dictionaries and is most commonly taught to second language learners), the 1 handshape moves from a location just below the ear to a location on the lower cheek near the mouth. However, this sign is commonly produced with movement from the chin location to the ear location or simply with one contact on the lower cheek. Observation might suggest that the final location of the sign (chin or ear) would be governed by the location of the preceding or following sign, so that the sign DEAF in the phrase DEAF FATHER might be signed from chin to ear, since the location of the following sign is the forehead, higher than the ear. Similarly, in the phrase DEAF PRIDE, one might expect that DEAF would be signed from ear to chin, as the sign that follows DEAF begins below the chin.

Contrary to expectations, Lucas's results (based on 486 examples produced by native signers in both formal and informal settings) indicated that the location of the following and preceding segments did not significantly affect the choice of a variant of DEAF. Rather, the key factor turned out to be the syntactic function of the sign itself, with adjectives being most commonly signed from chin to ear or as a simple contact on the cheek, and predicates and nouns being signed from ear to chin.

Another phonological variable, pinky extension, was the subject of a recent investigation by Hoopes (1998), who studied in detail the signing of one native signer. Some signs that in citation form have a handshape in which the pinky finger is closed and not extended variably allow the extension of the pinky. Examples include the signs THINK, LAZY, and CONTINUE. Hoopes's findings parallel Lucas's finding about the relative lack of importance of the location of the preceding or following sign. In both cases, the phonological factors that might seem to be most important— location in the case of DEAF and handshape in the case of pinky extension—in fact did not appear to condition the variation.

Turning to the area of fingerspelling, Blattberg et al. (1995) examined a subset of the data from Lucas's large-scale project on sociolinguistic variation in ASL (Lucas et al., 2001). They compared two groups of middle-class signers aged 15–25 and 55+ from Frederick, Maryland, and Boston. They found that adolescents and young adults used fingerspelling in either full or lexicalized forms, and that fingerspelling was produced in the area below the shoulder generally used for fingerspelling. The younger signers used fingerspelling primarily for proper nouns and for English terms that have no ASL equivalents. The older signers also used fingerspelling for these purposes, but their use of fingerspelling also resembled the use of locative signs. In addition, Maryland adults and the adolescents used fingerspelling much more frequently than their counterparts in Massachusetts. Finally, Mulrooney (2002) found clear evidence of a gender effect in fingerspelling, whereby men were more likely to produce noncitation forms (e.g., produced outside of the usual fingerspelling area) than women.

ASL discourse has been the topic of several recent investigations. Haas, Fleetwood, and Ernest (1995), for example, examined back-channeling, turn-taking strategies, and question forms in a conversation between Deaf-Blind individuals, comparing them to the same features in sighted ASL signing. They found that "in the tactile mode, Deaf-Blind signers use remarkably similar turn-taking and turn-yielding shift regulators as Deaf-sighted signers" (130). Touch is often substituted for eye-gaze, and "turn-yielding often uses a combination of dominant and non-dominant hands in yielding to the addressee. The dominant hand rests, and the non-dominant hand moves to 'read' the signer's dominant hand. Turn-claiming occurs with the dominant hand of the addressee repeatedly touching or tapping the non-dominant hand of the signer until the signer yields and moves their non-dominant hand to the 'reading' position." As for question forms, in this particular study, none of the question forms found seemed unique to tactile ASL. Collins and Petronio (1998), however, found that for yes/no questions, nonmanual signals that in sighted ASL include the raising of the eyebrows in Deaf-Blind signing are conveyed manually as either an outward movement of the signs or the drawn question mark.

Malloy and Doner (1995) looked at variation in cohesive devices in ASL discourse and explored gender differences in the use of these devices. Specifically, they looked at reiteration and expectancy chains. In their analysis of the use of reiteration and expectancy chains in the retelling of a story by two native signers (one male and one female), Malloy and Doner found that the male signer used reiteration more frequently than the female signer, but that the signers were similar in their use of expectancy chains.

African American signing has been the object of several investigations, including Aramburo (1989), Guggenheim (1993), Lewis, Palmer, and Williams (1995), and Lewis (1996). Aramburo and Guggenheim observed lexical variation during the course of structured but informal interviews. Lewis, Palmer, and Williams (1995) studied the existence of and attitudes toward African American varieties. Specifically, they described the differences in body movement, mouth movement, and the use of space in the signing of one African American signer who code-switched during the course of a monologue. In addition, they explored how interpreters handled the code-switching in spoken language from standard English to African American Vernacular English (AAVE). Lewis (1996) continued the examination of African American signing styles in his paper on the parallels between communication styles of hearing and deaf African Americans. His investigation took its departure from two observations: first, ASL users recognize the existence of what is often referred to as "Black signing" but have difficulty in explaining what it is that makes it "Black"; second, uniquely Black or "Ebonic" (Asante 1990) kinesic and nonverbal features exist, and these features occur in the communication of both hearing and Deaf African Americans. His investigation described some of these kinesic and nonverbal features—specifically, body postures and rhythmic patterns accompanying the production of signs—in the language used by a deaf adult African American woman. The frequently articulated perspective that African American signing differs markedly from white signing in all areas of structure—and not just lexically—is thus beginning to be explored.

The first national study of ASL that used standard sociolinguistic methods has recently been completed. From 1994 to 2001, Ceil Lucas of Gallaudet University led a team of researchers, including the first author of this chapter, in the first large-scale study of variation in ASL as it is used by Deaf people throughout the United States (Lucas et al. 2001). The study was based on conversations, interviews, and lexical elicitation tasks with 207 signers in seven different areas of the United States: Boston, Massachusetts; Frederick, Maryland; Staunton, Virginia; New Orleans, Louisiana; Olathe, Kansas/Kansas City, Missouri; Fremont, California; and Bellingham, Washington. Participants included working- and middle-class African American and white men and women ranging in age from 15 to 93. The project examined three phonological variables, a syntactic variable (presence or absence of subject pronouns), and a series of lexical items. The phonological variables were variation in the form of the sign DEAF, the location of a class of signs exemplified by the verb KNOW, and signs made with an 1 handshape in their citation, or standard, form.

The overall results of multivariate analysis of more than 10,000 tokens, reported in Lucas et al. (2001) and in a series of articles, indicated that variation in ASL, like variation in spoken languages, is systematic and subject to both internal and external constraints (Bayley, Lucas, and Rose 2000, 2002; Lucas et al. 2001; Lucas et al. 2002; Wulf et al. 2002). Internal constraints included such familiar linguistic constraints as the nature of the preceding and following segments (for the 1 handshape variable). Somewhat surprisingly, the grammatical function of the sign turned out to be the strongest constraint on phonological variation. The authors suggest that this result may be a consequence of modality differences between spoken and signed languages.

The external constraints found to be significant for one or more variables included constraints that are familiar from studies of spoken languages such as gender, ethnicity, social class, age, and region. However, a number of external constraints are also particular to the U.S. Deaf community and the effects of changes in Deaf education policy over the course of the twentieth century as well as to the earlier history of ASL. For example, the results revealed that signers in Staunton, Virginia, and Bellingham, Washington, were more similar to one another in their patterns of variation than either group was to signers in other regions. The authors suggest that this result provides an illustration of the importance of state residential schools for the Deaf, both as crucibles of Deaf culture and more importantly as centers for the transmission of ASL. The Washington State School for the Deaf was founded by teachers from Staunton in the mid-nineteenth century, and the results of that contact could still be observed in the signing of people educated at the two schools at the end of the twentieth century.

Although the project reported on in Lucas et al. (2001) was extensive, there is much more to be done before we have a full description of the varieties of ASL and other signed languages used in North America. In particular, Lucas et al. limited their study to African American and white participants. However, the North American Deaf community is much more diverse and includes people from a variety of language backgrounds, both signed and spoken. Although we do have some small-scale studies of language use in Latino families with Deaf children (e.g., Gerner de García 1995) and native American families that have developed systems of home-signs (Davis and Supalla 1995), the signing systems used in many minority communities have barely begun to be investigated. Also, although the project covered many areas of the United States, Lucas et al. (2001) were not able to collect data from all regions, nor were they able to investigate all variables of potential interest. Clearly, research on variation in ASL has just begun.

OTHER LANGUAGES IN THE UNITED STATES
AND CANADA

OTHER LANGUAGES IN THE UNITED STATES. Although Spanish and French have been the most widely studied languages in North America, other languages spoken in the United States have also received attention. Much of the research on immigrant languages has focused on language maintenance and shift and patterns of language use within language minority communities. However, a number of recent studies have focused on more traditional dialectological and linguistic concerns. In this section, we discuss a small sample of the studies of the languages of the major immigrant groups of the early twentieth century as well as some of the recent work on major immigrant languages of the last twenty years.

Among the languages of earlier immigrant groups, German has received the greatest amount of attention. German has been maintained to the greatest extent in small religious communities. Research includes a number of studies of these communities, among them the dialect of the Old Order Amish in Indiana (Thompson 1994) and Pennsylvania German of the Old Order Amish and Mennonites in a number of states (e.g., Louden 1988; Van Ness 1990). Salmons (1993) offers a recent overview of the current and historical situations of German dialects in North America, while Van Ness (1995) reviews four recent studies of U.S. German varieties, including Salmons (1993). Other recent work includes Gross (2000), who examined language attrition in the speech of six elderly German Americans who had lived in the United States for at least 40 years. Research on language shift and maintenance also includes Haller's (1988) study of ethnic language media and language loyalty among speakers of French, German, and Italian, which documents a decline in the influence of media in all three languages, and Costello's (1997) overview of different groups of German speakers in New York City.

Recent research also includes work on Czech, with a focus on structural changes in a language undergoing attrition (e.g., Henzl 1982; Eckert 1988; Smith 1991). Eckert (1988), for example, studied narratives from first-generation American Czechs in Nebraska. Despite similarities in age and background, speakers displayed highly variable degrees of proficiency. She concluded that age and immigrant generation did not predict ability to speak Czech. More recently, Dutkova-Cope (2001) studied Texas Czech, once one of the more widely spoken languages in the state. She examined two groups of second- to fourth-generation speakers born before and after 1945. Speakers born after 1945, when Czech ceased to be widely spoken in Texas Czech Moravian communities, used more overt pronouns (Czech is a pro-drop language), had fewer case distinctions, and less subject-verb agreement than those born before 1945. Resumptive pronouns were absent for both groups. Relativization, however, remained stable (Dutkova-Cope 2001, 59). In general, Dutkova-Cope found changes typical of those reported for dying languages by Dorian (1981) and others.

Among earlier immigrant languages, Yiddish, whose presence predates the American revolution, has also received attention. Fishman (1991), for example, estimates the number of speakers at 300,000, most of whom are concentrated in New York City and surrounding areas. Although secular communities are no longer transmitting Yiddish intergenerationally, a growing number of Ultra-Orthodox, particularly Hasidic, Jews are transmitting the language to the next generation and using it at home and even in some local businesses. Indeed, Kliger and Peltz (1997) describe the extensive use of Yiddish in Hasidic neighborhoods in Brooklyn, where the language has been strengthened by the arrival of Jewish immigrants from the former Soviet Union. Fishman (2001) updates his earlier account and finds that Yiddish continues to remain a vital force in the lives of the Ultra-Orthodox, although its use has continued to decline among more secular Jews.

During the past two decades, Asia has been a main source of immigrants to North America and, as we indicated in the beginning of this chapter, the number of speakers of many East Asian languages is increasing in both Canada and the United States. Huebner and Uyechi (forthcoming) survey the language situation of the highly diverse communities that are grouped under the term "Asian Americans." According to Huebner and Uyechi, like earlier immigrants, Asians and their U.S.-born descendants are shifting to English. However, researchers have observed different rates at which the shift to English is accomplished. By the mid-1970s, Filipinos, Japanese, and Koreans who arrived during the 1960s were most likely to have shifted to English as their usual language (Crawford 1992). Chinese, many of whom live in ethnic enclaves, were least likely to have adopted English as a main language.

A number of studies of Chinese language maintenance and shift have appeared in the past two decades. It should be borne in mind, however, that Chinese includes a large number of mutually unintelligible "dialects" that share a common writing system and that the Chinese immigrant population in the United States includes people from very different social strata. Many Chinese immigrants are poor with a relatively low educational level; others, however, are highly educated professionals, often graduates of leading U.S. universities, who have settled in the United States after completing graduate degrees. One study (Xia 1992), which focuses on a number of factors that contribute to Chinese maintenance, including increased immigration from China, concentrated patterns of settlement, the desire for cultural maintenance, and marriage patterns, provides a relatively optimistic view. As Huebner and Uyechi (forthcoming) note, however, a number of other studies, among them Li (1982), Veltman (1983), and Fishman et al. (1986), regard immigration as the primary factor in the continuing Chinese language presence in the U.S. and suggest that Chinese are likely to follow the historical pattern of ethnic language loss. More recently, Luo and Wiseman (2000) studied the roles of familial and peer influence on Chinese American children's ethnic language maintenance. They found that Chinese-speaking peer influence was the most important factor in ethnic language retention. Finally, Chiang (2000) examined the effect of a Chinese language school on language maintenance among second-generation U.S.-born Chinese. Chiang found that young people's acceptance of their families' expectations for high achievement in the larger society diverted their interests from maintaining their ethnic language and culture.

In a series of recent studies, He (2000, 2001, 2003) examined in detail language practices in Chinese heritage language schools, which constitute an important resource for language maintenance, particularly in areas without large Chinese communities. She analyzed the structure of teacher directives as well as the role of children as agents in the process of language socialization. He's work suggests several directions for future research, including reacquisition of immigrant languages by members of the second generation and the close examination of actual language practices in sites where ethnic language maintenance is attempted.

Other Asian languages have also been studied. Kondo (1998), for example, examined the social-psychological factors that affect language maintenance by second-generation Japanese Americans (*Shin Nisei*) in Hawaii. She found that Japanese mothers play a major role in their children's language maintenance, although children's language behavior interacts with their changing social identities. The issue of preservation of cultural norms also figures prominently in some families' attempts at language maintenance. For example, Smith-Hefner (1990) reports that the concern of Boston Cambodian parents that their children use honorifics appropriately was a factor in their promoting Khmer language maintenance. Finally, identity is also a major concern in Kuwahara's (1998) ethnographic study of Cambodian, Mien, Vietnamese, Thai, Chinese, and Mexican inner-city second-generation youth. Kuwahara examines how participants' uses of features of their native languages, standard English, and African American Vernacular English function as indices of their shifting identities.

Although studies of Asian languages in the United States, such as those reviewed here, have contributed substantially to our understanding of language use in new immigrant communities, it is clear that a great deal of work remains to be done. Much of the focus to date has been on language maintenance and shift. Relatively few studies have analyzed in detail the languages of speakers in the communities concerned. He's (2000, 2001, 2003) research on language in Chinese heritage schools, of course, represents an exception, as does Kuwahara's (1998) analysis of the varieties of English used by second-generation youth from a variety of language backgrounds. Such analysis, including studies of code-switching between English and the typologically diverse languages spoken by Asian immigrants, constitutes a needed area of research.

OTHER LANGUAGES IN CANADA. In stark contrast to the abundance of publications devoted to Canadian French (and, to a somewhat lesser extent, Canadian English), very little has been published on other (nonindigenous) languages in Canada. Indeed, Michol Hoffman's (2001, forthcoming) studies of the speech of young Salvadoran immigrants to Toronto are the only variationist works known to us. The bulk of the extant literature deals with the relationship between languages whose peak periods for immigration are now past, and the majority languages, English and/or French.

Several studies focus on bilingual discourse strategies, involving language choice and code-switching. For instance, Miwa Nishimura investigates patterns of language choice in the speech of several Canadian-born Japanese living in Toronto (1992) as well as syntactic and pragmatic aspects of code-switching (1995, 1997). Normand Labrie's monograph on the use of Italian, French, and English by members of the Montreal Italian community (Labrie 1991; see as well Labrie 1987 and Labrie and Deshaies 1989) involves sociolinguistic interview data (collected in the mid-1980s) for 32 Montreal residents, 16 father-and-son pairs. The phenomena investigated include patterns of language choice, code-mixing, code-switching, and the use of integrated borrowings. Among the extralinguistic factors considered are generation, language of education, intra- versus inter-group communication, and context of the interaction (home versus workplace).

Other studies deal with structural effects of language contact on the minority language. Linguistic research on Italian in Toronto, home of the largest Italian community outside of Italy, has centered on the influence of English on Italian, such as the incorporation of English loanwords into Italian (Danesi 1984, 1985; Clivio 1986) and the influence of English norms on pragmatic aspects of Italian usage (Frescura 1996). Auer (1991) compares the situation of Italian as an immigrant language in Canada and Germany. He considers structural effects on Italian, finding that the majority language has made deeper inroads in Canada than in Germany. Other differences between the two contexts include the finding of more positive attitudes toward Italian on the part of adolescents and postadolescents in Germany than in Canada.

Some research has been devoted to languages spoken in small enclave communities outside of Canada's major urban centers. Schaarschmidt (1995, 2002) deals with change in Doukhobor Russian, spoken in the interior of British Columbia. A number of changes are attributed to external influence from Ukrainian from the time of initial settlement of the Doukhobors in Saskatchewan, and more recently, from English, the current contact language. In addition, some changes are explained in terms of language-internal motivation. Timothy (1995) is concerned with the decline of Finnish language and culture in rural Thunder Bay in northwestern Ontario. He describes the situation of small, isolated communities where Finnish once thrived and which have, due largely to patterns of work, education, and intermarriage, become ones in which the youngest generation is largely English monolingual.

A third theme is language maintenance, attrition, and loss. Guardado's (2002) study of language socialization involves language use in four Hispanic families living in Vancouver, with the finding that parents' promotion of a sense of Hispanic cultural identity contributed strongly to language maintenance while the failure to actively promote positive attitudes toward the first language resulted in language loss. Chumak-Horbatsch (1987, 1999) investigates decline in Ukrainian language use in Toronto through a longitudinal study of intergenerational language transmission. A 1987 study of ten mother-child pairs found that Ukrainian was the only home language and the children, aged three at the time, were fluent speakers. Contrary to the general tendency toward language decline beyond the first generation of immigrants, these second-generation mothers were actively involved in preserving the language and had maintained it as the home variety. A second study (Chumak-Horbatsch 1999) investigates language use for five of the original mother-child pairs some ten years later. At that time, language use in the home involved both English and Ukrainian, on the part of both mothers and children, and the children showed clear decline in linguistic ability, a situation the author argues does not bode well for the future of Ukrainian in Toronto. In a study of language attitudes, Sachdev et al. (1987) examined the perceptions as to the present and future vitality of Chinese in Canada in a sample of first- (born in Hong Kong) and second-generation Canadian Chinese. Among the rather complex results of this study was a tendency of second-generation respondents to inflate, by comparison to "objective" measures, the ethnolinguistic vitality of the language. Finally, Prokop (1990) gives a comprehensive overview of the German presence in Alberta in media, businesses, clubs, and organizations, and in the school and university system. He shows that while the group has played a significant role in the province's history, the future of the language is bleak. In other research on German in Alberta, McKinnie (2000) turns to individual usage, examining the code-switching patterns of two elderly Edmonton residents.

Maintenance of the Portuguese language in Toronto has also been documented in ethnographically oriented research. Goldstein (1995, 1997) studies the language of the production lines of a small Toronto factory which employs Portuguese immigrants. In one strand of this research (Goldstein 1995), she shows how Portuguese is maintained as the language of the production floor by female workers who engage in little intergroup interaction, and how ESL-in-the-workplace classes do not take into consideration the local conditions of language use.

A new area of research for Canada involves language socialization and new immigrant communities (see Bayley and Schecter 2003). Lamarre and Paredes (2003) study the perceptions of young Montreal trilinguals who speak English and French and another language, the first language of their foreign-born parents (e.g., Arabic), while Pon, Goldstein, and Schecter (2003) are concerned with the classroom experiences of Hong Kong–born Chinese Canadians. Other interesting new research includes Giampapa's (2001) study of the discursive construction of multiple identities—Canadian, Italian-Canadian, Italian—on the part of eight young adults of Italian descent in Toronto. Such research constitutes an important step in investigating language and ethnicity in the rapidly changing landscape of Canada's urban centers. Research on bilingual and multilingual language use, from a variety of perspectives, including variationist, constitutes an area of needed research in Canada.

CONCLUSION

In a very brief report in PADS 71, *Needed Research in American English (1983)*, Eichhoff (1984), writing on behalf of the ADS Committee on "Non-English Dialects," called for greater research on these varieties, many of which were rapidly disappearing. Research on the languages in North America other than English has made a great deal of progress during the past two decades. However, given the increasingly diverse linguistic landscapes of both Canada and the United States that we outlined at the beginning of this chapter, much remains to be done, both to document the immigrant dialects spoken by earlier generations whose numbers are rapidly diminishing and to understand the changes that are taking place in the languages of new immigrants under conditions of language and dialect contact. Traditionally, the American Dialect Society has focused on the varieties of English spoken in the United States and, to a lesser extent, in Canada and the Caribbean. In the multilingual world of the twenty-first century, however, American dialects cannot be limited to English varieties, or even to the varieties of French and Spanish that have long coexisted with English. As North America becomes more linguistically diverse, the study of language and dialect contact, not only between English and other languages, but also between different varieties of the languages spoken or signed by language minorities, provides numerous opportunities to investigate language maintenance and shift, language change, the relationship of language to sociocultural identity, and language acquisition and reacquisition.

NOTES

Many colleagues have provided references and suggestions for this chapter. We wish to thank especially Sandra Clarke, David Heap, Thom Huebner, Pia Lane, Ceil Lucas, Anna Moro, Raymond Mougeon, Terry Nadasdi, Naomi Nagy, Carmen Silva-Corvalán, and James Walker. Both authors contributed equally to the chapter.

1. Several volumes on Ontario and Quebec French that are not reviewed here should also be noted (e.g., Mougeon and Beniak 1989; Paradis and Deshaies 1991; Erfurt 1996; Labrie and Forlot 1999). In addition to the research reviewed in this chapter, work on Acadian French includes individual studies of variation (e.g., Flikeid 1992; Beaulieu 1993; Beaulieu, Cichocki, and Balcom 2001) and English loan-words (e.g., Harriott and Cichocki 1993; Turpin 1998), as well as edited collections (e.g., Dubois and Bourdreau 1996) and volumes dedicated to individual provinces (e.g., Phlipponneau 1991).

2. See the special issue of Plurilinguismes edited by Klinger (1996) for an additional collection of articles on Louisiana French.

3. In accordance with convention, ASL signs are written in capitals. DEER, for example, refers to the ASL sign, not to the English word.

REFERENCES

Amastae, Jon, and Lucía Elías-Olivares, eds. 1982. *Spanish in the United States: Sociolinguistic Aspects.* Cambridge: Cambridge Univ. Press.

Amastae, Jon, and David Satcher. 1993. "Linguistic Assimilation in Two Variables." *Language Variation and Change* 5: 77–90.

Ancelet, Barry Jean. 1988. "A Perspective on Teaching the 'Problem Language' in Louisiana." *French Review* 61: 345–56.

Andersen, Roger W., and Yasuhiro Shirai. 1996. "The Primacy of Aspect in First and Second Language Acquisition: The Pidgin-Creole Connection." In *Handbook of Second Language Acquisition*, ed. William C. Ritchie and Tej K. Bhatia, 527–70. San Diego, Calif.: Academic.

Aramburo, Anthony J. 1989. "Sociolinguistic Aspects of the Black Deaf Community." In *The Sociolinguistics of the Deaf Community*, ed. Ceil Lucas, 103–19. San Diego, Calif.: Academic.

Asante, Molefi Kete. 1990. "African Elements in African American English." In *Africanisms in American Culture*, ed. Joseph E. Holloway, 19–23. Bloomington: Indiana Univ. Press.

Auer, Peter. 1991. "Italian in Toronto: A Preliminary Comparative Study on Language Use and Language Maintenance." *Multilingua* 10: 403–40.

Auger, Julie. 1998. "Le redoublement du sujet en français informel québécois: Une approche variationiste." *Canadian Journal of Sociolinguistics* 43: 37–63.

Bayley, Robert. 1999. "The Primacy of Aspect Hypothesis Revisited: Evidence from Language Shift." *Southwest Journal of Linguistics* 18.2: 1–22.

Bayley, Robert, Ceil Lucas, and Mary Rose. 2000. "Variation in American Sign Language: The Case of DEAF." *Journal of Sociolinguistics* 4: 81–107.

———. 2002. "Phonological Variation in American Sign Language: The Case of 1 Handshape." *Language Variation and Change* 14: 19–53.

Bayley, Robert, and Lucinda Pease-Alvarez. 1996. "Null and Expressed Pronoun Variation in Mexican-Descent Children's Spanish." In *Sociolinguistic Variation: Data, Theory, and Analysis: Selected Papers from NWAV 23 at Stanford*, ed. Jennifer Arnold, Renée Blake, Brad Davidson, Scott Schwenter, and Julie Solomon, 85–99. Stanford, Calif.: Center for the Study of Language and Information, Stanford Univ.

———. 1997. "Null Pronoun Variation in Mexican-Descent Children's Narrative Discourse." *Language Variation and Change* 9: 349–71.

Bayley, Robert, and Sandra R. Schecter, eds. 2003. *Language Socialization in Bilingual and Multilingual Societies*. Clevedon, Eng.: Multilingual Matters.

Bayley, Robert, Sandra R. Schecter, and Buenaventura Torres-Ayala. 1996. "Strategies for Bilingual Maintenance: Case Studies of Mexican-Origin Families in Texas." *Linguistics and Education* 8: 389–408.

Bayley, Robert, and José Zapata. 1993. *"Prefiero español porque I'm more used to it": Code-Switching and Language Norms in South Texas*. Working Paper WP-02. San Antonio: Hispanic Research Center, Univ. of Texas at San Antonio.

Beauchemin, Normand. 1983. *Concordance du corpus de l'Estrie*. Sherbrooke: Univ. de Sherbrooke.

Beaulieu, Louise. 1993. "Une analyse sociolinguistique du pronom *Wh* inanimé dans les relatives libres dans le français acadien du nord-est du Nouveau-Brunswick." *Linguistica Atlantica* 15: 39–67.

Beaulieu, Louise, and Patricia Balcom. 1998. "Le statut de pronoms personnels sujets en français acadien du nord-est du Nouveau-Brunswick." *Linguistica Atlantica* 20: 1–27.

Beaulieu, Louise, Wladyslaw Cichocki, and Patricia Balcom. 2001. "Variation dans l'accord verbal en français acadien du nord-est du Nouveau-Brunswick." In *Proceedings of the Annual Meeting of the Canadian Linguistics Association,* ed. John T. Jensen and Gerard Van Herk, 1–12. Ottawa: Univ. of Ottawa.

Belazi, Hedi M., Edward J. Rubin, and Almeida J. Toribio. 1994. "Code Switching and X-Bar Theory: The Functional Head Constraint." *Linguistic Inquiry* 25: 221–37.

Beniak, Édouard, Stephen Carey, and Raymond Mougeon. 1984. "A Sociolinguistic and Ethnographic Approach to Albertan French and Its Implications for French-as-a-Second-Language Pedagogy." *Canadian Modern Language Review* 41: 308–14.

Beniak, Édouard, Raymond Mougeon, and Daniel Valois. 1985. *Contact des langues et changement linguistique: Étude sociolinguistique du français parlé à Welland (Ontario).* Quebec: Centre international de recherche sur le bilinguisme.

Bergen, John J., ed. 1990. *Spanish in the United States: Sociolinguistic Issues.* Washington, D.C.: Georgetown Univ. Press.

Bills, Garland D. 1997. "New Mexican Spanish: Demise of the Earliest European Variety in the United States." *American Speech* 72: 154–71.

Bills, Garland D., Eduardo Hernández Chávez, and Alan Hudson. 1995. "The Geography of Language Shift: Distance from the Mexican Border and Spanish Language Claiming in the Southwestern U.S." *International Journal of the Sociology of Language* 114: 9–27.

Bills, Garland D., and Neddy A. Vigil. 1999. "Ashes to Ashes: The Historical Basis for Dialect Variation in New Mexico Spanish." *Romance Philology* 53: 43–67.

Blattberg, S., L. Byers, E. Lockwood, and R. Smith. 1995. "Sociolinguistic Variation in American Sign Language: Phonological Variation by Age Group in Fingerspelling." In Byers, Chaiken, and Mueller, 157–82.

Blondeau, Hélène. 2001. "Real-Time Changes in the Paradigm of Personal Pronouns in Montreal French." *Journal of Sociolinguistics* 5: 453–74.

Bridges, Byron. 1993. "Gender Variation with Sex Signs." Unpublished MS.

Brodie, Mollyann, Annie Steffenson, Jaime Valdez, Rebecca Levin, and Roberto Suro. 2002. *2002 National Survey of Latinos.* Menlo Park, Calif.: Henry J. Kaiser Family Foundation; Washington, D.C.: Pew Hispanic Center. Available from http://www.kff.org/content/2002/20021217a.

Brown, Becky. 1986. "Cajun/English Codeswitching: A Test of Formal Models." In Sankoff, 399–406.

———. 1993. "The Social Consequences of Writing Louisiana French." *Language in Society* 22: 67–102.

———. 2003. "Code-Convergent Borrowing in Louisiana French." *Journal of Sociolinguistics* 7: 3–23.

Byers, Laura, Jessica Chaiken, and Monica Mueller, eds. 1995. *Communication Forum 1995*. Washington, D.C.: Dept. of ASL, Linguistics, and Interpretation, Gallaudet Univ.

Cameron, Richard. 1996. "A Community-Based Test of a Linguistic Hypothesis." *Language in Society* 25: 61–111.

Canale, Michael, Raymond Mougeon, and Monique Bélanger. 1978. "Analogical Levelling of the Auxiliary *être* in Ontarian French." In *Contemporary Studies in Romance Linguistics*, ed. Margarita Suñer, 41–61. Washington, D.C.: Georgetown Univ. Press.

Carreira, María M. 2002. "The Media, Marketing, and Critical Mass: Portents of Linguistic Maintenance." *Southwest Journal of Linguistics* 21.2: 37–54.

Cedergren, Henrietta J. 1986. "Metrical Structure and Vowel Deletion in Montreal French." In Sankoff, 293–300.

Cedergren, Henrietta J., and David Sankoff. 1974. "Variable Rules: Performance as a Statistical Reflection of Competence." *Language* 50: 233–55.

Chevalier, Gisèle. 2002. "L'effet de génération dans l'usage de 'comme.'" *Revue québécoise de linguistique* 30: 13–40.

Chiang, Min-Hsun. 2000. "A Study of the Chinese Language School and the Maintenance of Ethnic Language in the Second-Generation, American-Born Chinese." Ph.D. diss., Univ. of Texas at Austin.

Chomsky, Noam. 1981. *Lectures on Government and Binding*. Dordrecht: Foris.

———. 1986. *Barriers*. Cambridge, Mass.: MIT Press.

———. 1995. *The Minimalist Program*. Cambridge, Mass.: MIT Press.

Chumak-Horbatsch, Roma. 1987. "Language Use in a Ukrainian Home: A Toronto Sample." *International Journal of the Sociology of Language* 63: 99–118.

———. 1999. "Language Change in the Ukrainian Home: From Transmission to Maintenance to the Beginnings of Loss." *Canadian Ethnic Studies* 31.2: 61–75.

Clermont, Jean, and Henrietta Cedergren. 1979. "Les 'R' de ma mère sont perdus dans l'air." In *Le français parlé: Études sociolinguistiques*, ed. Pierrette Thibault, 13–28. Edmonton, Alta.: Linguistic Research.

Clivio, Gianrenzo. 1986. "Competing Loanwords and Loanshifts in Toronto's Italiese." In *Alto Polo: Italian Abroad; Studies on Language Contact in English-Speaking Countries*, ed. Camilla Bettoni, 126–146. Sydney: Frederick May Foundation for Italian Studies, Univ. of Sydney.

Coles, Felice Ann. 1993. "Language Maintenance Institutions of the Isleño Dialect of Spanish." In Roca and Lipski, 121–33.

Collins, Steve, and Karen Petronio. 1998. "What Happens in Tactile ASL?" In *Pinky Extension and Eye Gaze: Language Use in Deaf Communities*, ed. Ceil Lucas, 18–37. Washington, D.C.: Gallaudet Univ. Press.

Cook, Eung-Do. 1998. "Aboriginal Languages: History." In *Language in Canada*, ed. John Edwards, 125–43. Cambridge: Cambridge Univ. Press.

Costello, John R. 1997. "German in New York." In *The Multilingual Apple: Language in New York City*, ed. Ofelia García and Joshua A. Fishman, 71–91. Berlin: de Gruyter.

Crawford, James. 1992. *Hold Your Tongue: Bilingualism and the Politics of "English Only."* Reading, Mass.: Addison-Wesley

———. 2000. *At War with Diversity: US Language Policy in an Age of Anxiety.* Clevedon, Eng.: Multilingual Matters.

Danesi, Marcel. 1984. "Italo-Canadian: A Case in Point for Loanword Studies." *Geolinguistics* 10: 79–90.

———. 1985. *Loanwords and Phonological Methodology.* Studia Phonetica 20. Ville LaSalle, P.Q.: Didier.

Davis, Jeffrey, and Samuel Supalla. 1995. "A Sociolinguistic Description of Sign Language Use in a Navajo Family." In Lucas 1995b, 77–106.

Deshaies, Denise. 1986. "Variation linguistique: Le cas des pronoms personnels du français." In Sankoff, 312–23.

d'Introno, Francesco. 1996. "Spanish-English Code-Switching: Conditions on Movement." In *Spanish in Contact: Issues in Bilingualism*, ed. Ana Roca and John B. Jensen, 187–201. Somerville, Mass.: Cascadilla.

Di Sciullo, Anne-Marie, Pieter Muysken, and Rajendra Singh. 1986. "Government and Code-Mixing." *Journal of Linguistics* 22: 1–24.

Dorian, Nancy C. 1981. *Language Death: The Life Cycle of a Scottish Gaelic Dialect.* Philadelphia: Univ. of Pennsylvania Press.

Drapeau, Lynn. 1998. "Aboriginal Languages: Current Status." In *Language in Canada*, ed. John Edwards, 144–59. Cambridge: Cambridge Univ. Press.

Dubois, Lise, and Annette Bourdreau, eds. 1996. *Les Acadiens et leur(s) langue(s): Quand le français est minoritaire; Actes de colloque.* Moncton, N.B.: Éditions d'Acadie.

Dubois, Sylvie. 1992. "Extension Particles, Etc." *Language Variation and Change* 4: 179–205.

————. 1997. "Field Methods in Four Cajun Communities in Louisiana." In Valdman, 47–70.

————. 2000. "French Language's Status and Preservation in Louisiana, U.S.A., and in the Maritime Provinces, Canada." Paper presented at International Symposium on Aspects of Interculturality—Canada and the United States, Vienna, 12–14 Apr. Published as "Le statut du français et les politiques linguistiques dans les provinces maritimes canadiennes et en Louisiane," in *Kanada und die USA: Interkulturelle Perspektiven*, ed. Waldemar Zacharasiewicz and Fritz Peter Kirsch, 123–37. Vienna: Zentrum für Kanada-Studien, Univ. Wien, 2002.

————. 2003. "Letter-Writing in French Louisiana: Interpreting Variable Spelling Conventions, 1685–1840." *Written Language and Literacy* 6: 31–70.

————. Forthcoming. "Pratiques orales en Louisiane." In *La phonologie du français contemporain: Variation et espace francophone*, ed. Jacques Durand, Bernard Laks, and Chantal Lyche. Special issue of *Tribune internationale des langues vivantes*.

Dubois, Sylvie, and Barbara Horvath. 1999. "When the Music Changes, You Change, Too: Gender and Language Change in Cajun English." *Language Variation and Change* 11: 287–313.

Dubois, Sylvie, and Megan Melançon. 2000. "Creole Is, Creole Ain't: Diachronic and Synchronic Attitudes toward Creole Identity in South Louisiana." *Language in Society* 29: 237–58.

Dubois, Sylvie, and David Sankoff. 1997. "L'absence de flexion sur les emprunts à l'anglais dans le français acadien." In *Explorations du lexique*, ed. Julie Auger and Yvan Rose, 163–76. Quebec: Centre international de recherche en aménagement linguistique.

Dutkova-Cope, Lida. 2001. "Texas Czech: The Language of Texans Who Say They Speak 'a Different Kind of Czech.'" *Southwest Journal of Linguistics* 20.1: 29–69.

Eckert, Eva. 1988. "First-Generation American Czech: A Sociolinguistic Survey." *Language Problems and Language Planning* 12.2: 97–109.

Eichhoff, Juergan. 1984. "Non-English American Languages." In *Needed Research in American English (1983)*, Publication of the American Dialect Society 71, ed. Thomas L. Clark, 67–70. University: Univ. of Alabama Press.

Elías-Olivares, Lucía. 1979. "Language Use in a Chicano Community: A Sociolinguistic Approach." In *Sociolinguistic Aspects of Language Learning and Teaching*, ed. J. B. Pride, 120–34. Oxford: Oxford Univ. Press.

———, ed. 1983. *Spanish in the U.S. Setting: Beyond the Southwest.* Rosslyn, Va.: National Clearinghouse for Bilingual Education.

Erfurt, Jürgen, ed. 1996. *De la polyphonie à la symphonie: Méthodes, théories et faits de la recherche pluridisciplinaire sur le français au Canada.* Leipzig: Leipziger Universitätsverlag.

Fishman, Joshua A, Michael H. Gertner, Esther G. Lowy, and William G. Milan. 1986. "Ethnicity in Action: The Community Resources of Ethnic Language in the United States." In *The Rise and Fall of the Ethnic Revival: Perspectives on Language and Ethnicity,* ed. Joshua A. Fishman, Michael H. Gertner, Esther G. Lowy, and William G. Milán, 195–282. Berlin: de Gruyter.

———. 1991. *Reversing Language Shift: Theoretical and Empirical Foundations of Assistance to Threatened Languages.* Clevedon, Eng.: Multilingual Matters.

———. 2001. "A Decade in the Life of a Two-in-One Language: Yiddish in New York City (Secular and Ultra-Orthodox)." In *Can Threatened Languages Be Saved? Reversing Language Shift, Revisited: A Twenty-first Century Perspective,* ed. Joshua A. Fishman, 74–100. Clevedon, Eng.: Multilingual Matters.

Flikeid, Karin. 1984. *La variation phonétique dans le parler acadien du nord-est du Nouveau-Brunswick: Étude sociolinguistique.* Bern: Lang.

———. 1989. "'Moitié anglais, moitié français?' Emprunts et alternance de langues dans les communautés acadiennes de la Nouvelle Ecosse." *Revue québécoise de linguistique théorique et appliquée* 8: 177–228.

———. 1992. "The Integration of Hypercorrect Forms into the Repertoire of an Acadian French Community: The Process and Its Built-in Limits." *Language and Communication* 12: 237–65.

Flikeid, Karin, and Louise Péronnet. 1989. "N'est-ce pas vrai qu'il faut dire 'J'avons été'? Divergences régionales en acadien." *Français moderne* 57: 219–28.

Flores, Nydia. 2002. "Subject Personal Pronouns in Spanish Narratives of Puerto Ricans in New York City: A Variationist Study." Ph.D. diss., City Univ. of New York.

Frescura, Marina. 1996. "Face Orientations in Reacting to Accusatory Complaints: Italian L1, English L1, and Italian as a Community Language." *Pragmatics and Language Learning* 6: 79–104.

Gaborieau, Antoine. 1985. *À l'écoute des franco-manitobains.* Saint-Boniface, Man.: Éditions des Plaines.

García, Maryellen. 1995. "*En los sábados, en la mañana, en veces:* A Look at *en* in the Spanish of San Antonio." In Silva-Corvalán, 196–213.

———. 1999. "*Nomás* in a Mexican-American Dialect." In *Advances in Hispanic Linguistics: Papers from the Second Hispanic Linguistics Symposium*, ed. Javier Gutiérrez-Rexach and Fernando Martínez-Gil, 16–27. Somerville, Mass.: Cascadilla.

Gérin, Pierre, ed. 1990. *Le glossaire acadien*. By Pascal Poirier. Moncton, N.B.: Éditions d'Acadie.

Gerner de García, Barbara. 1995. "Communication and Language Use in Spanish-Speaking Families with Deaf Children." In Lucas 1995b, 221–52.

Gesner, B. Edward. 1986. *Bibliographie annotée de linguistique acadienne*. Quebec: Centre international de recherches sur le bilinguisme.

Giampapa, Frances. 2001. "Hyphenated Identities: Italian-Canadian Youth and the Negotiation of Ethnic Identities in Toronto." *International Journal of Bilingualism* 5: 279–315.

Goldstein, Tara. 1995. "'Nobody Is Talking Bad': Creating Community and Claiming Power on the Production Lines." In *Gender Articulated: Language and the Socially Constructed Self*, ed. Kira Hall and Mary Bucholtz, 375–400. London: Routledge.

———. 1997. *Two Languages at Work: Bilingual Life on the Production Floor*. Berlin: de Gruyter.

Gross, Steven. 2000. "The Role of Abstract Lexical Structure in First Language Attrition: Germans in America." Ph.D. diss., Univ. of South Carolina.

Guardado, Martin. 2002. "Loss and Maintenance of First Language Skills: Case Studies of Hispanic Families in Vancouver." *Canadian Modern Language Review* 58: 341–63.

Guggenheim, Laurie. 1993. "Ethnic Variation in ASL: The Signing of African Americans and How It Is Influenced by Conversational Topic." In Winston, 51–76.

Haas, C., E. Fleetwood, and M. Ernest. 1995. "An Analysis of ASL Variation within Deaf-Blind Interaction: Question Forms, Backchanneling, and Turn-Taking." In Byers, Chaiken, and Mueller, 103–40.

Hakuta, Kenji, and Daniel D'Andrea. 1992. "Some Properties of Bilingual Maintenance and Loss in Mexican Background High-School Students." *Applied Linguistics* 13: 72–99.

Hakuta, Kenji, and Lucinda Pease-Alvarez. 1994. "Proficiency, Choice, and Attitudes in Bilingual Mexican-American Children." In *The Cross-Linguistic Study of Bilingual Development*, ed. Guus Extra and Ludo Verhoeven, 145–64. Amsterdam: North-Holland.

Haller, Hermann W. 1988. "Ethnic-Language Mass Media and Language Loyalty in the United States Today: The Case of French, German, and Italian." *Word* 39: 187–200.

Hallion, Sandrine. 2000. "Étude du français parlé au Manitoba." 3 vols. Ph.D. diss., Univ. Aix-Marseille.

Harriott, Philip, and Wladyslaw Cichocki. 1993. "Accentedness Ratings of English Loanwords by Acadian Listeners." *Revue québécoise de linguistique* 22: 93–106.

Haugen, Einar. 1950. "The Analysis of Linguistic Borrowing." *Language* 26: 210–31.

He, Agnes Weiyun. 2000. "Sequential and Grammatical Organization of Teacher's Directives." *Linguistics and Education* 11: 119–40.

———. 2001. "The Language of Ambiguity: Practices in Chinese Heritage Language Classes." *Discourse Studies* 3: 75–76.

———. 2003. "Novices and Their Speech Roles in Chinese Heritage Language Classes." In Bayley and Schecter, 128–46.

Heller, Monica. 1992. "The Politics of Codeswitching and Language Choice." *Journal of Multilingual and Multicultural Development* 13: 123–42.

———. 1994. *Crosswords: Language, Education, and Ethnicity in Ontario.* Berlin: de Gruyter.

———. 1995. "Language Choice, Social Institutions, and Symbolic Domination." *Language in Society* 24: 373–405.

Heller, Monica, and Laurette Lévy. 1994. "Les contradictions des mariages linguistiquement mixtes: Stratégies des femmes franco-ontariennes." *Langage et société* 67: 53–88.

Henzl, Vera M. 1982. "American Czech: A Comparative Study of Linguistic Modifications in Immigrant and Young Children's Speech." In *The Slavic Languages in Émigré Communities*, ed. Roland Sussex, 33–46. Carbondale, Ill.: Linguistic Research.

Hochberg, Judith G. 1986. "Functional Compensation for /s/ Deletion in Puerto Rican Spanish." *Language* 62: 609–21.

Hoffman, Michol. 2001. "Salvadorean Spanish /-s/ Aspiration and Deletion in a Bilingual Context." *University of Pennsylvania Working Papers in Linguistics* 7.3: 115–27.

———. Forthcoming. "Sounding Salvadorean: Phonological Variables in the Spanish of Salvadorean Youth in Toronto." Ph.D. diss., Univ. of Toronto.

Holloway, Charles E. 1997. *Dialect Death: The Case of Brule Spanish.* Amsterdam: Benjamins.

Hoopes, Rob. 1998. "A Preliminary Examination of Pinky Extension: Suggestions Regarding Its Occurrence, Constraints, and Function." In *Pinky Extension and Eye Gaze: Language Use in Deaf Communities*, ed. Ceil Lucas, 3–17. Washington, D.C.: Gallaudet Univ. Press.

Huebner, Thom, and Linda Uyechi. Forthcoming. "Asian American Voices: Language in the Asian American Community." In *Language in the USA: Perspectives for the Twenty-first Century*, ed. Edward Finegan and John R. Rickford. Cambridge: Cambridge Univ. Press.

Hurtado, Aida, and Raul Rodríguez. 1989. "Language as a Social Problem: The Repression of Spanish in South Texas." *Journal of Multilingual and Multicultural Development* 10: 401–19.

Jacobson, Rodolfo. 1982. "The Social Implications of Intra-sentential Code Switching." In Amastae and Elías-Olivares, 182–208.

Joshi, Aravind K. 1985. "Processing of Sentences with Intrasentential Code Switching." In *Natural Language Parsing: Psychological, Computational, and Theoretical Perspectives*, ed. David R. Dowty, Lauri Karttunen, and Arnold M. Zwicky, 190–205. Cambridge: Cambridge Univ. Press.

King, Ruth. 1985. "Linguistic Variation and Language Contact: A Study of the French Spoken in Four Newfoundland Communities." In *Papers from the Fifth International Conference on Methods in Dialectology*, ed. H. J. Warkentyne, 211–32. Victoria, B.C.: Dept. of Lingusitics, Univ. of Victoria.

———. 1994. "Subject-Verb Agreement in Newfoundland French." *Language Variation and Change* 6: 239–53.

———. 2000. *The Lexical Basis of Grammatical Borrowing: A Prince Edward Island French Case Study*. Amsterdam: Benjamins.

King, Ruth, and Terry Nadasdi. 1997. "Left Dislocation, Number Marking, and Canadian French." *Probus* 9: 267–84.

———. 1998. "How Auxiliaries *be/have* in Acadian French." In *Papers from the Annual Meeting of the Atlantic Provinces Linguistic Association*, ed. Gisèle Chevalier. Moncton, N.B.: Univ. de Moncton.

———. 1999a. "On Variable Use of Traditional Acadian Morphology in Prince Edward Island French." In *Proceedings of the Annual Meeting of the Canadian Linguistic Association*, ed. John Jensen and Gerard van Herk, 169–78. Ottawa: Univ. of Ottawa.

———. 1999b. "The Expression of Evidentiality in French-English Bilingual Discourse." *Language in Society* 28: 355–65.

———. Forthcoming. "Back to the *futur* in Acadian French." *Journal of French Language Studies*.

King, Ruth, and Robert Ryan. 1989. "La phonologie des parlers acadiens de l'Île-du-Prince-Édouard." In *Le français parlé hors Québec: Aperçu sociolinguistique*, ed. Raymond Mougeon and Édouard Beniak, 227–44. Quebec: Presses de l'Univ. Laval.

Kleinfeld, Mala Silverman, and Naomi Warner. 1996. "Variation in the Deaf Community: Gay, Lesbian, and Bisexual Signs." *Multicultural Aspects of Sociolinguistics in Deaf Communities*, ed. Ceil Lucas, 3–35. Washington, D.C.: Gallaudet Univ. Press.

Kliger, Hannah, and Rakhmiel Peltz. 1997. "Yiddish in New York." In *The Multilingual Apple: Language in New York City*, ed. Ofelia García and Joshua A. Fishman, 93–116. Berlin: de Gruyter.

Klinger, Thomas A. 1992. "A Descriptive Study of the Creole Speech of Pointe Coupée Parish, Louisiana." Ph.D. diss., Indiana Univ.

――――, ed. 1996. *La Louisiane*. Special issue of *Plurilinguismes* 11.

Klinger, Thomas A., Michael Picone, and Albert Valdman. 1997. "The Lexicon of Louisiana French." In Valdman, 145–82.

Kobel, David. 2003. "Language Mixing in the Media: Re-examining Code-Switching on the Radio." M.A. thesis, Univ. of Texas at San Antonio.

Kondo, Kimi. 1998. "Social-Psychological Factors Affecting Language Maintenance: Interviews with *Shin* Nisei University Students in Hawaii." *Linguistics and Education* 9: 369–408.

Kuwahara, Yuri Lea. 1998. "Interactions of Identity: Inner-City Immigrant and Refugee Youths, Language Use, and Schooling." Ph.D. diss., Stanford Univ.

Laberge, Suzanne. 1977. "Étude de la variation des pronoms sujets définis et indéfinis dans le français parlé à Montréal." Ph.D. diss, Univ. de Montréal.

Labrie, Normand. 1987. "Les comportements langagiers d'italophones de Montréal: Un modèle d'analyse linguistique." *Revue québécoise de linguistique théorique et appliquée* 6.2: 9–23.

――――. 1991. *Choix linguistiques, changements et alternances de langue: Les comportements multilingues des italophones de Montréal*. Quebec: Centre international de recherches en aménagement linguistique.

Labrie, Normand, and Denise Deshaies. 1989. "Diglossie et alternance de code: Un examen des concepts en fonction des comportements bilingues." *Revue québécoise de linguistique théorique et appliquée* 8.2: 57–72.

Labrie, Normand, and Gilles Forlot, eds. 1999. *L'enjeu de la langue en Ontario français*. Sudbury, Ont.: Prise de Parole.

Lamarre, Patricia, and Josefina Rossell Paredes. 2003. "Growing Up Trilingual in Montreal: Perceptions of College Students." In Bayley and Schecter, 62–82.

Lambert, W. E., and D. M. Taylor. 1996. "Language in the Lives of Ethnic Minorities: Cuban American Families in Miami." *Applied Linguistics* 17: 477–500.

Landry, Rodrigue, Réal Allard, and Jacques Henry. 1996. "French in South Louisiana: Towards Language Loss." *Journal of Multilingual and Multicultural Development* 17: 442–68.

Lemieux, Monique, and Henrietta J. Cedergren, eds. 1985. *Les tendances dynamiques du français parlé à Montréal.* 2 vols. Quebec: Office de la langue française, Gouvernement du Québec.

Lewis, John. 1996. "Parallels in Communication Styles of Hearing and Deaf African Americans." Unpublished MS.

Lewis, John, Carrie Palmer, and Leandra Williams. 1995. "Existence of and Attitudes toward Black Variations of Sign Language." In Byers, Chaiken, and Mueller, 17–48.

Li, Wen Lang. 1982. "The Language Shift of Chinese-Americans." *International Journal of the Sociology of Language* 38: 109–24.

Lipski, John M. 1987. "Language Contact Phenomena in Louisiana *Isleño* Spanish." *American Speech* 62: 320–31.

———. 1990. *The Language of the Isleños: Vestigial Spanish in Louisiana.* Baton Rouge: Louisiana State Univ. Press.

Louden, Mark Laurence. 1988. "Bilingualism and Syntactic Change in Pennsylvania German." Ph.D. diss., Cornell Univ.

Lucas, Ceil. 1995a. "Sociolinguistic Variation in ASL: The Case of DEAF." In Lucas 1995b, 3–25.

———, ed. 1995b. *Sociolinguistics in Deaf Communities.* Washington, D.C.: Gallaudet Univ. Press.

Lucas, Ceil, Robert Bayley, Ruth Reed, and Alyssa Wulf. 2001. "Lexical Variation in African American and White Signing." *American Speech* 76: 339–60.

Lucas, Ceil, Robert Bayley, Mary Rose, and Alyssa Wulf. 2002. "Location Variation in American Sign Language." *Sign Language Studies* 2: 407–40.

Lucas, Ceil, Robert Bayley, and Clayton Valli. 2001. *Sociolinguistic Variation in American Sign Language.* Washington, D.C.: Gallaudet Univ. Press.

Luo, Shiow-Huey, and Richard L. Wiseman. 2000. "Ethnic Language Maintenance among Chinese Immigrant Children in the United States." *International Journal of Intercultural Relations* 24: 307–24.

Malloy, C., and J. Doner. 1995. "Variation in ASL Discourse: Gender Differences in the Use of Cohesive Devices." In Byers, Chaiken, and Mueller, 183–205.

Mansfield, Doris. 1993. "Gender Differences in ASL: A Sociolinguistic Study of Sign Choices by Deaf Native Signers." In Winston, 86–98.

Martineau, France, and Raymond Mougeon. 2003. "A Sociolinguistic Study of the Origins of *ne* Deletion in European and Quebec French." *Language* 79: 118–52.

McKinnie, Megan. 2000. "'What Do You Want Me to Say, in Deutsch oder in English?' Code-Switching and Borrowing Strategies for Two Post-WWII German-Speaking Immigrants in Edmonton." In *German-Canadian Yearbook*, vol. 16, ed. H. Froeschle and L. Zimmerman, 171–88. Toronto: Historical Society of Mecklenburg Upper Canada.

Metzger, Melanie. 1993. "Pronoun Variation in Formal and Informal Discourse." In Winston, 132–49.

Mithun, Marianne. 1999. *The Languages of Native North America.* Cambridge: Cambridge Univ. Press.

Moriello, Becky, and Walt Wolfram. Forthcoming. "New Dialect Formation in the Rural South: Emerging Hispanic English Varieties in the Mid-Atlantic." *University of Pennsylvania Working Papers in Linguistics.*

Mougeon, Raymond, and Édouard Beniak. 1989. *Le français canadien parlé hors Québec: Aperçu sociolinguistique.* Quebec: Presses de l'Univ. Laval.

———. 1991. *Linguistic Consequences of Language Contact and Restriction: The Case of French in Ontario, Canada.* Oxford: Clarendon.

———, eds. 1994. *Les origines du français québécois.* Sainte-Foy, P.Q.: Presses de l'Univ. Laval.

Mougeon, Raymond, Cora Brent-Palmer, Monique Bélanger, and Wladyslaw Cichocki. 1982. *Le français parlé en situation minoritaire: Fréquence d'emploi et maîtrise du français parlé par les élèves des écoles de langue française dans des communautés franco-ontariennes.* Quebec: Centre international de recherche sur le bilinguisme.

Mougeon, Raymond, and Terry Nadasdi. 1998. "Sociolinguistic Discontinuities in Minority Speech Communities." *Language* 74: 40–55.

Mougeon, Raymond, Terry Nadasdi, Katherine Rehner, and Dorin Uritescu. 2002. "Acquisition of the Internal and External Constraints of Variable Schwa Deletion by French Immersion Students." Paper presented at the 14th International Sociolinguistics Symposium, Ghent, 6–9 April.

Mougeon, Raymond, and Katherine Rehner. 2001. "Variation in the Spoken French of Ontario French Immersion Students: The Case of *juste* vs. *seulement* vs. *rien que.*" *Modern Language Journal* 85: 398–415.

Mulrooney, Kristin. 2002. "Variation in ASL Fingerspelling." In *Turn-Taking, Fingerspelling, and Contact in Signed Languages,* ed. Ceil Lucas, 3–23. Washington, D.C.: Gallaudet Univ. Press.

Myers-Scotton, Carol. 1993. *Duelling Languages: Grammatical Structure in Codeswitching.* Oxford: Clarendon.

Nadasdi, Terry. 1995. "Subject Doubling, Matching, and Minority French." *Language Variation and Change* 7: 1–14.

―――. 2000. *Variation grammaticale et langue minoritaire: Le cas des pronoms clitiques en français ontarien.* Munich: Lincom Europa.

―――. 2001. "Agreeing to Disagree: Variable Subject-Verb Agreement in Immersion French." *Canadian Journal of Applied Linguistics* 4: 79–101.

Nadasdi, Terry, Raymond Mougeon, and Katherine Rehner. Forthcoming. "Emploi du 'futur' dans le français parlé des élèves d'immersion français." *Journal of French Language Studies.*

Nagy, Naomi, and Hélène Blondeau. 1999. "Double Subject Marking in L2 Montreal French." *University of Pennsylvania Working Papers in Linguistics* 6.2: 93–108.

Nagy, Naomi, Hélène Blondeau, and Julie Auger. Forthcoming. "Second Language Acquisition and 'Real' French: An Investigation of Subject Doubling in the French of Montreal Anglophones." *Language Variation and Change.*

Neumann, Ingrid. 1985. *Le créole de Breaux Bridge, Louisiane.* Kreolische Bibliothek 8. Bamberg: Buske.

Nishimura, Miwa. 1992. "Language Choice and In-Group Identity among Canadian Niseis." *Journal of Asian Pacific Communication* 3: 97–113.

―――. 1995. "The Use of Japanese Topics in Bilingual Discourse in Japanese and English." In *The Twenty-first LACUS Forum 1994,* ed. Mava Jo Powell, 39–47. Chapel Hill, N.C.: Linguistic Association of Canada and the United States.

―――. 1997. *Japanese/English Code-Switching: Syntax and Pragmatics.* New York: Lang.

Noetzel, Sibylle, and Sylvie Dubois. 2003. "Locative Prepositions '*dans la Louisiane, dans les États-Unis.*'" Paper presented at the Fourth International Symposium on Bilingualism, Arizona State Univ., Tempe, 2 May.

Otheguy, Ricardo, and Ana Celia Zentella. 2002. *Coding Manual for the Analysis of Transcripts in the Study of Subject Personal Pronoun Variation in*

Spanish in New York. New York: Research Institute for the Study of Language in Urban Society, City Univ. of New York.

Paradis, Claude, and Denise Deshaies. 1990. "Rules of Stress Assignment in Québec French: Evidence from Perceptual Data." *Language Variation and Change* 2: 135–54.

———. 1991. *Recherches sur le français québécois*. Special issue of *Revue québécoise de linguistique théorique et appliquée* 10.3.

Parodi, Claudia, and Otto Santa Ana. 2002. "The Los Angeles Spanish Koiné." Paper presented at the Reunión de Pronombristas: Workshop on the Sociolinguistic Study of Spanish Personal Pronouns, Research Institute for the Study of Language in an Urban Society, City Univ. of New York, 9 Feb.

Péronnet, Louise. 1991. "Système de modalités verbales dans le parler acadien du sud-est du Nouveau-Brunswick." *Journal of the Atlantic Provinces Linguistic Association* 13: 85–98.

———. 1992. *Le parler acadien du sud-est du Nouveau-Brunswick: Éléments grammaticaux et lexicaux*. New York: Lang.

Péronnet, Louise, Rose-Mary Babitch, and Wladyslaw Cichocki. 1998. *Atlas linguistique du vocabulaire maritime acadien*. Sante-Foy, P.Q.: Presses de l'Univ. Laval.

Pfaff, Carol W. 1982. "Constraints on Language Mixing: Intrasentential Code Switching and Borrowing in Spanish/English." In Amastae and Elías-Olivares, 264–97.

Phlipponneau, Cathérine, ed. 1991. *Vers un aménagement linguistique de l'Acadie du Nouveau-Brunswick*. Moncton, N.B.: Centre de recherche en linguistique appliquée, Univ. de Moncton.

Picone, Michael D. 1994. "Code-Intermediate Phenomena in Louisiana French." In *CLS 30-1: Papers from the Thirtieth Regional Meeting of the Chicago Linguistics Society*, vol. 1, *The Main Session*, ed. Katherine Beals, Jeanette Denton, Robert Knippen, Lynette Melmar, Hisam Suzuki, and Erica Zeinfeld, 320–24. Chicago: Chicago Linguistics Society.

———. 1997a. "Enclave Dialect Contraction: An External Overview of Louisiana French." *American Speech* 72: 117–53.

———. 1997b. "Code-Switching and Loss of Inflection in Louisiana French." In *Language Variety in the South Revisited*, ed. Cynthia Bernstein, Thomas Nunnally, and Robin Sabino, 152–62. University: Univ. of Alabama Press.

Poirier, Claude, ed. 1998. *Dictionnaire historique du français québécois: Monographies lexicographique de québécismes*. Sainte-Foy, P.Q.: Presses de l'Univ. Laval.

Pon, Gordon, Tara Goldstein, and Sandra R. Schecter. 2003. "Interrupted by Silences: The Contemporary Education of Hong-Kong-Born Chinese Canadians." In Bayley and Schecter, 114–27.

Poplack, Shana. 1980. "'Sometimes I'll Start a Sentence in Spanish and *termino en español*': Toward a Typology of Code-Switching." *Linguistics* 18: 581–618. Repr. in Amastae and Elías-Olivares, 230–63.

———. 1981. "Syntactic Structure and Social Function of Codeswitching." In *Latino Language and Communicative Behavior*, ed. Richard P. Durán, 169–84. Norwood, N.J.: Ablex.

———. 1985. "Contrasting Patterns of Codeswitching in Two Communities." In *Methods V: Papers from the Fifth International Conference on Methods in Dialectology*, ed. Henry J. Warkentyne, 363–86. Victoria, B.C.: Univ. of Victoria Press.

———. 1988. "Language Status and Language Accommodation along a Linguistic Border." In *Language Spread and Language Policy: Issues, Implications, and Case Studies*, ed. Peter H. Lowenberg, 90–118. Washington, D.C.: Georgetown Univ. Press.

———. 1989. "The Care and Handling of a Mega-corpus: The Ottawa-Hull French Project." In *Language Change and Variation*, ed. Ralph W. Fasold and Deborah Schiffren, 411–51. Amsterdam: Benjamins.

———. 1996. "The Sociolinguistic Dynamics of Apparent Convergence." In *Towards a Social Science of Language: Papers in Honor of William Labov*, vol. 1, *Variation and Change in Language and Society*, ed. Gregory R. Guy, Crawford Feagin, Deborah Schiffrin, and John Baugh, 285–308. Amsterdam: Benjamins.

Poplack, Shana, David Sankoff, and Christopher Miller. 1988. "The Social and Linguistic Processes of Lexical Borrowing and Assimilation." *Linguistics* 26: 47–104.

Poplack, Shana, and Danielle Turpin. 1999. "Does the *futur* Have a Future in (Canadian) French?" *Probus* 11: 133–64.

Prokop, Manfred. 1990. *The German Language in Alberta: Maintenance and Teaching*. Edmonton: Univ. of Alberta Press.

Rehner, Katherine. 2002. "The Development of Aspects of Linguistic and Discourse Competence by Advanced Second Language Learners of French." Ph.D. diss., Univ. of Toronto.

Rehner, Katherine, and Raymond Mougeon. 1999. "Variation in the Spoken French of Immersion Students: To *ne* or Not to *ne*, That Is the Sociolinguistic Question." *Canadian Modern Language Review* 56: 124–54.

Rehner, Katherine, Raymond Mougeon, and Terry Nadasdi. 2003. "The Learning of Sociostylistic Variation by Advanced FSL Learners: The Case of *nous* versus *on.*" *Studies in Second Language Acquisition* 25: 127–56.

Reyes, Rogelio. 1982. "Language Mixing in Chicano Spanish." In Amastae and Elías-Olivares, 154–65.

Roca, Ana, ed. 2000. *Research on Spanish in the United States: Linguistic Issues and Challenges.* Somerville, Mass.: Cascadilla.

Roca, Ana, and John M. Lipski, eds. 1993. *Spanish in the United States: Linguistic Contact and Diversity.* Berlin: de Gruyter.

Rochet, Bernard. 1993. "Le français parlé en Alberta." *Francophonies d'Amérique* 3: 5–24.

———. 1994. "Le français à l'ouest de l'Ontario: Tendances phonétiques du français parlé en Alberta." In *Langue, espace, société: Les variétés du français en Amérique du nord,* ed. Claude Poirier, 433–55. Sainte-Foy, P.Q.: Presses de l'Univ. Laval.

Rodriguez, Liliane. 1984. *Mots d'hier, mots d'aujourd'hui.* Saint-Boniface, Man.: Éditions des Plaines.

Rottet, Kevin. 1998. "Clause Subordination Structures in Language Decline." *Journal of French Language Studies* 8: 63–95.

———. 2001. *Language Shift in the Coastal Marshes of Louisiana.* New York: Lang.

Rottet, Kevin, and Dan Golembeski. 2000. "Vers une étude comparée des lexiques français d'Amérique du Nord: L'influence lexicale anglaise en français canadien et en français acadien." In *Contacts de langues et identités culturelles,* ed. Danièle Latin and Claude Poirier, 99–112. Saint-Nicholas, P.Q.: Agence Universitaire de la Francophonie, Presses de l'Univ. Laval.

Rousseau, Pascale, and David Sankoff. 1978. "Advances in Variable Rule Methodology." In *Linguistic Variation: Models and Methods,* ed. David Sankoff, 57–69. New York: Academic.

Russo, Marijke, and Julie Roberts. 1999. "Linguistic Change in Endangered Dialects: The Case of Alternation between *avoir* and *être* in Vermont French." *Language Variation and Change* 11: 67–85.

Sabourin, Conrad F., and Rolande M. Lamarche. 1985. *La francité canadienne.* Vol. 1, *Aspects linguistiques.* Montreal: Univ. de Montréal.

Sachdev, Itesh, Richard Bourhis, Sue-wen Phang, and John D'Eye. 1987. "Language Attitudes and Vitality Perceptions: Intergenerational Effects amongst Chinese Canadian Communities." *Journal of Language and Social Psychology* 6: 287–307.

Salmons, Joseph C., ed. 1993. *The German Language in America, 1683–1991.* Madison: Max Kade Institute for German American Studies, Univ. of Wisconsin.

Sankoff, David, ed. 1986. *Diversity and Diachrony.* Amsterdam: Benjamins.

Sankoff, David, Henriette J. Cedergren, William Kemp, Pierce Thibault, and Diane Vincent. 1989. "Montreal French: Language, Class, and Ideology." In *Language Change and Variation,* ed. Ralph W. Fasold and Deborah Schiffren, 107–18. Amsterdam: Benjamins.

Sankoff, David, Gillian Sankoff, Suzanne Laberge, and Marjorie Topham. 1976. "Méthodes d'échantillonnage et utilisation de l'ordinateur dans l'étude de la variation grammaticale." *Cahiers de linguistique de l'Université du Québec* 6: 85–126.

Sankoff, Gillian, Hélène Blondeau, and Anne Charity. 2001. "Individual Roles in a Real-Time Change: Montreal (r → R) 1947–1995." In *'R-atics: Sociolinguistic, Phonetic, and Phonological Characteristics of /r/,* ed. Hans Van de Velde and Roeland van Hout, 141–58. Special issue of *Études et travaux* 4.

Sankoff, Gillian, and Henrietta J. Cedergren. 1973. "Some Results of a Sociolinguistic Study of Montreal French." In *Linguistic Diversity in Canadian Society,* ed. Regna Darnell, 61–88. Edmonton, Alta.: Linguistic Research.

Sankoff, Gillian, and Pierrette Thibault. 1980. "The Alternation between the Auxiliaries *avoir* and *être* in Montreal French." In *The Social Life of Language,* ed. Gillian Sankoff, 311–46. Philadelphia: Univ. of Pennsylvania Press.

Sankoff, Gillian, Pierrette Thibault, Naomi Nagy, Hélène Blondeau, Marie-Odile Fonollosa, and Lucie Gagnon. 1997. "Variation and the Use of Discourse Markers in a Language Contact Situation." *Language Variation and Change* 9: 191–218.

Santa Ana, Otto, and Claudia Parodi. 1998. "Modeling the Speech Community: Configuration and Variable Types in the Mexican Spanish Setting." *Language in Society* 27: 23–51.

Schaarschmidt, Gunter. 1995. "Aspects of the History of Doukhobor Russian." *Canadian Ethnic Studies* 27: 197–205.

———. 2002. "Canadian Doukhobor Russian: Losses and Influences." Paper presented at the 47th annual conference of the International Linguistic Association, Toronto, 5–7 Apr.

Schecter, Sandra R., and Robert Bayley. 1997. "Language Socialization Practices and Cultural Identity: Case Studies of Mexican-Descent Families in California and Texas." *TESOL Quarterly* 31: 513–41.

———. 2002. *Language as Cultural Practice: Mexicanos en el Norte*. Mahwah, N.J.: Erlbaum.

Shapiro, E. 1993. "Socioeconomic Variation in American Sign Language." In Winston, 150–75.

Shroyer, Edgar H., and Susan P. Shroyer. 1984. *Signs across America: A Look at Regional Differences in American Sign Language*. Washington, D.C.: Gallaudet College Press.

Silva-Corvalán, Carmen. 1982. "Subject Expression and Placement in Mexican-American Spanish." In Amastae and Elías-Olivares, 93–120.

———. 1994. *Language Contact and Change: Spanish in Los Angeles*. New York: Oxford Univ. Press.

———. Forthcoming. "Spanish in the Southwest." In *Language in the USA: Perspectives for the 21st Century*, ed. Edward Finegan and John R. Rickford. Cambridge: Cambridge Univ. Press.

———, ed. 1995. *Spanish in Four Continents: Studies in Language Contact and Bilingualism*. Washington, D.C.: Georgetown Univ. Press.

Smith, Connie S. 1991. "The Demise of Czech in Two Texas Czech Communities." Ph.D. diss., Univ. of Texas at Austin.

Smith-Hefner, Nancy J. 1990. "Language and Identity in the Education of Boston-Area Khmer." *Anthropology and Education Quarterly* 21: 250–68.

St.-Amand, Anne, and Shana Poplack. 2002. "A Real-Time Window on Nineteenth Century Vernacular French: The Récits du Français Québécois d'Autrefois." Paper presented at the annual meeting of the Canadian Linguistic Association, Toronto, 25–28 May.

Statistics Canada. 2002. "Population: Languages" (Web site). Ottawa. Available at http://www.statcan.ca.

Thibault, Pierrette, and Michelle Daveluy. 1989. "Quelques traces du passage du temps dans le parler des Montréalais, 1971–1984." *Language Variation and Change* 1: 19–46.

Thibault, Pierrette, and Diane Vincent. 1990. *Un corpus de français parlé, Montréal 84: Historique, méthodes et perspectives de recherches*. Quebec: Dépt. de langues et linguistique, Univ. Laval.

Thomas, Alain. 1986. *La variation phonétique: Cas du franco-ontarien*. Ville La Salle, P.Q.: Didier.

Thompson, Chad. 1994. "The Languages of the Amish of Allen County, Indiana: Multilingualism and Convergence." *Anthropological Linguistics* 38: 69–91.

Timothy, Dallen J. 1995. "The Decline of Finnish Ethnic Islands in Rural Thunder Bay." *Great Lakes Geographer* 2.2: 45–58.

Toribio, Almeida Jacqueline. 2002. "Spanish-English Code-Switching among U.S. Latinos." *International Journal of the Sociology of Language* 158: 89–119.

Toribio, Almeida Jacqueline, and Edward J. Rubin. 1996. "Code-Switching and Generative Grammar." In *Spanish in Contact: Issues in Bilingualism*, ed. Ana Roca and John B. Jensen, 203–26. Somerville, Mass.: Cascadilla.

Turpin, Danielle. 1998. "'Le français, c'est le last frontier': The Status of English-Origin Nouns in Acadian French." *International Journal of Bilingualism* 2: 221–33.

U.S. Bureau of the Census. 1984. *1980 Census of Population: Detailed Population Characteristics, United States.* Washington, D.C.: GPO.

———. 1993. *1990 Census of Population: Social and Economic Characteristics, United States.* Washington, D.C.: GPO.

———. 2003. "File QT-P16: Language Spoken at Home: 2000." Washington, D.C.: GPO.

Valdés, Guadalupe. 1982. "Social Interaction and Code-Switching Patterns: A Case Study of Spanish/English Alternation." In Amastae and Elías-Olivares, 209–29.

Valdman, Albert, ed. 1997. *French and Creole in Louisiana.* New York: Plenum.

Valdman, Albert, and Thomas Klinger. 1997. "The Structure of Louisiana Creole." In Valdman, 109–44.

Valdman, Albert, Thomas Klinger, Margaret Marshall, and Kevin Rottet. 1998. *Dictionary of Louisiana Creole.* Bloomington: Indiana Univ. Press.

Van Ness, Silke. 1990. *Changes in an Obsolescing Language: Pennsylvania German in West Virginia.* Tübingen: Narr.

———. 1995. "Review Article: The Current Status of Research on German Dialects in North America." *American Speech* 70: 401–14.

Vasquez, Olga A., Lucinda Pease-Alvarez, and Sheila M. Shannon. 1994. *Pushing Boundaries: Language and Culture in a Mexicano Community.* New York: Cambridge Univ. Press.

Veltman, Calvin. 1983. *Language Shift in the United States.* Berlin: de Gruyter.

———. 1988. *The Future of the Spanish Language in the United States.* New York: Hispanic Policy Development Project.

Vincent, Diane. 1992. "The Sociolinguistics of Exemplification in Spoken French in Montreal." *Language Variation and Change* 4: 137–62.

Vincent, Diane, Marty Laforest, and Guylaine Martel. 1995. "Le corpus de Montréal 1995: Adaptation de la méthode d'enquête sociolinguistique pour l'analyse conversationnelle." *Dialangue* 6: 29–46.

Vincent, Diane, and David Sankoff. 1992. "Punctors: A Pragmatic Variable." *Language Variation and Change* 4: 205–16.

Weinreich, Uriel. 1968. *Languages in Contact: Findings and Problems*. The Hague: Mouton.

Willis, Lauren. 2000. "Être ou ne plus être: Auxiliary Alternation in Ottawa-Hull French." M.A. thesis, Univ. of Ottawa.

Winston, Elizabeth, ed. 1993. *Communication Forum 1993*. Washington, D.C.: Dept. of ASL, Linguistics, and Interpretation, Gallaudet Univ.

Wulf, Alyssa, Paul Dudis, Robert Bayley, and Ceil Lucas. 2002. "Variable Subject Presence in ASL Narratives." *Sign Language Studies* 3: 54–76.

Xia, Ningsheng. 1992. "Maintenance of the Chinese Language in the United States." *Bilingual Review* 17.3: 195–209.

Zentella, Ana Celia. 1981. "'*Tá bien*, you could answer me *en qualquier idioma*': Code Switching in Two New York Puerto Rican Bilingual Classrooms." In *Latino Language and Communicative Behavior*, ed. Richard P. Durán, 109–31. Norwood, N.J.: Ablex.

——. 1982. "Code-Switching and Interactions among Puerto Rican Children." In Amastae and Elías-Olivares, 354–85.

——. 1997. *Growing Up Bilingual: Puerto Rican Children in New York*. Malden, Mass.: Blackwell.

10. LANGUAGE CHANGE IN VARIATION AND FORMAL SYNTAX

RALPH W. FASOLD

Georgetown University

Sociolinguistic variation analysts have long been interested in language change, including syntactic change. In formal theory, there are a number of linguists who are examining how syntactic change occurs. However, there is a need for more research that attempts to meld the two strands together. On the one hand, linguists working on syntactic change from a formal theory perspective are largely limited to an "I[nternal]-Language" approach, meaning that they are severely restricted in solving what Weinreich, Labov, and Herzog (1968) call "the actuation problem," in other words, what makes a change start. That is, while they have done excellent work on detecting historical changes and uncovering the effects one change will induce in another part of the syntactic system, only the effects of earlier changes, and possibly language contact phenomena, seem to be available to them as impetuses for actuation.[1]

THE NATURE OF VARIATION: VARIATION RESEARCH AND FORMAL SYNTAX

From the beginning of research on language variation and change (e.g., Labov 1969), researchers have proposed that variation is INHERENT. This means specifically that alternative means of expression are an integral part of the human language capacity, rather than arising from separate grammars in which the same individuals are proficient. This was expressed early on by VARIABLE RULES, which formally built variation into rewrite rules of the sort described by Chomsky and Halle (1968). The original variable rule

231

assigned a "more-or-less" value to optional elements in rule environments. In other words, a rule would apply more frequently when there were more, and more powerful, elements present in its environment. The environment included not only linguistic elements, such as phonological environment and stress, but relevant aspects of the speaker's social identity, such as age, gender, and social status. With the development of the VARBRUL programs (Cedergren and Sankoff 1974; Rand and Sankoff 1990), a mathematical procedure became available that allows the probabilities contributed by various elements of the environment to be estimated and evaluated for significance. These probabilities were taken to be part of speakers' competence and therefore an inherent part of their grammar.

In formal syntactic work, the goal of the Chomskyan transformational tradition has been to discover principles from which it can be determined whether a given construction is or is not a sentence in the language. While there has always been an emphasis on grammars as biologically based, transformational grammars have relatively little to do with the actual production of utterances by particular speakers under specific circumstances.[2] Variation in this tradition, then, means that alternative expressions are BOTH in conformity with the principles of grammars. This entails the notion of PARAMETERS, which may be "set" in one way or another, each setting producing an outcome that does not violate the general principles of natural language grammars. However, it is assumed that parameters are binary, and also that they must be set one way or the other in a particular grammar. This entails that if a given speaker allows sentences reflecting BOTH settings of a parameter, then that speaker has at least two grammars, one with the parameter set one way and one with it set the other. In other words, variation in this tradition is not distinguished from bilingualism; such speakers have two or more nearly identical grammars and can produce utterances reflecting either or any of them.[3]

In effect, the emphasis on inherent variability has slowly faded in variation research. Part of the reason for this is the replacement of Chomsky-Halle-1968-style rewrite rules with the ascendancy of optimality theory in phonology, a theory in which the variable rule model of inherent variability fits less well.[4] Another part of the reason is that variable rule analysis using VARBRUL gradually and implicitly came to be seen for what it is—a statistical method for analyzing unevenly distributed nominal data. Furthermore, seldom, if ever, was SYNTACTIC variation associated with syntactic rewrite rules, even when rewrite rules were part of current transformational theory (Fasold 1991). Most variation work about syntax is about the presence and selection of "grammaticalized" lexical items or constructions. For a very recent example, we can take Dannenberg's (2002) monograph on Lumbee Native American English in North Carolina, *Sociolinguistic Constructs of Ethnic Identity: The Syntactic Delineation of an American Indian English.* The syntactic features she addresses in this variety are elements like "perfective *be,*" as in "You look more like an Indian than anyone I'm seen yet" (37), and the form *be* or *bes,* as in "And that's when the blessed train bes running, every time we get out of class" (55). The study is largely about the occurrence and meaning of these items, not about whether or how they are integrated into speakers' grammar(s) of English. Even work like Jacobson's (1983) corpus-based study about the placement of *probably,* as in *He probably will buy a new car* versus *He will probably buy a new car,* seems clearly to be about whether *probably* is adjoined to IP or VP, with concomitant subtle meaning differences. The meaning differences are so subtle that the case could serve as a good candidate for a syntactic variable, but the choice between the variants, in terms of transformational theory, is how different options in clause construction are chosen.

Interestingly enough, the variation and formal syntax research programs have unwittingly converged on this issue. In spite of the presence of parameters in the theory, Chomsky's MINIMALIST PROGRAM depends on several properties of the lexicon to motivate larger-scale syntactic characteristics, such as (1) the presence or absence in the lexicon and privileges of occurrence of such silent elements as "small pro," (2) selectional restrictions on lexical and functional entries, and (3) syntactic features of functional categories to induce movement (more accurately, overt versus covert movement). To take an example, the difference between Middle

English *He complained not* and Modern English *He didn't complain,* assuming that *not* is located between the main verb and the inflection, depends on whether or not I^0, the inflection functional entry, has features that are so strong that they must be satisfied by moving the verb to the inflection position, or so weak that they can be satisfied covertly. In other words, if during the transition period, a speaker used both *He complained not* and *He didn't complain* type constructions, this could be analyzed as the presence in the lexicon of both strong-feature and weak-feature I^0 elements, and the variation attributed to the speaker's choice between them, rather than to a speaker being competent in two grammars, each with a differently set parameter.[5] Similarly, the distribution of *probably* studied by Jacobson can naturally be taken to reflect the choice of one of two homophonous entries for *probably*, one selectively restricted to being adjoined to IP and the other to VP, or alternatively, one entry with two selectional frames, between which a speaker can choose.

The needed research here, as I see it, is on three issues: (1) do variation research and formal syntax research really agree that the root cause of syntactic variation stems from choices from the lexicon? (2) If not, should it be maintained that syntactic variation is inherent in some other sense, and can that sense be given some theoretical substance? And (3) also if not, can the notion that speakers of a changing language might be "diglossic" (Lightfoot 1999, 92) with respect to two grammars with oppositely set parameters be made more precise (in particular, need they be two— largely overlapping—mental grammars, or can the opposite parameter–setting apply only to a subsection of the grammar)?

LANGUAGE CONTACT AND SYNTACTIC CHANGE

The best possibilities for fruitful future research between variation analysis and formal syntactic theory would be the contribution of variation studies to external explanations of actuation. The literature on formal studies of syntactic change includes numerous references to broad-brush external influences—language contact and dialect divergence. The effect of language contact on the VERB

SECOND (V2) phenomenon between Old English and the northern dialect of Middle English is developed in Kroch and Taylor (1997). The following is a substantially oversimplified account of Kroch and Taylor's quite complicated analysis. They argue that Old English was an "IP-V2" language, meaning that the position to which verbs moved was the head of IP, I^0. The northern dialect of Middle English, by contrast, was "CP-V2," with the verb moving to the C^0 position. Discovering to which position the verb has moved is not quite straightforward, but a revealing piece of evidence is the clitic behavior of pronouns in Old English. Pronouns, according to Kroch and Taylor (1997, 305) "move to the CP-IP boundary" and then cliticize to whatever is to its left.[6] If the tensed verb has moved only to I^0, then this verb will not be at the "CP-IP boundary" and the pronoun will have moved to its left, cliticizing to any form that may be occupying the Specifier position of CP. If the verb has moved to C^0, then the verb will be the first thing to the left of the "CP-IP boundary" and the pronoun will cliticize to that. I have illustrated how this would work out in figures 1 and 2, using examples from texts of glosses of the Latin Vulgate Bible from Skeat (1881–87). Figure 1 is based on the Early West Saxon translation of Mark 8:18 and figure 2 on the Rushworth text from the latter half of the tenth century (Kroch and Taylor 1997, 320–21).[7] Kroch and Taylor assume that the translators interpreted the words for 'eyes' in the original as topicalized, therefore located in Spec CP. With no overt pronoun in the Latin original, they would have placed the pronoun according to their native syntactic system.[8] In the older text, with IP-V2 syntax, that would mean the pronoun would have to go to the left of the tensed verb. In the newer text, with CP-V2 syntax, the translator would be led to place the pronoun to the right of the tensed verb, now in C^0.

If Kroch and Taylor have interpreted the evidence correctly, the question arises as to why Old English went from IP-V2 to CP-V2. Their hypothesis is that the change stems directly from language contact, as they put it, following "modern sociolinguistic approaches to the relationship between language change and second-language acquisition" (Kroch and Taylor 1997, 318). The E-language fact that triggered the change was "the imperfect second-language

FIGURE 1

West Saxon Gloss of Mark 8:18 "Have eyes (do you not see)?"

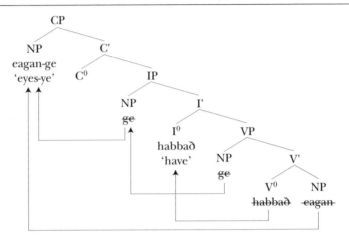

FIGURE 2

Rushworth Gloss of Mark 8:18 "Have eyes (do you not see)?"

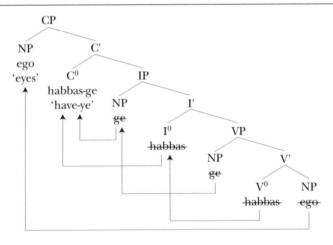

learning of English by the Norse invaders of the ninth to eleventh centuries" (Kroch and Taylor 1997, 318). Specifically, they hypothesize that these speakers replaced the Old English inflectional endings with /ð/, which did not occur word-finally in their native language, with /s/. This had a profound effect on the verb inflection system of Old English as they acquired it, reducing the number of persons and numbers for which verbs were inflected distinctly. This, in turn, reduced the Old English inflection system from a richly inflected system to poorly inflected one. Learners of this variety of English would still hear evidence for V2 but would assume that the verb was not being attracted to the poorly inflected I^0, but rather that C^0 had a strong syntactic feature that drew the verb there. If Kroch and Taylor are right about this, taking into account the kind of context information that variation analysts routinely do yields a richer understanding of a syntactic change. The change was triggered by a contact-induced effect on morphonology. On the other hand, an understanding of the workings of syntax in terms of formal theory allows us to understand how the morphonological change could lead to seemingly unrelated changes in subject-verb order in topicalized constructions.

LANGUAGE USAGE AFFECTING SYNTACTIC CHANGE

Although Kroch is undoubtedly correct in his pessimism about the availability of facts of this kind in historical records (see n. 1), occasionally there are hints that language usage phenomena might provide a contributing impetus to change in very subtle ways. Lightfoot (1999, 111–43) discusses the syntactic effects of another morphological change in the history of English, the loss of case. He shows that a number of syntactic changes resulted from case loss, but we will concentrate here on the development of Middle English SPLIT GENITIVES into the Modern English possibility of expressing genitives in the manner of *Smith's hypothesis* or *the hypothesis of Smith*. Middle English allowed such constructions as:

ÆLFREDES godsune CYNINGES
of-Alfred godson of-king
"King Alfred's godson"
["The Peterborough Chronicle" 1122–54, entry for 890]

With nouns overtly inflected for case—here nouns in small capitals have genitive case—we find that a noun like *godsune* could assign case (also thematic role) to its left and to its right in Middle English, making such split genitives possible. Interestingly, as required by current understanding of syntactic theory, case and thematic role assignment occur together. This means that there is no

> þæs CYNINGES *godsune* FRANCES
> the of-king godson of-France
> "The King of France's godson"

This is so because there is no relationship between *godsune* and *Frances*. The notion 'of France' is a relationship of the king, not of the godson, so genitive case cannot be assigned to the right of *godsune*.

In Middle and Early Modern English, split genitives still occur but have a strikingly different form. We find forms like:

> *the Kynges sone of Troie*
> "the King of Troy's son"
> [Chaucer, *Troilus and Cressida*, 111, 1715]

Notice that this case is like the one PROHIBITED in Old English, since, like *godson* in 'the king of France's godson', *sone* has no thematic relationship with *Troie*—it is the King of Troy that we are talking about. It turns out that this can be understood as a consequence of the loss of case. The old genitive endings sounded a lot the same, but with the case system being lost, they eventually began to be interpreted by new child learners of English as something different, not a case ending, but a genitive clitic, the head of the determiner phrase, as in figure 3. This new clitic assigns genitive case to *Alfred* instead of morphologically expressed genitive case being assigned directly by *godson*.

At the same time, forms such as—

> *the Grekes hors Synoun*
> the Greek's horse Sinon
> "Sinon the Greek's horse"
> [Chaucer, *The Squire's Tale*, 209]

FIGURE 3
English Genitive Ending as a Clitic

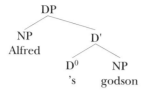

—are possible. Here, *Synoun* is the name of the Greek, not the horse. Although the genitive looks like the old case ending, it seems fairly clear that in the speakers' mental grammars it is a clitic as in figure 3 (Lightfoot 1999, 120). The reason is the proper name *Synoun* has no overt case ending, although theoretically it must actually have case. In fact, it has (abstract) genitive case. Due to its appositional relationship with *the Grekes*, it can share the case assigned by *'s* (spelled *es*).

The same is not true in *the Kynges sone of Troie*. *Troie* is not in apposition with *Kynges* so it cannot share its case. Unless something develops to assign a case to *Troie*, the split genitive would theoretically be ungrammatical. Quite evidently, something has developed, the dummy preposition *of*.

But where did *of* come from? A possible answer to this question is suggested by the apparent fact (Lightfoot 1999, 122) that the Middle English expressions with *of* always involved the thematic roles Locative or Source. There are expressions meaning *King's son of Troy*, but not *King's son of great courage*, so they can mean *the son of the king of (the place) Troy*, but they do not mean *the son of the king who possesses great courage*. Lightfoot further suggests that at least a supporting role might have been played by another "split" phenomenon, SPLIT NAMES. These are forms like:

Simundeschamberleyn Ward
'chamberlain of Simon Ward'
[1318 *Patent Rolls* (Elmstead Ess.)]

These look similar, with respect to case assignment, to the earlier expressions of the form *Alfred's godson king* since *Simund* and *Ward*

refer to the same person, like *Alfred* and *king*, and surnames furthermore often referred to social roles, for example, *Ward* meant
'guard'. It seems these would have been grammatical under the
older grammar, since the surname is, in a sense, in apposition to
the given name.

At the same time, there were split names involving French
names, of the form:

> *Alicesbailiff de Watevill*
> 'bailiff of Alice de Watevill'
> [1323 *Patent Rolls* (Panfield Ess.)]

Sometimes, the French preposition *de* was dropped or replaced by
of, as in:

> *Julianesservant of Weston*
> 'servant of Julian of Weston'
> [1348 *Patent Rolls* (Tetbury Gl.)]

As Lightfoot (1999, 124) points out, "Given that *of* is a Case
marker, then it must have a distinctive thematic role; Locative/
Source is a good candidate given the structure of names such as
[*Julianesservant of Weston*], all of which indicate the place from
which [people like *Julian*] originate." Eventually, *of* in this form
became generalized to an assigner of case on its own. At this point,
people no longer said things like *Julian's servant of Weston* or *the
King's son of Troy*, but *Julian Weston's servant* and *the King of Troy's son*.
Since the clitic is now the head of DP (fig. 3) it can allow complex
noun phrases in DP's Specifier position, making *the King of Troy's
son* possible.[9] Speakers could also say things like *Chris's heart of gold*
meaning what it now means, not something like *Chris Gold's heart* or
Chris from Gold's heart. *Of* assigns not only case, but conjointly a
separate thematic role.

Finally, we are ready to say something about the role of language use. Ekwall (1943, 16, 17; cited in Lightfoot 1999, 123) says
of split names that they were particularly profuse in the English
Patent Roles of the time, and "we may assume that the split genitives
represent local usage and everyday speech. Many of the descriptions, especially those which contain a pet form of a personal

name, have a very homely and colloquial ring." To put it in the vernacular, perhaps split names were a cool way of talking and this way of talking played an important role in the development of Modern English genitives. One may wonder if a modern discourse analysis of the use of split names in the relevant texts, using approaches that would not have been available to Eckwall in the 1940s, might reveal the social value of using this form of naming and perhaps even something about the kind of people most likely to use it. In any event, it appears that a combination of sociolinguistic method with formal analysis has the potential to deepen understanding of the E-language practices that can contribute to a (in this case broad) set of related syntactic changes.

THE CONSTANT RATE EFFECT

Another area where more research might be needed connecting variation and formal syntax involves something of a controversy between scholars with excellent credentials in variation research. Kroch (1989, 1994) has taken issue with Bailey's (1973) hypothesis that syntactic change would begin in the most favoring environment; the new form would become more frequent there, then spread to the second most favoring environment and so on. This implicational wave movement was reflected in the original theory of variable rules. Kroch argues that the data do not support this pattern of at least syntactic change. Rather, a new structure will appear in all the relevant environments at once and move to completion at a constant rate. It may well be that as the change moves to completion, the newer form may be more frequent in some environments than others, but that does not affect the rate of change. Using an analysis exploiting logarithms, Kroch has been able to isolate the rate of change from these variations in frequency and show the CONSTANT RATE EFFECT in numerous cases, and these results have been replicated by Santorini (1993), among others. As far as I know, no one has challenged the constant rate effect hypothesis in the past decade or so. In particular, there have been no defenses of the wave model. If there is evidence that can support the wave model in the face of the challenge by Kroch and his colleagues, this would provide a fertile area for new research. It is possible, of course, that the fact that this research has apparently not been done in so long means that the constant rate effect can be considered established, at least for the moment.

THE BLOCKING EFFECT: EXPLAINING THE S-CURVE

It has long been noticed that innovation in language (and elsewhere) proceeds in the form of an elongated S when frequency of the new form is plotted over time, as in figure 4. That is, the new form appears infrequently at first, then rapidly becomes more frequent, finally slowing its advance toward categoricality when the frequency becomes very high. Although this strong tendency has often been observed, explaining it, in particular, the middle part of the S where frequency increases very rapidly, has not been easy. It has been suggested by Kroch (1994) and Lightfoot (1999, 97–101) that the BLOCKING EFFECT, noted in the case of morphological doublets, might be the answer.

The blocking effect is the name given to such phenomena as the fact that, although children may experiment with regular verb forms where the adult form has an irregular form (*bringed* instead of *brought*), they do not continue with the two forms indefinitely

FIGURE 4
The S-Curve Illustrated

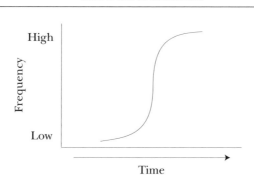

(the adult form wins out); and that irregular nominalized forms, like *authenticity*, block out what would otherwise be the regular form, *authenticness*. Kroch (1994) cites work by Ann Taylor (1994) which shows that regular-irregular doublets in past tense verb forms exist in the history of English, but that they have a limited history and no form that had two variants in Middle English has survived to the present day. Still, it seems to be a problem that they exist at all. Kroch's answer, endorsed by Lightfoot, is that the different forms either (1) take on different meanings, thereby losing their status as variants, or (2) are sociolinguistically assigned to different dialects or registers, where they can survive for a time helping to express extralinguistic social meaning for speakers, but one form will in this case ultimately yield to the other. An example of the first type, popularized by Steven Pinker's *The Language Instinct* (1994), is the pair *flew* and *flied*. The form *flew* is a general-use verb, as in *The birds flew away*, and *flied* is a technical term in baseball, as in *The batter flied out to left field*.

There are, however, at least two problems with this understanding of the blocking effect. The first is, if it is to account for the steep part of the S-curve, it would seem to imply that the steep part is steep indeed. If the steep section lasts for generations, then the S-curve (and the blocking effect) would not seem to be a (psycho)linguistic fact at all. If individual speakers can tolerate variant pairs with the same meaning for their entire lives, then the blocking effect cannot straightforwardly be a consequence of limitations on individual linguistic competence (or individual competence at all).[10] In fact, when S-curves are constructed for historical texts, the steep section often covers centuries. For example, Santorini (1992) extends the blocking effect to pairs of syntactic structures (as Kroch and Lightfoot do) in her study of a word order change in Yiddish. Her figure 1 (Santorini 1992, 617) is a quite clear S-curve, but the steep part extends from something like 1560 until the first years of the nineteenth century, about 250 years. According to Kroch (1994, 186), a search of citations in the *Oxford English Dictionary* (1989) indicates that past-tense verb-form doublets survive an average of 300 years. A consideration that mitigates this problem is given by Kroch: "This figure is, of course, misleadingly long, since it reflects citations in any dialect and takes no account of conscious or unconscious archaism."

Kroch's answer implicitly appeals to the response to the second problem. The second problem is that a theory that allows for doublets to last indefinitely, as long as they belong to different dialects or registers, would seem to eviscerate any explanatory power the blocking effect might offer. It would seem that any counterexample—in the form of a long-lived doublet—can be explained away by asserting that each member of the doublet belongs to a different dialect, even if both dialects are part of a single speaker's competence. If the theory cannot be falsified, it is a poor theory. However, Kroch's understanding of what the blocking effect predicts would not be falsified by long-lived doublets (Kroch 1994, 196).

The blocking effect, as we have seen, does not prevent doublets from arising in a language by sociolinguistic means; that is, by dialect and language contact and perhaps other processes. Instead, the effect appears to be a global economy constraint on the storage of formatives, which resists addition to the lexicon of forms equivalent to ones already learned. This effect may be inviolable in primary language acquisition by young children, but it can clearly be overridden as speakers learn a wider range of styles and social dialects in the course of maturation. Nevertheless, over long periods of time, the constant pressure of economy on acquisition seems to win out over sociolinguistic variation in the history of doublet forms.

In other words, there is a limit, perhaps like the limit on storage space in people's attics, that causes doublets to fall into disuse as new ones come along, like people cleaning out their attic in order to make space for new items. This view of the blocking effect is, in principle, falsifiable. Whether or not the effect is "inviolable in primary language acquisition" might possibly be established by acquisition experimentation, though it is far from obvious how one would distinguish the "primary" constraint from the "sociolinguistic means" that allow doublets to creep in. The whole notion could in principle be refuted if it can be shown that there is a case in which doublets have survived too long, but this would depend on a long period of excellent language records, and, in any case, almost nothing is known about what might constitute "too long."

But collaborative research between variation researchers and formal syntacticians might be carried out following a suggestion from Kroch (1989, 199–200): "General principles derived from the study of living languages in the present will hold of archaic ones as well. This assumption allows the historical syntactician to, in the words of Labov [1974], 'use the present to explain the past.'" It would seem that variation researchers, skilled at examining forms in relation to styles and social and regional dialects, could quite readily examine evidence on doublets in records of living languages to see if they can reasonably be assigned to different dialects or registers. With advice from formal syntacticians on what to look for, this could also include doublets of syntactic constructions, which both Kroch and Lightfoot believe are also subject to the blocking effect.

EXAMINATION OF A POTENTIAL CHANGE IN PROGRESS

In the final section, I turn to some of my own work on reflexives as an example of a mechanism that could potentially lead to change in forms subject to a principle that has been part of syntactic theory for quite some time, the BINDING THEORY. The binding theory says that "anaphors"—reflexives and reciprocals—are subject to three subprinciples. The one that is of interest to the example we are about to examine is Principle A, which governs the privilege of occurrence of reflexives.[11] Oversimplifying a bit, Principle A states that reflexives can occur only if their antecedent is the subject of the clause in which they are located. So it is possible to say *Dana likes herself,* but not *Dana's father likes herself* (*Dana* is not the subject, *Dana's father* is), and also not *Dana hopes her brother likes herself* (*Dana* is a subject, but not of the clause containing *herself*).

A problem arises when reflexives apparently occur in violation of Principle A. A number of these have been pointed out by Zribi-Hertz (1989) and Baker (1995). For example:

> Tell him$_i$, please, that we wish him no harm; but that it will be better for himself$_i$ if he goes away from Germany at once. [Isherwood 1935, 196; cited in Zribi-Hertz 1989, 707]

> Maggie$_i$ looked at him. Did he mean herself$_i$—herself$_i$ and the baby? [Woolf 1937, 188; cited in Zribi-Hertz 1989, 707]

> But when the second moment had passed, when she$_i$ found every doubt, every solicitude removed, compared her situation with what so lately it had been,—saw him honourably released from his former engagement, saw him instantly profiting by the release, to address herself$_i$ and declare an affection as tender, as constant as she had ever supposed it to be,—she was oppressed, she was overcome by her own felicity. [Austen 1811, 343; cited in Baker 1995, 70]

In all of these examples it is perfectly clear that Principle A is not respected; the antecedent of the reflexive is not only not the subject of the reflexive's clause, it is not even in the local clause. Yet these are admirable sentences written by eminent writers. It is not only in literary works that such examples occur. I have collected several that I have observed, including:

> They can have their silhouettes drawn which they$_i$ then fill in with writing and pictures that describe themselves$_i$. [description of the Boston Children's Museum on Monitor Radio, broadcast on 30 Apr. 1990]

> According to Harvey$_i$, the two men stole $80 from his friend and about $20 from himself$_i$. [student newspaper article about a mugging, 30 Oct. 1992]

It is clear that it is sometimes possible to observe reflexives in positions not allowed by Principle A. Zribi-Hertz (1989) argues that Principle A is an artifact of formal syntacticians taking sentences out of context to examine for acceptability. Instead, in her analysis, reflexives are not structurally controlled at all, but are allowed wherever their antecedents are participants whose point of view is being represented, which she called "a subject of consciousness." In an isolated sentence, the subject of the local clause is very likely to be taken as the subject of consciousness, and this is what has misled formal syntacticians. Baker (1995) criticizes Zribi-Hertz's analysis as both overspecifying and underspecifying the distribution of reflexives. He cites a number of examples from literary works in which reflexives neither respect Principle A nor refer to a subject of consciousness, and others in which a PRONOUN (not a reflexive) has a subject of consciousness as antecedent. Further problems arise when we observe the results in research by a former student of mine, Keller Magenau (1994), who tested a number of the citations in Zribi-Hertz (1989), giving as much context as Zribi-Hertz does in the article, for acceptability with groups of nonlinguist English speakers and found that majorities considered them unacceptable. Somewhat later I asked subscribers to two electronic lists on the Internet to respond to a survey on the acceptability of three sentences. It was a forced-choice test between a sentence that conformed to the binding theory and one that did not. One example was a garden-variety example like what might be found in an introductory textbook, and the other was one of the Zribi-Hertz examples. The 54 respondents overwhelmingly preferred the binding-theory-compliant choice to the other in both cases, and the Zribi-Hertz example was evaluated statistically identically with the standard binding theory example. If the binding theory is irrelevant and subject of consciousness is the key, these results are hard to interpret.

Baker went on to develop his own analysis of the cases that do not conform to the binding theory. He concluded that these reflexive forms are allowed only in contexts in which the antecedent is contrasted with another participant and is also "discourse prominent." Discourse prominence is determined by a list of factors, including subject of consciousness. Baker's analysis is not altogether satisfactory since his definitions involve disjunctions, but no one has yet proposed a convincing analysis, although it is fairly clear that discourse-pragmatic principles are at work here.

In the course of his analysis, Baker noticed that this usage of reflexives seemed to parallel the use of a combination of a full noun or a nominative pronoun plus a reflexive, producing the following distribution (adapted from Baker 1995, 80):

the students	the students themselves
they	they themselves
them	themselves

Baker does not take the next step, which I propose here—that *themselves* is structurally identical to the other two forms, except that the pronoun is covert. I assume that the structure is something like those in figure 5. Given this analysis, a structure like the one in figure 5b carries its own conformity to Principle A, since the reflexive is always bound by pro.

This analysis carries two problems. First, it is not clear how to guarantee that the structure in figure 5b is possible only if pro has ACCUSATIVE case, since there is no *Themselves did it*. This problem is not unique to the present analysis; there needs to be some account of why *them themselves* is degraded, while *they themselves* and *the students themselves* are perfectly fine. It cannot just be the reluctance to repeat *them* since *us ourselves* and *me myself* are just as troublesome. I have no proposals to offer for either problem here, but I suspect that the solution to the *us ourselves* problem will apply to pro + *Xself/ves*.

The second problem is the same as the one raised in connection with the blocking effect. If the present analysis is accepted, the apparent consequence is that Principle A would be rendered unverifiable, since a reflexive would seem to conform to Principle A in any (accusative) environment whatsoever, provided it represented the structure in 5b. In other words, while the Zribi-Hertz example quoted above is ungrammatical if it has the structure *Did he mean* [$_{DP}$ *herself*], but it is grammatical if it has the structure *Did he mean* [$_{DP}$ pro [$_{NP}$ *herself*]], despite the fact that the two are indistinguishable when uttered. Any instance of a reflexive apparently not in compliance with Principle A could be claimed to be a case of the structure in figure 5b, and the hypothesis is unfalsifiable.

FIGURE 5

Structure for *they themselves* and Problematic Cases of *themselves*

There are several things that can be said in this regard. First, the cases cited above from Zribi-Hertz (1989), Baker (1995), and my own observations exist and need to have some account. One possibility would be to say that there are homophonous sets of reflexives, one anaphoric in the sense of the binding theory and the other not, but this solution has all of the drawbacks of the one proposed here, and the disadvantage that it does not regularize Baker's paradigm above, nor does it allow the problematic examples to be understood as conforming to the binding theory, despite appearances. Another possibility would be to say that the binding theory is invalid, but that would give up the wide range of cases it has been found to account for over the years and would not explain why even examples that seem perfectly reasonable in their literary contexts are nonetheless found to be degraded under acceptability testing by native speakers with no stake in the binding theory.

However, this very fact raises problems of its own. An utterance like *I think my goldfish loves myself (not you)* should be perfectly grammatical, and even acceptable in the right discourse-pragmatic context, yet even I find it severely degraded even if I try to build up the appropriate context. I have no doubt most English speakers would agree. If a grammatical sentence is unacceptable, even in a favorable context, how can it be considered grammatical? Of course, it must be remembered that grammaticality is not the same as acceptability and that in principle grammatical sentences can be rendered unacceptable by a variety of factors unrelated to their grammaticality. In this case, what may be in play could be a particularly virulent kind of garden path effect, which I call the "bad meaning drives out good" effect. When we are presented with a sentence like *I think my goldfish loves myself*, the meaning corresponding to the structure that violates Principle A suggests itself so strongly that we cannot see the interpretation associated with the grammatical reading, unless, perhaps, it is presented in an elaborate context with the skill of a Jane Austen or a Virginia Woolf.

Furthermore, these cases are not the only ones illustrating the "bad meaning drives out good" effect. Consider the following pair of sentences:

> Live free or die. [the motto of the State of New Hampshire]
> Live freely or die.

The two are both meaningful and have different meanings, the first associated with a small-clause structure—[*Live* [PRO *free*]]— and the other in which *freely* is an adverb in construction with the imperative verb *live*. If, on the other hand, you are presented with the example:

> Drive careful

and your version of English requires *-ly* on most adverbs, you will hear this as ungrammatical, although it has a perfectly unexceptionable meaning on the grammatical small-clause reading, something like 'drive while being a careful person'. Yet it is hard to convince people who are not linguists that this reading is possible.[12] The "bad" adverbial reading presents itself so strongly that the small-clause reading is driven out. I know of at least one similar example which we will not examine here, so that we can return as soon as possible to the issue of needed research combining formal syntax and variation research to solve problems of syntactic change.

The final thing I would say in defense of the criticism that this analysis is not falsifiable is that, in principle, it IS falsifiable. To claim that the internally bound structure is involved in a case in which a reflexive seems not to respect Principle A, it must be arguable that it conforms to whatever discourse-pragmatic principles make these forms reasonable, principles along the lines of those proposed by Zribi-Hertz and Baker. I say, "in principle" because applying this test is hampered by the imprecision with which the discourse-pragmatic principles have so far been stated.

If we assume that one way in which syntax can change is by the choice of functional or substantive elements with one property or another, then we can imagine how English reflexives might come into variation in such a way that they cease to be marked [+ anaphoric], that is, cease to be subject to Principle A, for future learners of English. The way this would happen is if the discourse contexts favoring the selection of the *pro Xself* forms became a "cool" way of talking in some segment of the English-speaking world. Imagine that these people went out of their way to frame their discourse in such a way as to emphasize discourse prominence (in Baker's sense). Imagine further that this led to a proliferation of utterances with apparently unbound *pro Xself* forms that are indistinguishable from anaphoric reflexives. At this point, a new generation of learners might not hear sufficient instances of reflexives that respect Principle A and might learn the plain reflexive as a form used to express discourse prominence. There would now be no forms left in English to which Principle A would apply. This would not mean Principle A is no longer a part of Universal Grammar, just that there are no forms to which it applies. Bickerton (1991) argues just this for Haitian Creole, where the form *li* occurs where both pronouns and reflexives are called for by the binding theory. Burzio (1991) further argues convincingly that if a reflexive is not available, pronouns can freely substitute. In this way, he takes forms like *me* in Italian, which are not distinct on pronominal versus reflexive meanings, not to be homophones but to be the pronoun in all cases.

A future version of English which had undergone such a change would sound very different from early twenty-first-century English. Present-day linguists, if they could be transported forward in time, might well be totally perplexed about what had happened to the binding theory. The answer, of course, would be that nothing had happened to the binding theory; something quite explicable had happened to English *-self* forms.

Sociolinguists, variationists, and discourse analysts, if some can be found who have an interest in melding their work with the work in the formal analysis of syntactic change, could construct a research program of looking for cases like these, in which puzzling things seem to be happening to previously well-behaved forms. Their work could make clear the E-language forces that are actuating a change and even throw light on possible outcomes. I can envision some exciting collaboration along these lines.

NOTES

1. Anthony Kroch, who knows as much as anyone about the variation literature, says that a major reason why there is no appeal to functional (i.e., E[xternal]-Language) phenomena in studies of past syntactic change is that the required information is not generally available in historical records: "Unfortunately, the evidence that would be needed to actually show that some linguistic factor had a causal effect in advancing a change . . . under any functional model as far as we can see, would seem to be of a kind unavailable to historians" (1989, 240).

2. As Newmeyer (2002) has said, "Transformational grammars specify possible languages, not probable languages." His point could be expanded to state that transformational grammars specify (some) possible utterances, not probable utterances.

3. This view is explained clearly in Kroch (1994, 181–84) and Lightfoot (1999, 92–101).

4. However, recently phonologists have begun investigating the possibility that probabilities may play a role in phonological theory. (See, e.g., Bod, Hay, and Jannedy 2003.)

5. It seems to me that it is possible that parameters may not be needed at all. It would be crucial to determine whether syntactic differences that would otherwise have to be attributed to several pairs of lexical entries always co-occur, and their co-occurrence cannot be understood as one change logically implicating the other, or as the result of usage conventions. I cannot go further into this issue here, but see Baker (2001) for a contrary view.

6. It is not entirely clear to me specifically what Kroch and Taylor mean by moving to the CP-IP boundary. For convenience, I am assuming Spec IP, but that may not be correct.

7. Both texts are in Old English, but, as Kroch and Taylor argue, the Rushworth text reflects the CP-V2 grammar that became a feature of the northern dialect of Middle English. I use these examples instead of actual Middle English ones for the convenience of having translations of the same text for maximum comparison. Although these texts are interlinear glosses of the Latin, they are still instructive, because Latin is pro drop and Old English is not, forcing the translators to decide where to place the pronouns (Kroch and Taylor 1997, 321).

8. The Latin original is *oculos habentes non uidetis* 'eyes having not see-you'.

9. In fact, once *of* starts assigning its own case and thematic role, split names and split genitives become impossible, because the second part of the split would then get two cases, one from their appositional relationship to the first part, and a second from *of*, violating a grammatical principle (Lightfoot 1999, 124).

10. In fact, Lightfoot (1999, 103) reports an example from Kaufman (1995) involving randomly connecting buttons with thread by pairs that also produces an S-curve and has nothing to do with language.

11. Principle A is also usually taken to apply to reciprocals, but we will limit the discussion to reflexives here.

12. I have tried again and again to convince my wife, not a linguist, that the sign "Drive careful" that we saw near a construction site on the road is perfectly grammatical in the most sophisticated English. I have not succeeded.

REFERENCES

Austen, Jane. 1811. *Sense and Sensibility.* London: Egerton. Repr., ed. Ros Ballaster. New York: Penguin, 1995.

Bailey, Charles-James N. 1973. *Variation and Linguistic Theory.* Arlington, Va.: Center for Applied Linguistics.

Baker, C. L. 1995. "Contrast, Discourse Prominence, and Intensification, with Special Reference to Locally Free Reflexives in British English." *Language* 71: 63–101.

Baker, Mark C. 2001. *The Atoms of Language: The Mind's Hidden Rules of Grammar.* New York: Basic Books.

Bickerton, Derek. 1991. "On the Supposed 'Gradualness' of Creole Development." *Journal of Pidgin and Creole Languages* 6: 25–58.

Bod, Rens, Jennifer Hay, and Stefanie Jannedy, eds. 2003. *Probabilistic Linguistics.* Cambridge, Mass.: MIT Press.

Burzio, Luigi. 1991. "The Morphological Basis of Anaphora." *Journal of Linguistics* 27: 81–105.

Cedergren, Henrietta, and David Sankoff. 1974. "Variable Rules: Performance as a Statistical Reflection of Competence." *Language* 25: 257–82.

Chomsky, Noam, and Morris Halle. 1968. *The Sound Pattern of English.* New York: Harper and Row.

Dannenberg, Clare J. 2002. *Sociolinguistic Constructs of Ethnic Identity: The Syntactic Delineation of an American Indian English.* Publication of the American Dialect Society 87. Durham, N.C.: Duke Univ. Press.

Ekwall, Eilert. 1943. *Studies on the Genitive of Groups in English.* Lund: Gleerup.

Fasold, Ralph W. 1991. "The Quiet Demise of Variable Rules." *American Speech* 66: 3–21.

Isherwood, Christopher. 1935. *Mr. Norris Changes Trains.* London: Hogarth. Repr. London: Methuen, 1987.

Jacobson, Sven. 1983. "A Variable Rule for the Placement of *probably.*" In *Papers from the Second Scandinavian Symposium on Syntactic Variation, Stockholm, May 15–16, 1982,* ed. Sven Jacobson, 31–40. Stockholm: Almqvist and Wiksell.

Kauffman, Stuart. 1995. *At Home in the Universe: The Search for Laws of Self-Organization and Complexity.* New York: Oxford University Press.

Kroch, Anthony. 1989. "Reflexes of Grammar in Patterns of Language Change." *Language Variation and Change* 1: 199–244.

———. 1994. "Morphosyntactic Variation." In *Papers from the Thirtieth Regional Meeting of the Chicago Linguistic Society, 1994,* vol. 2, *The Parasession on Variation in Linguistic Theory,* ed. Katharine Beals, Jeannette Denton, Robert Knippen, Lynette Melnar, Hisami Suzuki, and Erica Zeinfeld, 180–201. Chicago: Chicago Linguistic Society.

Kroch, Anthony, and Ann Taylor. 1997. "Verb Movement in Old and Middle English: Dialect Variation and Language Contact." In *Parameters of Morphosyntactic Change,* ed. Ans van Kemenade and Nigel Vincent, 326–52. Cambridge: Cambridge Univ. Press.

Labov, William. 1969. "Contraction, Deletion, and Inherent Variability of the English Copula." *Language* 45: 715–62.

———. 1974. "The Use of the Present to Explain the Past." In *Proceedings of the Eleventh International Congress of Linguists: Bologna-Florence, Aug. 28–Sept. 2, 1972,* ed. Luigi Heilmann, 825–51. Bologna: Il Molina.

Lightfoot, David. 1999. *The Development of Language: Acquisition, Change, and Evolution.* Malden, Mass.: Blackwell.

Magenau, Keller. 1994. "Anaphora: A Formal and Functional Phenomenon." Unpublished MS.

Newmeyer, Frederick. 2002. "Typology and Universal Grammar." Lecture delivered at Georgetown University, Washington, D.C., 22 Oct.

Oxford English Dictionary. 1989. 2d ed. 20 vols. Oxford: Clarendon.

"The Peterborough Chronicle." 1122–54. MS Laud 636. Bodleian Library, Oxford. MS E of the *Anglo-Saxon Chronicle.*

Pinker, Steven. 1994. *The Language Instinct.* New York: HarperCollins.

Rand, David, and David Sankoff. 1990. *GoldVarb: A Variable Rule Application for Macintosh. Version 2.* Available from http://www.crm.umontreal.ca/~sankoff/GoldVarbManual.Dir.

Santorini, Beatrice. 1992. "Variation and Change in a Yiddish Subordinate Clause Word Order." *Natural Language and Linguistic Theory* 10: 595–640.

———. 1993. "The Rate of Phrase Structure Change in the History of Yiddish." *Language Variation and Change* 5: 257–83.

Skeat, Walter W. 1881–87. *The Holy Gospels in Anglo-Saxon, Northumbrian, and Old Mercian Versions.* Cambridge: Cambridge Univ. Press.

Taylor, Ann. 1994. "Variation in Past Tense Formation in the History of English." *University of Pennsylvania Working Papers in Linguistics* 1: 143–59.

Weinreich, Uriel, William Labov, and Marvin I. Herzog. 1968. "Empirical Foundations for a Theory of Language Change." In *Directions for Historical Linguistics: A Symposium,* ed. W. P. Lehmann and Yakov Malkiel, 95–188. Austin: Univ. of Texas Press.

Woolf, Virginia. 1937. *The Years.* London: Hogarth. Repr. London: Triad Grafton, 1987.

Zribi-Hertz, Anne. 1989. "Anaphor Binding and Narrative Point of View: English Reflexive Pronouns in Sentence and Discourse." *Language* 65: 695–727.

CONTRIBUTORS

SHARON ASH received her B.A. in biology from Bryn Mawr College and her Ph.D. in linguistics from the University of Pennsylvania. She is currently associate director of the Linguistics Laboratory at the University of Pennsylvania and coauthor of the *Atlas of North American English* (with William Labov and Charles Boberg, Berlin: de Gruyter, forthcoming).

RICHARD W. BAILEY is Fred Newton Scott Collegiate Professor of English at the University of Michigan. From 1987 to 1989, he was president of the American Dialect Society. His biography of a nineteenth-century American philologist and murderer has recently appeared: *Rogue Scholar: The Sinister Life and Celebrated Death of Edward H. Rulloff* (Ann Arbor: Univ. of Michigan Press, 2003).

ROBERT BAYLEY is professor of sociolinguistics in the Division of Bicultural-Bilingual Studies at the University of Texas at San Antonio. His research concerns language use in Mexican American families and communities and variation in American Sign Language, English, and Spanish. He is coauthor of *Sociolinguistic Variation in American Sign Language* (with Ceil Lucas and Clayton Valli, Washington, D.C.: Gallaudet Univ. Press, 2001) and *Language as Cultural Practice: Mexican en el norte* (with Sandra R. Schecter, Mahwah, N.J.: Erlbaum, 2002) and is coeditor of *Language Socialization in Bilingual and Multilingual Societies* (with Sandra R. Schecter, Clevedon: Multilingual Matters, 2003).

CONNIE C. EBLE teaches English at the University of North Carolina at Chapel Hill and is editor of *American Speech*. Her *Slang and Sociability* (Chapel Hill: Univ. of North Carolina Press, 1996) describes the slang of American undergraduates since the 1970s.

PENELOPE ECKERT is professor of linguistics at Stanford University. Her research examines the relation between language use and

social identity and most particularly the role of phonological variation in the coconstruction of styles and identities. In this work, she
combines ethnographic methods for data collection with quantitative analyses of social and linguistic constraints on variation. Her
recent work has focused on adolescents and preadolescents, and
she has done extensive ethnographic sociolinguistic work in and
around schools. She is author of the high-school ethnography *Jocks
and Burnouts* (New York: Teachers College Press, 1989), as well as
Linguistic Variation as Social Practice (Malden, Mass.: Blackwell, 2000),
a sociolinguistic study of the relation between language and participation in high-school social categories, and is coauthor of *Language and Gender* (with Sally McConnell-Ginet, Cambridge: Cambridge Univ. Press, 2003).

RALPH W. FASOLD holds M.A. and Ph.D. degrees in linguistics from
the University of Chicago. He is past chair of the Department of
Linguistics at Georgetown University and is now professor emeri-
tus. He is the author of four books and editor or coeditor of six
others. Among them are *The Sociolinguistics of Society* (1984) and
The Sociolinguistics of Language (1990), published in Blackwell Publishers' Sociolinguistics Series, for which he is also one of two
North American consultant editors. Together, these books constitute a survey of sociolinguistics and have been used as textbooks
both in the United States and abroad. His research in sociolinguistics
furnishes some of the early linguistic analysis of African American
Vernacular English, including a monograph, *Tense Marking in Black
English* (Arlington, Va.: Center for Applied Linguistics, 1972). He
is a past member of the International Group for the Study of
Language Standardization and Vernacular Literacy, a consortium
of linguists in Britain, France, and several other countries. Fasold's
research interests also include the principles governing the distribution of reflexives in English, German, and other languages.

JOAN HOUSTON HALL came to the University of Wisconsin–Madison
in 1975 as assistant editor for the *Dictionary of American Regional
English* (Cambridge, Mass.: Belknap Press of Harvard Univ. Press, 4
vols. to date, 1985–). She became editor in 1979 and, following the
death of Frederic Cassidy in 2000, was named his successor as chief

editor. She is vice-president and president-elect of the American Dialect Society.

BARBARA JOHNSTONE (Ph.D., University of Michigan, 1981) is professor of rhetoric and linguistics at Carnegie Mellon University. She is author of *Stories, Community, and Place: Narratives from Middle America* (Bloomington: Indiana Univ. Press, 1990), *The Linguistic Individual* (New York: Oxford Univ. Press, 1996), and two textbooks, *Qualitative Methods in Sociolinguistics* (New York: Oxford Univ. Press, 2001) and *Discourse Analysis* (Malden, Mass.: Blackwell, 2002). Her research interests have to do with how the individual and the social are related and with the ways people evoke and shape places in discourse. Almost all her work has involved the study of conversation and text in, and discourse about, American English. She is currently exploring how dialect, discourse, and place evoke and create each other in the Pittsburgh area.

RUTH KING is professor of linguistics and women's studies at York University, Toronto. Her research areas include sociolinguistics, language contact, and language and gender. She has published extensively on variation and change in Acadian French. She is lead author of *Talking Gender* (Toronto: Copp Clark Pitman, 1991) and author of *The Lexical Basis of Grammatical Borrowing* (Amsterdam: Benjamins, 2000).

WILLIAM A. KRETZSCHMAR, JR. (Ph.D., University of Chicago, 1980), is professor of English and linguistics at the University of Georgia. His publications include *The Oxford Dictionary of Pronunciation for Current English* (with Clive Upton and Rafal Konopka, Oxford: Oxford Univ. Press, 2001); *Introduction to Quantitative Analysis of Linguistic Survey Data* (with Edgar Schneider, Thousand Oaks, Calif.: Sage, 1996); and *Handbook of the Linguistic Atlas of the Middle and South Atlantic States* (with Virginia McDavid, Theodore Lerud, and Ellen Johnson, Chicago: Univ. of Chicago Press, 1994). The primary outlet for his linguistic atlas research is the Linguistic Atlas Web site, http://us.english.uga.edu. He is also directing corpus and text-encoding activities funder by a National Cancer Institute grant to study tobacco documents, and text analysis, as shown by his special issue of *Language and Literature* (10.2 [2001]) on literary dialect analysis with computer assistance. He served as editor of the *Journal of English Linguistics* for 15 years. He now serves as editor for three linguistic atlases (LAMSAS, LANCS, LAWS) and a board member for several others; as an executive board member for the international Text Encoding Initiative Consortium; and as an advisory board member or consultant for various professional journals and dictionaries, including the new online *Oxford English Dictionary*. He has done consulting work over the years for forensic, industrial, and academic clients.

MICHAEL B. MONTGOMERY's work on the history of American English focuses on two related areas: colonial American English and transatlantic connections (especially with Ireland and Scotland). His chapter "British and Irish Antecedents" appeared in John Algeo's *English in North America* (Cambridge: Cambridge Univ. Press, 2001, 86–153), vol. 6 of *The Cambridge History of the English Language*.

DENNIS R. PRESTON, University Distinguished Professor of Linguistics Michigan State University (Ph.D., University of Wisconsin-Madison, 1969), has been a visiting professor at the Universities of Indiana Southeast, Hawaii, Arizona, and Michigan and has held Fulbright Senior Research Awards in Poland and Brazil. He was codirector of the 1990 TESOL Summer Institute and director of the 2003 Linguistic Society of America Institute, both at MSU. He was president of the American Dialect Society (2001–2) and has served on the executive boards of that society and the International Conference on Methods in Dialectology; on the editorial boards of *Language*, the *International Journal of Applied Linguistics*, the *Journal of Pan-Pacific Association of Applied Linguistics*, and the *Journal of Sociolinguistics*; and as a reader for numerous other journals, publishers, and granting agencies. His work focuses on sociolinguistics, dialectology, and ethnography, and he has been concerned with minority language and variety education in schools. He has directed two NSF research grants in folk linguistics and one in language variation and change. He is invited frequently for presentations in both academic and popular venues. His most recent books are *A Handbook of Perceptual Dialectology*, volume 2 (with Daniel Long, Amsterdam: Benjamins, 2002), and *Folk Linguistics* (with Nancy Niedzielski, Berlin: de Gruyter, 2000). He will appear in the McNeil/Leher Productions supplement to *The Story of English* entitled *Do You Speak American?* due for PBS broadcast in 2004. He was awarded the medal of the university by Adam Mickeiwicz University in Poland in 1986 and was made a fellow of the Japan Society for the Promotion of Science in 1998. He is a recipient of the MSU Distinguished Faculty Award and the Paul Varg Alumni Award of the College of Arts and Letters.

PUBLICATION OF THE AMERICAN DIALECT SOCIETY

Editor: RONALD R. BUTTERS, *Duke University*
Managing Editor: CHARLES E. CARSON, *Duke University*

THE AMERICAN DIALECT SOCIETY

Membership is conferred upon any person interested in the aims and activities of the Society. Dues for 2004 are $50 for regular members, $25 for students, and $22 extra for members outside the United States. Life membership is available to individuals for $1,000. Members receive all publications: *American Speech*, its monograph supplement Publication of the American Dialect Society (PADS), and the *Newsletter*. Institutional subscriptions are also available. Address payments to Duke University Press, Journals Fulfillment, Box 90660, Durham NC 27708-0660; phone 888-387-5687 or 919-687-3602. Questions concerning membership or the Society should be addressed to the Executive Secretary, Allan Metcalf, Department of English, MacMurray College, Jacksonville IL 62650 (e-mail: AAllan@aol.com).

STATEMENT FOR AUTHORS

The object of the American Dialect Society, as stated in its constitution, "is the study of the English language in North America, together with other languages influencing it or influenced by it." The monograph series Publication of the American Dialect Society (PADS) publishes works by ADS members in (1) regional dialects, (2) social dialects, (3) occupational vocabulary, (4) place-names, (5) usage, (6) non-English dialects, (7) new words, (8) proverbial sayings, and (9) the literary use of dialect. Models for these kinds of studies may be found in issues of PADS. PADS does not publish articles on general grammar without dialect emphasis or articles on literary figures not known as dialect writers.

The general policy of PADS is to devote each issue to two or three long articles or, more commonly, to a single study of monograph length. Shorter articles and book reviews should be submitted to *American Speech*, the journal of the American Dialect Society.

Manuscripts submitted to PADS and *American Speech* should be styled following *The Chicago Manual of Style* (14th ed., 1993). Documentation must be given in the text itself using the author-date system (chap. 16), with the list of references at the end prepared in the humanities sytle (chap. 15).

Manuscripts for *American Speech* and PADS may be submitted to Charles E. Carson, Managing Editor, American Dialect Society Publications, Duke University Press, Box 90018, Durham NC 27708-0018. Telephone: (919) 687-3670. E-mail: carson@duke.edu.